AFRICAN
AMERICAN
SOCIOLOGY

D1596847

AFRICAN AMERICAN SOCIOLOGY

A Social Study
of the
PAN-AFRICAN DIASPORA

Editors
James L. Conyers, Jr.
Alva P. Barnett

Nelson-Hall Publishers/Chicago

Project Editor: Steven M. Long
Designer: Jane Rae Brown
Typesetter: E. T. Lowe
Printer: Bang Printing
Cover Painting: *Thru the Time Warp*, by C. Mansfield

African American sociology : a social study of the Pan African diaspora /
    editors, James L. Conyers, Alva Barnett.
        p.   cm.
    Includes bibliographical references and index.
    ISBN 0-8304-1525-4 (alk. paper)
    1. Black nationalism—United States. 2. Pan-Africanism.
3. African diaspora. 4. Afro-Americans—Social conditions—1975–
5. Sociology—United States. 6. Afro-Americans—Study and teaching.
7. Afro-Americans—Intellectual life. I. Conyers, James L. II. Barnett, Alva.
E185.625.A383   1998   97-43072
                                                                  CIP

Manufactured in the United States of America

10 9 8 7 6 5 4 3 2 1

TM   The paper used in this book meets the
     minimum requirements of American
     National Standard for Information
     Sciences—Permanence of Paper for
     Printed Library Materials, ANSI
     Z39.48-1984.

To the memory of the late Dr. Gerald L. Davis "19–06" and Louise Giles, your spirit, memory, and energy live with us always.

ACKNOWLEDGMENTS

With each book that comes to print, writers must often reflect back on their support from families, networks, and communities. This collection of essays is the result of Alva P. Barnett and myself brainstorming, debriefing, holding extensive conversations, and making critical commentary to produce an exhaustive work of scholarship examining the social interaction and function of continental and diaspora Africans. Our families have played an integral role in the support and our continued learning. First of all, my mother Agnes Conyers and my wife Jacqueline Conyers are the breadth and depth of support for my reflectivity and analysis of describing and evaluating the black experience in a historical and cultural context. My children, Chad, Khalfani, and Kamau, are my young lions who test my common-sense approach and applicability of new knowledge to praxis. To my father and mother Mr. and Mrs. Barnett, who continue to be educators to many and my brothers along with extended family—thank you for your blessings, support, and encouragement throughout this life.

Mentors who have been extremely valuable and supportive of our research endeavors are Dr. Julius E. Thompson, Dr. James B. Stewart, Dr. Delores Aldridge, and the late Dr. Gerald L. Davis. The friendship and brotherhood of: Zane Corbin, Qawi Jamison, Anthony Robinson, Henry Bernard Robinson, Gregory Mainor, Abdullah Mainor, Mustafa Aziz Rasool, Mustafa Harper, Joseph E. Taylor, and James Bullock, has existed for over a decade on the basis of respect, trust, and comradery.

Others, to whom we would like to give a shout-out of thanks, appreciation, and those whose scholarly works have influenced our continued learning are the following: Dr. John Henrik Clarke, Dr. Molefi Kete Asante, Dr. Abu Abarry, Dr. Jerry W. Ward, Jr., Dr. Shawn Donaldson, Dr. Nancy Belck, Dr. John Wanzenried, Dr. Mark Rousseau, Dr. Boyd Litrell, Dr. Bruce Garver, Dr. James Johnson, Dr. Philip Secret, Dr. Nancy Dawson, Dr. Lewis Gordon, Dr. Robert Edwards, Dr. Bernard Bell, Dr. Emily Grosholz, Dr. H. Lewis Suggs, Dr. Keith, Parker, Dr. Alonzo Smith, Dr. Mary Mudd, Professor Barbara Hewins-Maroney, Dr. David Hinton, Dr. Clyde Robertson, Dr. B. J. Reed, Dr. John Flocken, Professor Abdu Nanji, Dr. James Turner, Dr. Darlene Clark Hine, Dr. Houston Baker, Dr. Nell Painter, Dr. John Blassingame, Dr. Jack Ravage, Dr. Bing Howell, Mike Innis-Thompson, Thomas Hughes, Scott Nelson, Mr. Russell and Bettye Jackson, Mr. John Brown, Frederick Pierce, Inger Pierce, Gwen Woods, Shaheed Woods, Khalis Rashchard Hakim Woods, Gladys Cox, John Sharkey, Glenn Dee, Frank Dee, Kenneth Butts, Professor Andrew Smallwood, Joye Knight, Amir Abdurahman, Dr. Learthen Dorsey, Cynthia Robinson, George Dillard, Brenda Council, Imam Na'im Muhammad, Preston Love, Larry Menyweather-Woods, Lous Thomas, David Kimble, Constanza Sampson, Malachi Crawford, James Shaw, Robert Nash, Tia Harrison, and Dr. Lordes Gouveia. A special thanks goes to Steven M. Long, Associate Editor at Nelson-Hall, for his patience, tenacity, discipline, and humor during the process of nurturing the production of this book into publication. Also, I would like to thank Jackie Lynch for her typing and editorial services. Again, it is with the support of others, the sacred circle, that we gain mental, physical, and spiritual strength and upliftment to move onward and upward.

CONTENTS

PART I

Nationalism and the Africana Diaspora

ix

CONTENTS

PART II

Social Welfare and Critical Analysis

CONTENTS

PART III

The African Diasporic Experience Through Autobiography and Black Studies Narratives

LIST OF CONTRIBUTORS

MOLEFI K. ASANTE   a professor of African American Studies at Temple University, holds a Ph.D. in Communications from UCLA. His books include: *Afrocentricity: The Theory of Social Change; The Afrocentric Idea; Kemet, Afrocentricity, and Knowledge; A Historical and Cultural Atlas of African Americans;* and *African Culture.* Asante is architect of the first doctoral program in African American Studies in the United States and one of the leading theoreticians of the Afrocentric paradigm.

ALVA P. BARNETT   is an associate professor of social work at the University of Nebraska at Omaha. She holds a Ph.D. in social work from the University of Pittsburgh. Her research and expertise is in the field of medical health care, social policy, and social work practice. She is also the co-editor of the forthcoming book, *Africana History, Culture, and Social Policy.* Published in the United States and abroad, she has been published in the *Western Journal of Black Studies, The Urban League Review,* and book chapters in *The Black Adolescent Parent* and *The Black Family.*

FRANK CHAPMAN   holds an M.A. from Washington University in St. Louis. He is the executive director of National Alliance Against Racist and Political Oppression, as well as the author of numerous articles published in the *Journal of Negro Education* and *Freedom Ways.*

JUANITA FLETCHER-CONE	holding a M.D. from Howard University, is a member of National Medical Association, the Jacksonville Chamber of Commerce, and the national Council of Negro Women. Currently, she is in private practice in Jacksonville, Florida.
CECIL W. CONE	holds a Ph.D. in Theology from Emory University. He was formerly pastor of Union A.M.E. Church; Executive Director of OIC in Little Rock, Arkansas; and held the positions of dean and president of Edward Waters College. He has conducted research in the area of African American religion and spirituality and has received numerous awards within the state of Florida for social and civic service. Presently, he is pastor of Mt. Olive A.M.E. Church in Jacksonville, Florida.
JAMES L. CONYERS, Jr.	chair of the Department of Black Studies and associate professor of Black Studies and Sociology at the University of Nebraska at Omaha, holds a Ph.D. in African American Studies from Temple University. His books include *The Evolution of African American Studies;* co-editor of the forthcoming work *Africana History, Culture, and Social Policy;* and editor of *African American Historiography; Africana Studies: A Disciplinary Quest for Both Theory and Methods; Charles H. Wesley: The Intellectual Tradition of A Black Historian; Black American Intellectualism and Culture; Carter G. Woodson: An Historical Reader;* and *Black Lives: Essays in African American Biography.* Additionally, he has published numerous articles and book reviews in the leading Black Studies journals.

ROBERT L. HARRIS is an associate professor of African American History, Africana Studies, and Research Center at Cornell University. His research interest is on African Americans and the United Nations and is the author of *Teaching African American History* and several articles on African American history and culture published in Black Studies and history journals. Also, he is the editor of the African American History and Culture series for Twayne Publications.

DORRAINE HOOKS earned her Masters of Science in Human Relations from the University of Oklahoma. Currently, she is a doctoral student in the department of Public Administration at the University of Nebraska at Omaha. Her research area of interest is in African American religion, social policy, and history.

AUDREYE JOHNSON an associate professor of social work at the University of North Carolina at Chapel-Hill, earned her Ph.D. in social welfare from the University of Denver. She has received numerous awards for social and civic service in the areas of African American history, culture, and social welfare. Her research area of interest is in social work practice, with an emphasis on African American culture. She is a founding member of the National Association of Black Social Workers and is the director and creator of the annual Black Experience Workshop at the University of North Carolina at Chapel-Hill.

WILLIAM LOREN KATZ received an M.A. in History and Education from Syracuse University. He is a freelance writer of non-fiction, with emphasis on African American history, culture, and minority race relations. His books include *Eyewitness: The Negro in American History; Five Slave Narratives; Teacher's Guide to American Negro History; American Minorities and Majorities; A Syllabus of United States History for Secondary Schools; The Black West; A History of Black Americans; An Album of Reconstruction; An Album of the Civil War; The Constitutional Amendments; Minorities in American History; Making Our Way; Black People Who Made the Old West; The Great Depression.* In addition, he has edited over ten published documents that are relative to African American history and culture. He is the author of seventeen books and numerous articles that examine African American history and culture. Currently, he is a scholar in residence at the New school for Social Research.

VENITA KELLEY   is an assistant professor of Communications and African American Studies at the University of Nebraska at Lincoln. With a Ph.D. in Communications from the University of Kansas, her research interests are in the field of intercultural communications, African American Studies, and Women Studies.

DARRYLL M. H. LEWIS   an associate professor of Law and Society at the University of Nebraska at Omaha, holds a Juris Doctorate from Creighton University. He has published numerous scholarly articles, with a curricula emphasis in race and discrimination in the work place.

GUY MARTIN   works in the International Relations Institute of Cameroon. His research area of emphasis is on the developmental process of African Studies.

JEROME H. SCHIELE an associate professor and chair of the Ph.D. program in the School of Social Work at Clark-Atlanta University, also holds a D.S.W. in Social Work from Howard University. His research area of interest is in the field of social work with an emphasis on African Americans and Afrocentric Theory. He has published articles in *Social Work, The Journal of Black Studies,* and *The Journal of Sociology and Social Welfare,* and is currently working on a forthcoming book titled *Human Services and the Afrocentric Paradigm.*

ANDREW P. SMALLWOOD an instructor of Black Studies at the University of Nebraska at Omaha, is currently a doctoral candidate at Northern Illinois University in Adult Education. His research areas of expertise are in African American history and psychology.

STERLING STUCKEY professor emeritus of History at Northwestern University in Evanston, Illinois, has written several books that include *The Ideological Origins of Black Nationalism; Chains of Slavery; Separate But Equal; Quest for Equality;* and co-author of *A People Uprooted.* He is contributor to magazines and newspapers such as *New York Times Book Review; Negro Digest;* and the *Massachusetts Review.*

JULIUS E. THOMPSON is the director of the Black Studies Program and associate professor of History and Black Studies at the University of Missouri at Columbia. His books include, *Percy Greene and the Jackson Advocate; The Black Press in Mississippi; Hiram Revels: A Biography;* and he has recently completed a literary biography of *Dudley Randall and the*

xvi

Broadside Press, which is scheduled to be published in fall 1998.

AHATI N. N. TOURE — holds an M.A. in African American Studies from the State University of New York at Albany. He is also a journalist and freelance writer of non-fiction cultural studies, and currently resides in New York City.

CARLENE YOUNG — a sociologist and educational psychologist by training, is a professor of African American Studies at San Jose State University. She is one of the leading theoreticians in the discipline of Black Studies and was the former chair of the African American Studies department at San Jose State University. Additionally, she is a practicing clinical psychologist. Her publications can be found in the leading Black Studies journals.

INTRODUCTION

This study seeks to critically examine sociological implications of Africana phenomena, with direct emphasis on a social study of the Pan-African diaspora. The organizational structure of this study focuses on the following cognitive areas: black nationalism and Pan-Africanism; social policy and analysis; and autobiographical, biographical, and research studies on Africana studies.

Ironically, much of the sociological or group interactive studies conducted on African Americans are too descriptive, lacking any critical assessment of retention of black cultural autonomy and authenticity. Paradoxically, this study attempts to incorporate research query and intellectual thought, in the way of shaping and formatting the parameters of an African American collective consciousness. Moreover, this method becomes essential in presenting alternative ideological repertories, that examine African American group interaction. Therefore, the essential function and intersubjective aim of this study, is to describe and evaluate Africana phenomena, in the organizational form of a social study, within the Pan-African diaspora.

To be straight forward, this study seeks the alternative, whereas, the method is sociological; the theory is interdisciplinary, located within the disciplinary contours of African American Studies; and the analysis is holistic, employing research tools from within the social sciences and humanities. Accordingly, the central core, or the breadth and depth of this study, is to examine the sociological interaction of African American history, culture, memory, and ethos. Even more important, within the body of literature presented throughout this study, the reader may develop a rationale, logic, reason, and emotion for studying the historical and cultural experiences of Africana diasporic people from a prism of a black perspective.

PART I

Nationalism and the Africana Diaspora

CHAPTER 1 Molefi Kete Asante
Systematic Nationalism: A Legitimate Strategy for National Selfhood

CHAPTER 2 Frank Chapman
The Black Colony Theory Revisited

CHAPTER 3 Sterling Stuckey
The Cultural Philosophy of Paul Robeson

CHAPTER 4 James L. Conyers, Jr.
Black Nationalism and Pan-Africanism: A Social Study of African Americans Participation in United States Foreign Policy Towards Africa

CHAPTER 5 William Loren Katz
The Afro-American's Response to U.S. Imperialism

CHAPTER 6 Venita Kelley
African American Women Preachers: Fulfilling a Mandate and a Calling

CHAPTER 1

Systematic Nationalism: A Legitimate Strategy for National Selfhood

Molefi Kete Asante

The contemporary Marxists' credo these days is based upon histori-cally incorrect perceptions of American society and consequently af-fords no historically or experientially derived methods for us. Their belief in the inherent integrity of the working class is contradictory to our history in America. Furthermore, the current critiques of Pan-Africanism and nationalism by black Marxists are simplistic formulas derived from the 1860s. In an attempt to attack African cultural, po-litical, and economic unity at home and abroad, they have seriously distorted the political configuration of contemporary society and failed to account for the historically correct analyses of leading na-tional theoreticians.

Systematic nationalists as opposed to naive nationalists have al-ways considered Pan-Africanism without socialism to be self-defeat-ing because otherwise the exploitation of the people would simply continue at the hands of black exploiters. Thus, exploitation in any form by any type of economic order is vehemently denounced. What is disturbing, however, is that the Marxists believe that in order to achieve cultural and political solidarity among black people there has to be complete unification of the world's working classes. Not only is this a naive Marxist view, it is a view which has been roundly criti-cized for its inaccuracies. At least, nationalists have articulated clear and profound views in the last ten years (Madhubuti 1977). New works by Karenga and Madhubuti have sparked a lively debate on the nationalist question but more appropriately they have continued the activist tradition. However, the triumvirate of Marx-Lenin-Stalin has more validity in contemporary Afro-American Marxist thinking than Walker-Garvey-Muhammad because the Marxists are not conscious of the intellectual and activist postures derived from our history.

This article contends that the historically correct path for national selfhood has always been systematic nationalism. In effect, systematic nationalists believe that any ideology for a people's liberation must be derived from their social and historical context. This is not to say that no ideas from other theorists or theories are acceptable. Certainly, nationalism must be built upon the cardinal truth principles of political behavior expressed in African, Eastern, and Western philosophies. Our critical difference, however, must be in our history, that is, in what can be considered truth for us. Marxism is a method, systematic nationalism is a method. One method is designed to deal with class contradictions, the other speaks to race as a contradiction. Thus, the contributions of Marxism cannot be ignored; they must be placed in context (Agyeman 1978).

The systematic nationalist position is clear. The fundamental contradiction in American society is *racism*. If there is one fact on which blacks have historically been united, it is the reality of race in American society. Even Clark, the integrationist, saw accurately in *Dark Ghetto* (1965) the pervasiveness of racism, saying it has permeated the whole society. W. E. B. Du Bois, America's most prolific intellectual and a socialist, understood that socialist fraternity could not exist while human brotherhood was still a mockery. Du Bois did not allow his method to interfere with his nationalism or his Pan-Africanism. This was also true of Padmore (1972).

It is from racism as the fundamental contradiction that our most pressing political and social issues are derived. Whether we are discussing jobs, education, welfare, or foreign affairs, racism is a factor. Systematic nationalists understand and have always admitted that it is not the *only* contradiction; it is the *principal* contradiction for African Americans. A racially homogeneous capitalist nation would produce sharper economic contradictions than the United States. The African population within the American society acts as a buffer between what would conceivably be revolutionary working classes of whites and the capitalist classes according to orthodox Marxism. Such a cleavage, pragmatic and operative for a working-class revolution, is nearly obliterated by the presence of thirty million blacks who

4

are the victims of a psychosocial rage called racism. The fact that Africans are disproportionately represented in the working classes is also derived from racism. This has to be understood as a uniquely American situation. Applications of a methodological analysis developed under circumstances other than the American society must come under extreme review. To take Guinea, Somalia, or China as examples for the liberation of Africans in America is a distortion. Cuba itself has found that the revolution has not eradicated racism. Governments find it easier to manage economies than to manage racism.

Marxists are content to find refuge in the European past and in an organizational hierarchy ready-made for the platform rather than in the creative practice of struggle based upon our own historical content. Bookchin in *Post Scarcity Anarchism* (1971) was at least correct in his analysis of Marxism as a conservative ideology, because the authoritarian leader and hierarchy replace the patriarch and school bureaucracy; the discipline of the movement replaces the discipline of bourgeois society; the authoritarian code of political obedience replaces the state; the credo of "proletarian morality" replaces the mores of puritanism and work.

The truth of the matter is that nationalist thought has not been as structured as it should have been. Thus, brothers and sisters looking for a unified approach to revolutionary struggle have found Marxism easier to argue. The development of a systematic nationalism, born in African American history, provides an alternative strategy for liberation. The bankruptcy peddled by Marxists lacks the necessary revolutionary vision to see the intricacies of racist capitalism in American society. Systematic nationalism seeks freedom from Marxist racists as well as capitalist racists (Moore 1972).

Systematic nationalism does not destroy the validity of Marxism as a critique of industrial capitalism in the nineteenth century; it transcends Marxism as a critique for liberation struggles by minority people within imperialist nations. This fact has always been understood by classical thinkers such as Garvey and Malcolm X. A Marxist's analysis of class struggle was both appropriate and real for the nineteenth century. However, as even the black Marxists will admit, the traditional class struggle simply readjusts and strengthens the capitalist system by modifying wages, labor time, fringe benefits, and employment and position mobility. These are precisely the factors which work against the romantic notion of white and black workers in

America leading a socialist revolution. If socialism is ever achieved in the American society it will be through systematic nationalism, not a collective of multiracial workers. White industrial workers who earn ten and twelve dollars per hour find little to share with a brother or sister who cannot get a job because of racist oppression expressed in poor education, substandard housing, inadequate health care, and a defeatist attitude toward life. The white worker, indeed even the antiblack black worker, who earns twelve dollars an hour has difficulty sympathizing with a street corner brother who suffers from racist oppression. The reality of this fact alone shows the impoverished nature of a proletarian revolution in contemporary America. There are no revolutionary implications for America in traditional Marxist class conflict. In fact, conflict may be orchestrated to purge the system of radicals. Any casual analysis of the American labor scene will show that the unions, the organizations of the working classes, have become a part of the capitalist monopoly system. Workers in contemporary America are not serfs, indentured servants, and overworked Russian peasants; they are an incorporated part of the general capitalist governors of the estate, demonstrating the same disdain for the poor, blacks, and women. It is in this context that Marxism shows itself to be most bankrupt as a liberating doctrine for African Americans. Although various other conflicts do exist in the capitalist estate, they are pretty much handicapped by the rich capitalists and rich unionists sitting down to work out their conflicts.

Systematic nationalism has no illusions about the racism which exists in the American society. Bishop Henry Turner, Marcus Garvey, Malcolm X, and Elijah Muhammad proclaimed it in their pioneering analyses. They began in a fragmented way to build a foundation for systematic nationalism. Their perspectives, informed by our history, are more valuable to us than those of Marx or Engels. We do not claim their wisdom or correctness merely on skin criterion, but rather because their analyses of the black condition in America were hammered out on the anvil of historical experience.

THREE ASSUMPTIONS

All theoretical arguments of systematic nationalism flow from three overarching assumptions: *racism is the principal contradiction in non-homogeneous industrial societies; racism is a permanent psychosocial reality in nonhomogeneous industrial societies; outmigration of large populations of minorities is impracticable.*

According to systematic nationalism, racism will exist in any nonhomogeneous industrial society whether the economics is capital or social. History affords no example where this has not been the case. Thus, the systematic nationalist takes this position as a given. Furthermore, racism is a permanent, psychosocial reality in nonho-mogeneous industrial societies. Changes in class conditions or religions do not obliterate the psychosocial permanence of racism. The presents of a minority population periodically engenders prejudice and discrimination. Yet the outmigration of large minority populations is impracticable. African Americans will remain in the United States. Systematic nationalists see our struggle in terms of the three principal assumptions mentioned earlier.

Garvey (1967) saw racism as the principal contradiction in American society and articulated a black nationalism which would drive fear out of the minds of the people. Garvey's movement, contrary to some beliefs, was well organized. Consistent with later nationalist thinking Garvey imposed strict discipline, taught pride and self-respect, encouraged independence from the white society, and created unifying symbols. Unlike Elijah Muhammad, Garvey planned a "Back to Africa" movement because Africans would never be free in America. Nationalism, for him, was a technique to be utilized to liberate blacks from America. Hard thinking had left him in the impracticable position of demanding that Africans be allowed to return to Africa. It was impracticable in the first quarter of the twentieth century because blacks who were prepared to support nationalism were not as prepared to support emigration to the continent. Second, the cost was prohibitive. And third, as Garvey discovered, we did not have the equipment capabilities, at the time, necessary for transporting large numbers of people over long distances within a short period of time, comfortably. Thus, the physical migration which he preached had to be spiritual migration for the vast majority of his followers.

Garvey, as a messenger, had struck the bell of nationalism like no other black person in the Americas. What he taught in his message would be learned, modified, and applied by those who came after him.

Elijah Muhammad's nationalism was complex and intricate. Starting from the same base as did Garvey, Muhammad saw racism as a permanent psychosocial reality in America. Nevertheless, he did not counsel Africans to run to Africa. His realistic appraisal of the impracticability of back to Africa gave him enormous credibility in the light of the history of Garvey's movement a few years earlier. Thus, Muhammad never promised to take anyone to Africa. According to Muhammad, Africans had as much right to the land as did Europeans. Therefore, nationalism as expressed by the messenger, Elijah Muhammad, depended upon securing land in America for the black nation. The base of his nationalist ideology, like that of Garvey, was economic development. Systematic nationalism accepts economic development as a major tenet but argues that spiritual conquest precedes either economic or political conquest.

Malcolm X articulated the sentiments of nationalism but was never permitted to develop the structure upon which those sentiments were to rest. Thus, the Marxists who openly attack nationalism have been setting up ducks and bowling them over. They have not yet appreciated the classical nationalist doctrine understood by every nationalist from Garvey to Karenga and even hinted at in the white scholar Willhelm's *Who Needs the Negro?* (1970) Racism is for real. Systematic nationalism accepts that as a starting point to construct a practical theory to deal with African American life.

Karenga calls his brand of systematic nationalism *Kawaida;* the name may differ but the method is the same. The method is primarily *pragmatics.* What we can demonstrate from an analysis of history is that our philosophy stemming from the classical theorists—Blyden, Delaney, Turner, Garvey, and Muhammad—is based upon situational demands. Exploited people will eventually do what is necessary to achieve their liberation. Garvey and Muhammad defended pragmatics in the most powerful manner and regularly pointed out the erroneous deviations from the principal assumptions of systematic nationalism. Garvey's views are most profoundly set forth in *The Philosophy and Opinions of Marcus Garvey* (1976); Muhammad's views are expressed in the *Message to the Blackman* (1965). Neither Garvey nor Muhammad stopped with a statement of philosophy; they advanced philosophical thought by submitting it to practice. In fact, both saw pragmatics as the carrying out of the national consciousness through committed effort to recover identity. Deepening the philosophical interest in pragmatics Garvey initially, and Muhammad later, advanced science by anticipating in political sociology the discoveries in biology and engineering. Garvey proved that the American cultural and political sphere was a system. In this respect he anticipated the work to be done by Von Bertalanffy and others in systems theory. Garvey made minute observations of the American society as well as numerous observations of West Indian communities before announcing his discovery. It was not until 1916 that he pronounced the establishment of the Universal Negro Improvement Association in America. He had by this time seen the interconnectedness of economics, geography, culture, and the military. The United States had formed a racist system and it was impossible to get out of the system anything but detriment to nonwhite minorities. It was this awareness which caused Garvey (1967) to argue vehemently for nationalism.

Following Garvey's well-developed philosophy which was grounded in historical reality, Muhammad carried it to the next level. Incipient in Garvey was *cultural consciousness.* But it was Muhammad who attempted to reconstruct the past as a basis for a more exact science. With hindsight we can look back and criticize the constituents of Muhammad's system, but as Abdul Farrakhan once said to me, "the old man's conceptual scheme was perfect." Malcolm X first, and Farrakhan subsequently, took the mantle of national purpose to another level. However, it was Farrakhan who understood the messenger's objective. Malcolm X enriched the political theory and provided new insights into the nationalist rationale but never lived to develop the cultural component to accompany the political philosophy. It would have been a natural occurrence had he lived. Abdul Farrakhan has moved toward an extension of the doctrine in order to achieve nationalist aims.

Nationalists have always responded to the situation which deprived the black person of information, thus the theory is *data based.* It argues that once you give a black person information about his/her African and American past, you will create a nationalist. It is a theoretical prediction based upon historical data. Correctly understanding the problem is a necessity for a problem solution. Prior to Garvey and Muhammad, nationalism was naive and sentimental. It was not a system; it was the psychological longings and wishes of some very creative and gifted individuals who were tired of discrimination and racism. As Marx and Engels had done for the economically oppressed, Garvey and Muhammad did for the racially oppressed. That is why the systematic nationalist says socialism is to deal with class contradictions; nationalism, to deal with race contradictions.

Classical theory as propounded by Garvey and Muhammad explained the root causes of the African's dissatisfaction with American society. They refuted the notion advanced by white and white-oriented black theorists that the black person was alienated from American society by demonstrating that blacks had never been a part of that society. Alienation suggests that one has been affiliated. In our historical experiences we affiliated with one another and grew to appreciate our strength. Dissatisfaction existed and exists because we have been unjustly treated and the time for redress is long past. Political and economic institutions constitute architectonic structures based on American racism. For justice to be done to the black person would mean the redistribution of political and economic wealth, i.e., the dismantling of the racist system. Since that is not going to be willingly done, we have to insure that the various scaffolds of racism do not encapsulate our spirit.

AN APPROACH

Systematic nationalism is not dependent upon geography. In this respect it departs most sharply from traditional concepts of nationalism. It was impossible for Elijah Muhammad or Malcolm X to conceive of nationalism without land. Their views, while understandable in previous political situations, are not necessarily operative in contemporary societies. Nationalism is a *relationship* among people with a common heritage and with common expectations. The Moluccans of Holland, the Palestinians in the Middle East, the Africans in South Africa, and African Americans in the United States constitute nations to the degree that political and spiritual solidarity is achieved. Land acquisition is merely the ultimate stage of nationalism.

The consummation and crystalization of our aspirations into an organic and systemic instrument for emancipatory politics is the first objective of systematic nationalism. This process is accomplished through historically and culturally determined actions for national expression. It contradicts attempts at national oppression through the exploitative uses of culture, science, religion, and economics. Emancipatory politics is the keystone of nationalistic struggle. It liberates the mind from the duality of marginal existence. Nationalists are therefore capable of functioning in any situation. What is necessary, absolutely necessary, is an attachment to the national idea. Such an attachment is both historically and politically correct. The correctness of systematic nationalism stems from its assault on the twin evils of race and class exploitation. This, however, is not its philosophical grounding; it is rather its activist character. The philosophical base of systematic nationalism must always be emancipatory politics.

The response of systematic nationalism to the main components of contemporary American society begins with a realistic analysis of our current condition. American society of the twentieth century is a media society. This fact alone distinguishes the last quarter of the twentieth century from any other era in history. The authority to support this view is overwhelming. Nevertheless, many militant responses, both nationalistic and Marxist, to national exploitation and repression in America, have been rooted in premedia notions. Culture, religion, science, and economics are *communicative* facts. Symbols form societies, symbols integrate societies, and symbols wreck societies. Imagery and rhetoric have played a role in our previous attempts to address national oppression but never in terms which combine our symbolic and strategic powers What is the meaning of a nationalist in any venue in society? What responses are symbolic? Which are strategic? What responses are both? Furthermore, the ability to operate nationally, that is, as a nationalist, is not restricted by one's venue. A nationalist is not a nationalist at the mass meeting and not one at the university, church, or United Nations. Such practice is the antithesis of Kawaida, systematic nationalism. As a function of social analysis, it is clear that nationalism is not limited by geography. Emancipatory politics in a highly mobile society such as America or South Africa must operate in every place. However, the symbolic and strategic symbols must reflect the positive elements of systematic nationalism as a relationship between people who express a common origin, struggle, and common aspirations. Such a systematic method must be applied to every sector of the society. There are four areas which must be addressed in any nationalist system: culture, science, spirituality, and economics.

CULTURE

Systematic nationalism defines culture as the creative activity of the people expressing a relationship with nature and each other in a functionally and aesthetically rewarding manner. American culture is generally decadent and base, having little pragmatic or spiritual content. The nationalist rejects the insipid and shallow treatment of culture by most American artists and encourages the creation of morally powerful images, sounds, words, and movements. An emphasis on spirit and pragmatism is not a negation of aesthetics but rather a resurrection of the essence of any true aesthetics. Aesthetics is not determined by a superordinate seer who decides what is beautiful and valuable and what is not; it is determined by that which is most instructive to the people. The musician, choreographer, painter, or other artist who engages in banalities receives the absolute condemnation of the nationalist, just as a Greek organization's black pledge is condemned for irrelevancies. Systematic nationalism builds upon the historically determined paths of the ancestor artists. The creativity of our artists must be instructed by history. It is necessary for an artist to read history and politics in American society in order to express more authentically the struggle and victory of national expression. As politics must be emancipatory, so culture must also be liberating. Our artists are priests and their ministry must be nationalistic and conscious.

SCIENCE

Science is a structured approach to the solution of practical problems. Systematic nationalism itself is science. All science should derive from praxis; praxis provides the basis for theory. The idea that theory should precede praxis is erroneous; theory is refined by praxis, and praxis is perfected by the people's criticism. Science, therefore, is employed for the benefit of the nation. Serious science assumes a role in medicine, technology, economics, literary analysis, and Afrology. It does not consider unimportant subjects for mere intellectual exercise, which is a waste of human time. Systematic nationalism contends that the scientist must apply his/her skills to problem-solving among the people. This is the scientist's first task. Achievement of skills brings with it a nationalistic scientific responsibility for the building of the nation.

SPIRITUALITY

Spirituality satisfies the human thirst for fulfillment. Systematic nationalism argues that spirituality is necessary and useful. However, we recognize that spirituality is founded upon specific histories from which we are able to draw universal lessons. All spiritual exercises have grown from specific histories. Hinduism, Judaism, Christianity, Islam, Candomble, Shango, and Maoism have expressed the peculiar conditions of the people to whom they were initially addressed. Universal acceptance of the general principles have come after the acceptance by the nationals. Systematic nationalism seeks to maintain the spirituality, which emerges out of our unique history as a symbolic people. This view is expressed in varying ways in the writings of Marcus Garvey, Elijah Muhammad, and Maulana Karenga. What they all understand is that religion, in its most spiritual sense, is the act of people seeking their own standards of ethics. According to systematic nationalism, those standards can only be found in the people's specific history. As a vanguard people, a people with integrity and spirit, the Afro-Americans must establish spiritual purpose in the world.

ECONOMICS

Economics is the cooperative production and management of goods and services. A systematic nationalist's view of economics sees all production and management orchestrated for the benefit of the people. It is everywhere operative. Exploitation through cheap labor schemes, class distinctions, and unfair labor policies are condemned outright by systematic nationalism. An economic system which does not stifle the human personality and which is based upon the historical experience of our people is the acceptable system of economics. Individual initiative should not be denied, but individual ruthlessness must be vehemently opposed. As a leading contradiction in American society, class exploitation has made it necessary for systematic nationalism to posit communalism as a pragmatic alternative to class oppression.

A serious application of systematic nationalism to our social and economic perspectives would revolutionize our community. It must, however, be a committed and persistent application in every sector of the society. By the beginning of the twenty-first century, African Americans will have transformed intellectual and cultural life as our ancestors bequeathed the singular spiritual legacy of the American nation.

Bibliography

Agyeman, O. (1978). "The Supermarxists and Pan-Africanism." *Journal of Black Studies* (June).

Bookchin, M. (1971). *Post Scarcity Anarchism.* Berkeley, CA: Ramparts.

Clark, K. B. (1965). *Dark Ghetto.* New York: Harper & Row.

Garvey, M. (1967). *The Philosophy and Opinions of Marcus Garvey.* London: Frank Cass.

Karenga, M. (1976). *The Roots of the US-Panther Conflict.* San Diego, CA: Kawaida Publications.

Madhubuti, H. (1977). *Enemies: The Clash of Races.* Chicago: Third World Press.

Moore, C. (1972). *Were Marx and Engels White Racists?* Chicago: Third World Press.

Muhammad, E. (1965). *Message to the Blackman.* Chicago: Muhammad Temple No. 2.

Padmore, G. (1972). *Africa and World Peace.* London: Frank Cass.

Willhelm, S. (1970). *Who Needs the Negro?* Cambridge, MA: Schenkman.

CHAPTER 2

The Black Colony
Theory Revisited

Frank Chapman

According to the capsule review on its inside cover, Manning
Marable's latest book, *How Capitalism Underdeveloped Black America,*
is in the tradition of *How Europe Underdeveloped Africa* by Walter Rodney. But more to the point, it is also in the tradition of *The Political
Thought of James Forman,* Robert Allen's *Black Awakening in Capitalist
America* and other works which subscribe to the concept that Black
Americans constitute a colony. Writes Marable, ". . . Blacks are an integral and necessary part of an imperialist and powerful capitalist society, yet they exist in terms of actual socioeconomic and political
power *as a kind of Third World nation . . .*" (italics mine).

From the preface we learn the purpose of this work and are provided with an overview of Dr. Marable's point of view. For example,
"To be Black and socialist in America is to be nonconformist. . . ." And
Dr. Marable warns that if in some instances he appears "too harsh,
too extreme, too utopian, too subjective, very well. The times we live
in call for harsh measures, both behind the cloistered towers of university and in the streets. . . ." He assures us that for the black masses
to "return to their own history" it must be rewritten, "not in the language, style or outlook of the system. . . ." Finally,

> This book records the respective histories of the different social strata
> within Black political economy and society, from the political Brahmins
> of the elite to the industrial working class. The methodology is sociological;
> the questions raised, political and economic; the style polemical; the goal:
> to present a critique of the strengths and contradictions which comprise
> Black American labor and life, with the purpose of destroying the process
> of underdevelopment which has imprisoned us for almost four centuries.

WHAT IS UNDERDEVELOPMENT?

Now on to a consideration of the author's goal, methodology, and the political and economic questions he raises. Marable contends that the "underdevelopment" of Black people is the necessary precondition for the development (i.e., the "rapid accumulations of capital") of "white society." Hence, ". . . white affluence coexists with Black poverty; white state and corporate power is the product in part of Black powerlessness . . . ," and capitalist development in the United States is based on the "integration" of Black people as brutally exploited workers and consumers who have been denied equal partnership in the "American Social Contract. This different perspective raises a basic theoretical question: What is development, and what is its structural relationship to underdevelopment?"

Marable briefly discusses what he calls certain Western scholars' "liberal interpretations" of the term "developed nation." In the main, these scholars define a developed nation as one that is capitalist and white ruled, proposing that the path of "modernization" for non-white, third world nations is capitalist development based on models provided by Western Europe and the United States.

Marable rejects these approaches, which are put forth by such theorists of modernization as Robert L. Heilbroner and Irving Louis Horowitz,[1] on the grounds that their adherents suffer from "economic amnesia" and sometimes discount the relationship between political development and "socioeconomic factors" relating to modernization. Their "economic amnesia" consists in ignoring the historic fact that:

> For Western Europe, Great Britain and the United States domestic development meant the conquest of foreign markets, the stimulation of demand for Western goods within the Third World, the domination of indigenous political and social systems by bribery . . . and outright colonial occupation. Development was, more than all other factors combined, the institutionalization of the hegemony of capitalism as a world system. *Underdevelopment* was the direct consequence of this process: chattel slavery, sharecropping, peonage, industrial labor at low wages, and cultural chaos. The current economic amnesia of the West is therefore no accident, because it reveals the true roots of massive exploitation and human degradation upon which the current world order rest. The world "periphery" and capitalist "core" share a common history.[2]

16

In my view, Marable's critique of "modernization" theory misses the point. First of all, the main purpose of the modernizationists is to construct a rationale for imperialist "aid" to developing countries. Whether this "aid" takes the form of grants, loans, investments or bribes, it is aimed at perpetuating colonial domination, which produces superprofits via the siphoning off of resources and extensive exploitation of labor.

To challenge modernization theorists only from the standpoint of their "economic amnesia," i.e., their failure to recognize that capital came into the world dripping from every pore with blood and dirt, is to obscure the real objective of their thesis. Essentially, modernization theory assists state-monopoly capitalists in their effort to overcome the present acute crisis in the international capitalist division of labor. Aid—such as food deliveries—is a major component of their strategy in that it is used to put political pressure on young independent states, in tandem with the exploitation of third world labor based on up-to-date methods. Marable leaves out of account the changes wrought in the industrial structure of capitalist countries by the technological revolution, and ignores the fact that the countries of Asia, Africa and Latin America need markets for the products of their developing industries. In so doing, he misses the heart and soul of modernization theory: It is intended to provide a theoretical basis for the present neo-colonialist policies of the U.S. and other Western states.

So how does the theoretical question posed by the author get answered in terms of the structural relationship between development and underdevelopment? Unfortunately, Marable does not delineate his theoretical approach with enough clarity for us to fully appreciate why particular questions are raised, certain procedures are followed and a given perspective adopted. For example, in studying "the respective histories of the different social strata within Black political economy and society," what do the terms "periphery" and "core" mean, and how does one justify the use of such terms and the conceptual framework they imply? We might also ask what is meant by "Black political economy."

One would expect the author to answer these questions at the beginning of a study whose methodology is sociological. But this is precisely what Marable does not do. Instead, without explanation, he loosely uses the model of "third world periphery" and "capitalist core" to explain "how capitalism underdeveloped Black America" in the same manner that Rodney explained "how Europe underdeveloped

Africa." Given Rodney's and others' (e.g., Nader Entessar, *Political Development in Chile* 1980) criticisms of the orthodox Western view of the relationship between development and underdevelopment, we can provide some missing definitions that are clearly accepted by Marable, Rodney, etc.

Key to understanding what is meant by underdevelopment in relation to development is the concept of *dependency,* defined as follows by Theotonio dos Santos:

> By dependence we mean a situation in which the economy of certain countries is conditioned by the development and expansion of another economy to which the former is subjected. The relation of interdependence between two or more economies, and between these and world trade, assumes the form of dependence when some countries (the dominant ones) can expand and can be self-sustaining, while other countries (the dependent ones) can do this only as a reflection of that expansion, which can have a positive or a negative effect on their immediate development.[3]

This definition implies that the underdevelopment of a third world country is not determined by such internal factors as lack of industrial capital but by domination of its economic structure by the developed capitalist nations. Such domination generates a "class structure" within the country whereby a small minority ("the domestic elite") benefits from the system of foreign domination (i.e., colonialism), while the overwhelming majority experiences the cruelest oppression and the most abject poverty.

The sociological model of dependency so defined[4] is called the "Living pyramid":

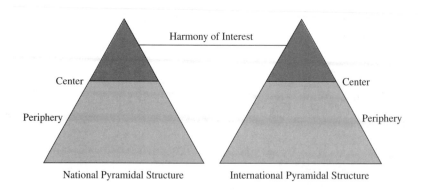

National Pyramidal Structure   International Pyramidal Structure

The Industrial nations of the capitalist world form the center of the international pyramidal structure, and its periphery consists of the dependent third world nations. The domestic elite—that is, the "urban and rural elites," the middle class, etc.—form the center of the *national* pyramidal structure (i.e., of each peripheral nation). The national periphery consists of the working class, peasants, unemployed and underemployed masses. The national center has a "harmony of interest" with the international center and, accordingly, gets its marching orders from the latter.

This model, with all of its underlying assumptions, is used by Marable to delineate the condition of Black people in the United States. But in order for the model to apply, Black people must be viewed as an oppressed, colonized nation. But, in fact, Black people are not a colony with a common territory and economy separated geographically from the "center" or colonizing country.[5] Colonies are generally rich in raw materials (diamonds, gold, uranium, etc.), and it is precisely for these that the colonies are plundered by the imperialist countries. It is this economic looting of the colonies which is the cause of their underdevelopment.

Marable mistakenly equates underdevelopment with the economic, social and political inequality of Black people. Indeed, this business about Black people being underdeveloped is reactionary in substance in that it denies that Black people are an integral part of the United States, and that institutionalized racism consistently denies them their full citizenship rights. Ironically, it also obscures the fact that black workers are exploited by the capitalists.

FROM UNDERDEVELOPMENT TO "SOCIALISM"

Having characterized Black America as "underdeveloped," Marable goes on to address the question of how to overcome or "smash" underdevelopment. Now if we consistently applied the "living pyramid" model depicted earlier, then the general answer would have to be that we overcome underdevelopment through "independence." The struggle for Black liberation would have to be a struggle for "independence"—for separate development.

Marable, however, is everything but consistent. Though he states that Black people are a "unique national minority within the world's second most racist state," who have been "pressured to become dependent on white liberals and moderates to articulate their agendas," he utters not a word about how Blacks scattered in ghettos throughout the country would wage a struggle for independence. In fact, what he says is that there is no road to political independence because Blacks are forced into political coalitions with whites in order to affect government policy and, thereby, are trapped in alliances as dependent clients.

It is unique to be a colonized, underdeveloped people forced into dependency and yet totally incapable of waging a struggle for independence. Obviously, something is wrong with this logic, but Dr. Marable is undisturbed. He has an answer, albeit one that is as illogical and devoid of common sense as his thesis.

Marable thinks that a program for abolishing racist/capitalist underdevelopment must be based on an examination of the "historical foundations of underdevelopment" and "a vision of an alternative, noncapitalist development." In pursuing his "vision," he takes inspiration from W. E. B. Du Bois, whom he describes as "the most outstanding proponent of democracy, socialism and Black equality."

According to Marable, the Du Bois program was as follows:
1. The fight for Black liberation is the "realization of democracy for all."
2. No real democracy has ever existed in the United States inasmuch as state power has never been in the hands of the masses.
3. Therefore, a "new democracy" that is "biracial" and "antisexist" must be constructed, and such a democracy would be committed to eliminating poverty and unemployment, while using the "state apparatus" to insure civil liberties for all and popular education. To accomplish the "new democracy," a great alliance between people of color and the working class everywhere is necessary.
4. Socialism must become the central vision for Black liberation.
5. Socialism will be constructed by restoring the New Deal and a welfare state.

20

Of course, in laying out Du Bois's program Marable conveniently forgets that at the end of his life, Du Bois joined the Communist party, stating on that occasion:

> Today I have reached a firm conclusion: Capitalism cannot reform itself; it is doomed to self-destruction. No universal selfishness can bring social good to all. Communism—the effort to give all men what they need and to ask of each the best they can contribute—this is the only way of human life. . . . In the end communism will triumph. I want to help bring that day.[6]

Whether or not one shares Du Bois's "firm conclusion," to leave it out of account is a transparent sleight-of-hand maneuver by Marable, perpetrated to convey the false picture that his notion of Black people being an underdeveloped colony is somehow complemented by Du Bois's monumental scholarly and political contributions to the struggle for Black equality.

Moreover, Marable's final claim, that Du Bois's "theoretical conclusions" "form the basic point of view for *How Capitalism Underdeveloped Black America*," is just simply nonsense. Du Bois's views never came within a thousand miles of the idea that Black Americans have colonial status.

Marable's solution to Black oppression in the United States is democratic socialism based on worker self-management. It is time to put the issue of socialism on the table, says Marable, as if we have been waiting for him to arrive in shining theoretical armor to pose the question of socialism to the workers. But what do we do *now*—about unemployment, poverty, disease, crime, housing, the military budget, repression, and so on? How do we fight, whom do we fight, and to what end? To place socialism on the agenda as an immediate objective is no answer.

How Capitalism Underdeveloped Black America is an eclectic hodgepodge of conflicting viewpoints and political approaches to Black people's struggles. In style, it is more egotistical than polemical. Rife with militant breast-beating and slandering of Black leaders and mass organizations, it combines theoretical shallowness with intellectual arrogance in an exercise that contributes nothing but confusion to our present endeavors and quest.

Notes

1. Robert L. Heilbroner, *The Great Ascent: The Struggle for Economic Development in Our Time* (1963). Irving Louis Horowitz. *Three Worlds of Development* (1966).
2. Actually, "periphery" and "core" are euphemisms developed by modernization theorists as substitute terms for imperialist financial and industrial centers in Europe and North America and colonies in Asia, Africa, and Latin America.
3. Theotonio dos Santos. "The Structure of Dependence" in *American Economic Review* 60 (May 1970): 231.
4. See, e.g., Marshall Wolfe, "Developments: Images, Conceptions, Criteria: Agents Choices," in *Economic Bulletin for Latin America* 18 (1973): 2.
5. See Henry Winston, *Class, Race and Black Liberation* (New York: International Publishers 1977), pp. 115–131.
6. *Black Titan: W. E. B. Du Bois: An Anthology by the Editors of Freedomways* (Boston: Beacon Press 1970), p. 305.

CHAPTER 3

The Cultural Philosophy of Paul Robeson

Sterling Stuckey

"I suppose" Paul Robeson wrote in 1933, "I am the only black man in the world who does not want to be white." Whether Robeson exaggerated is not the point; the sentiment set him apart from most of his contemporaries and cut to the core of a major historical problem of black people, the desire of many to be shaped in the image of their oppressor. It has been that psychic aberration, a direct product of centuries of oppression at the hands of whites, which has militated, in concert with the very forces which produced it, against black people devising a more dynamic culture, that is, a more liberating way of life and a method of preserving it from generation to generation.

Though very few scholars are aware of it, few people in this country's history have taken as serious an interest in cultural questions as Robeson. The 1930s was the period of his most profound insights into the nature of the black past and present, the time of his deepest reflections on the state of world cultural groupings. His philosophy of culture was projected in that decade in a series of brilliant essays and in newspaper interviews. And it is his thought at that time that is under examination in this essay, the thesis of which is that Robeson penetrated to the foundations of black culture, exposed the chief dangers of the culture of the larger society and accurately identified the essential ingredients of world cultures, while calling for the synthesis that would save mankind.

Early in the decade, in one of his essays, Robeson identified important elements of character of the people who created black culture in America—"a people upon whom nature has bestowed, and in whom circumstances have developed, great emotional depth and spiritual intuition." The value dispensation of the Afro-American—especially as reflected in his religion and art constitutes, Robeson contended, the only significant American culture since the inception of the country. More than any other single factor, however, a deep sense of inferiority, nurtured by white America, prevented large numbers of black people from being aware of the greatness of their culture.

Addressing himself to the question of the Negro's feelings of inadequacy, Robeson wrote that the sufferings undergone by the Negro had "left an indelible mark" on his soul, had caused him to become the victim of an inferiority complex which leads him to imitate white people.

> [It] has been drummed into him that the white man is the Salt of the Earth and the Lord of Creation, and as a perfectly natural result his ambition is to become as nearly like a white man as possible.

"I am convinced," the young scholar wrote, "that in this direction there is neither fulfillment nor peace for the Negro."

Robeson described the American Negro as that "tragic creature, a man without a nationality." Though he might claim to be American, to be French, to be British, *"You cannot assume a nationality as you would a new suit of clothes"* (italics mine). So wrote Robeson in 1934. With notable courage and insight, he pursued this line of investigation, remarking that the assumption of African nationality is "an extremely complicated matter, fraught with the greatest importance to me and some millions of coloured folk." The inferiority complex of large numbers of black people had helped complicate the matter. Such self-laceration was buttressed by the belief that they "had nothing whatever in common with the inhabitants of Africa"—a view which was reinforced by American educators who, with rare exceptions, carried in their heads grotesque but comforting stereotypes of African peoples and their history. Though blacks in this country were a race without nationality, the effects of such a condition were, in Robeson's opinion, not immutable. But more than viewing Africa from afar would be required if the Negro were to secure some of the benefits of a nation in the absence of nationhood in the literal sense.

> In illustration of this take the parallel case of the Jews. They, like a vast proportion of Negroes, are a race without a nation; but, far from Palestine, they are indissolubly bound by their ancient religious practices—*which*

they recognize as such. I emphasize this in contradiction to the religious practices of the American Negro, which, from the snake-worship practiced in the deep south to the Christianity of the revival meeting; are patently survivals of the earliest African religions; *and he does not recognize them as such.* Their acknowledgement of *their common origin, species, interest, and attitudes binds Jew to Jew; a similar acknowledgement will bind Negro to Negro.* (last italics added)

Robeson set himself the task of seeking, through "patient inquiry," to lay the foundations on which a new awareness of black culture and tradition could be based. He would investigate a great many questions regarding Africa and America and hoped, by 1938, to have reached the peak of a campaign "to educate the Negro to a comsciousness of the greatness of his own heritage."

His "patient inquiry" had doubtless begun some years before, for he reported during the same year (1934) that he had already "penetrated to the core of African culture when I began to study the legendary traditions, folksongs and folklore of the West African Negro." Robeson's encounter with West Africa cultures, then, was no mere academic exercise; he said it had been "like a homecoming" for him. He wanted to interpret the "unpolluted" African folk song, to do for it what he had done for the Spiritual, to make it respected throughout the world; all of which, he hoped, would make it easier for blacks in America not only to appreciate this aspect of their heritage but to play a role in exploring the "uncharted musical material in that source." The researches of Robeson into the folklore of West Africa were aided by his proficiency in several languages of the area, languages which, he thought, had come easily to him "because their rhythm is the same as that employed by the American Negro in speaking English."

Afro-Americans during the 1930s were often as dreadfully uninformed about African languages as they were about other aspects of African culture. Robeson's findings in this regard were for this reason of special interest to these blacks who thought, as many did, that Africans communicated their ideas solely through gestures and sign language! Robeson concluded from his initial studies of African languages that Swahili, for all its impurities, was "constructed in the same way as that language which gave us the wonder of Chinese poetry." (He would later become proficient in Chinese.) But he was not satisfied to point up such analogies, however thrilling they may have been to American Negroes of the thirties: "As a first step" in dispelling the "regrettable and abysmal ignorance of the value of its own heritage in the Negro race itself," he decided to launch a comparative study of the main language groups, Indo-European, African, and Asian, "choosing two or three principal languages out of each, and indicate their comparative richness at a comparable stage of development."

> It may take five years to complete this work but I am convinced that the results will be adequate to form a concrete foundation for a movement to inspire confidence in the Negro in the value of his own past and future.

By 1935, Robeson was saying, in the context of a discussion of African and Asian ties, that "Negro students who wrestle vainly with Plato would find a spiritual father in Confucius or Lao-tze. . . ." His meaning on this point would become clearer as he, in later years, spelled out the salient cultural components of the East and West. Meanwhile, in addition to studying African linguistics and drawing conclusions which, though known to the few specialists in the field, were revelations to many, he had long since concluded that blacks in this country were under quite substantial African influences (a position that he would retain, like almost all of his cultural views of the thirties, for decades to come). The dances, songs, and religion of the black man in America, he wrote, were the same as those of his "cousins" centuries removed in the depths of Africa, "whom he has never seen, of whose very existence he is only dimly aware." Robeson added that the American Negro's "peculiar sense of rhythm," his "rhythm-consciousness," as it were, "would stamp him indelibly as African."

Thus Robeson joined Du Bois and Woodson before him in affirming African "survivals," probing deeply into the specific, irreducible components of African influence, contending that the American Negro is too radically different in mental and emotional structures from the white man "ever to be more than a spurious and uneasy imitation of him . . ." The emotive, intuitive and aesthetic qualities of the Afro-American not only linked him to the African homeland but to the West Indian black as well. "The American and West Indian Negro," he argued, "worships the Christian God in his own particular way and makes him the object of his supreme artistic manifestation which is embodied in the Negro spiritual." He realized what few scholars knew at the time, that there was such a thing as black religion in the Caribbean and in the United States. As to what gives rise to the ties between people of African ancestry, Robeson ventured that "It would take a psycho-anthropologist to give it a name."

The achievement of Robeson's scholarship on African "survivals" is all the more evident when one takes into account the extreme backwardness of America's colleges and universities, of "higher" education, vis-à-vis Africa and her descendants in diaspora. When the decade of the thirties opened, even the most progressive and advanced white thinkers in America, scholars such as Franz Boas and Ruth Benedict, had not realized the role Africa was playing in helping to fashion the black ethos in America. Advocates of the "culturally stripped" thesis, Boaz and Benedict were joined by the Chicago School of Sociology, which was an influential promoter of the "tangle of pathology" view of black culture. But unlike Boaz and Benedict, almost all of the remaining intellectuals were unaware of the role of Africa in world history.

Apart from Melville Herskovits later in the decade, few indeed were the white scholars who were even close to understanding the continuing impact of Africa on blacks in this country. While one might quarrel with certain particulars of Robeson's position on African influences on the black experience in America, with the extent to which, for example, he ascribes African attributes to our dance and song, his views here, though doubtless somewhat overstated, now appear to be, on balance, more persuasive than ever. Recent researches into comparative African and Afro-American dance and song styles, especially the work of Alan Lomax, in the main support Robeson's findings of more than thirty years ago. (When his thinking on African influences has been more thoroughly researched, there is reason to believe that he will move to the fore as perhaps the most significant contributor to Negritude theory to come out of America.)

Since the rehabilitation of Africa was central to his campaign to heighten the consciousness of American Negroes, he had to confront the fundamental issue of the nature of black African history while continuing his investigation into various aspects of contemporary African cultures. The schools of the West, especially in the United States, stressing African backwardness, made these concerns inescapable for Robeson. He asserted in fact that the younger generation of Negroes looks toward Africa and wants to know what is *there* to interest them; they want to know, he added, what Africa has to offer that the West cannot provide.

> At first glance the question seems unanswerable. He sees only the savagery, devil-worship, witch doctors, voodoo, ignorance, squalor, and darkness taught in American schools. *Where these exist, he is looking at the broken remnants of what was in its day a mighty thing; something which perhaps has not been destroyed but only driven underground, leaving ugly scars upon the earth's surface to mark the place of its ultimate reappearance.* (italics added)

Still, much that was impressive was not hidden, certainly not from Robeson. In his writings, he called attention to the supreme artistry of West African sculpture, which had inspired leading European artists; hailed West African bronzes, which bore striking similarities to the finest examples of Javanese, Chinese, and Mexican art; recognized the intricacies of African musical rhythms, which were far more complex than anything attained by a Western composer; stressed the flexibility and sophistication of African languages, which could convey subtleties of thought far beyond what was suspected by those unacquainted with African linguistics; and emphasized the rich spiritual heritage of Africa, which is also associated with the great civilizations of the East.

As comprehensive and painstaking as his inquiry was (he had learned east coast languages, including Swahili and the Bantu group, and proceeded to learn several West African languages), convincing black Americans that what they had been taught about Africa was false would very likely prove to be more difficult than persuading them that their people had made important cultural contributions while in America. Robeson intimated that the more privileged, the better "educated," young blacks were less favorably disposed to revising their prejudices regarding their heritage than the great mass of older blacks.

> I found a special eagerness among the younger and, I am sorry to say, the more intelligent Negroes, to dismiss the Spiritual as something beneath their new pride in their race. It is as if they wanted to put it behind them as something to be ashamed of—something that tied them to a past in which their forefathers were slaves.

Those blacks who turned their backs on this folk music were, whether they realized it or not, contributing to their own destruction, for the

28

Spirituals were, in Robeson's view, "the soul of the race made manifest." This position was integrally related to his deep concern about the black artist giving emphasis to the art "of other people in our Negro programs, magnificent and masterly though they may be." He felt that concessions to European music would lead to the "eventual obliteration of our own folk music, the musical idioms of our race . . . the finest expression and the loftiest we have to offer."

Robeson, realizing the potentially fatal consequences of the failure of sizable numbers of black intellectuals (and others) to appreciate their folk heritage, had posited in an interview in 1931 that if black musical groups did not "arise all over the land to cherish and develop our old spirituals," blacks would have to leave the country and "go to Africa, where we can develop independently and bring forth a new music based on our roots."

Robeson's interest in cultural independence for blacks grew out of a deeply felt belief that the black man in America must be in a position "to set his own standards," which was "the pressing need." Urgent because American whites, generally closer than blacks to Europeans in life styles, were dangerously, perhaps fatally entrapped by European dependence upon abstractions and hostility toward emotive and intuitive values.

In 1936, Robeson described a critical problem of the West, one with dire implications for the whole of mankind—"the cost of developing the kind of mind by which the discoveries of science were made has been one which now threatens the discoverer's very life." In fact, he argued, Western man appears to have gained greater powers of abstraction "at the expense of his creative faculties."

> But because one does not want to follow Western thought into this dilemma, one none the less recognizes the value of its achievements. One would not have the world discount them and retrogress in terror to a primitive state. It is simply that one recoils from the Western intellectual's idea that, having got himself on to this peak overhanging an abyss, he should want to drag all other people—on pain of being dubbed inferior if they refuse—up after him into the same precarious position.

"That, in a sentence," wrote Robeson, "is my case against Western values."

So it was simply that America was uncongenial to meaningful, creative living; the Western world as a whole seemed, short of very drastic changes, an unlikely place in which new forms of freedom, a new humanity, could develop. The West had gone astray as far back as the time of the Renaissance, if not before:

> A blind groping after Rationality resulted in an incalculable loss in pure Spirituality. Mankind placed a sudden dependence on that part of his mind that was brain, intellect, to the discountenance of that part that was sheer evolved instinct and intuition; we grasped at the shadow and lost the substance and now we are not altogether clear what the substance was.

Having identified the main weaknesses of the West, Robeson asserted that the person who embraced Western values completely would, in time, find his creative faculties stunted and warped, would become almost wholly dependent on external gratification. Becoming frustrated in this direction, neurotic symptoms develop, and it is borne in upon the victim that life is not worth living. In chronic cases he might seek to take his life. "This is a severe price," said Robeson, "to pay even for such achievements as those of Western science."

As one reads Robeson's brief against Western values, it is evident that he does not place great faith in the ability of Western man, left to his own devices, to halt his momentum and pull back from the precipice. He provides an index into the depth of the European disorder by drawing our attention to the fact that as abstract intellectualism became enthroned in Europe the artistic achievements of that section of the world declined steadily. He found in European art "an output of self-conscious, uninspired productions" which people of discriminating taste recognize as "lifeless imitations" rather than "the living pulsing thing." This malady was not confined to the small minority described as artists, "but unfortunately what shows amongst these is only a symptom of a sickness that to some extent is affecting almost every stratum of the Western world."

The relationship of the artist to society was of major concern to Robeson, and the position he took is but one more illustration of his special angle of vision: "The whole problem of living can never be understood until the world recognizes that artists are not a race apart." Artists, Robeson added, do not have potentialities unknown to large numbers of other human beings, for creativity means more than the ability to make music, to paint, and to write. Each man has something of the artist in him; if this is uprooted "he becomes suicidal and dies."

Robeson contended that, given the opportunities for creative development, very large numbers of people could contribute to the sum of the artistic and spiritual achievements of a given society. He posited an organic tie between artist and society—a reciprocity of interests—that is distinctly non-Western.

Robeson remarked in 1936 that it has been a boon to the American Negro that he has managed, despite his presence in the white man's deadly spiritual world, and despite centuries of oppression, to retain a world view that is still largely non-Western, predicated on sensibilities similar to those of his African ancestors and to those people who live in cultures which place a higher priority on concrete symbols than upon abstractions:

> For it is not only the African Negro, and so-called primitive peoples, who think in concrete symbols—all the great civilizations of the East (with possibly the exception of India) have been built up by people with this type of mind. It is a mentality that has given us giants like Confucius, Mencius, and Lao-tze. More than likely it was this kind of thinking that gave us the understanding and wisdom of a person like Jesus Christ. It has given us the wonders of Central American architecture and Chinese art. It has, in fact, given us the full flower of all the highest possibilities in man—with the single exception of applied science. That was left to a section of Western man to achieve and on that he bases his assertion of superiority.

The American Negro's great asset, then, is his "immense emotional capacity," though, Robeson added, emotive powers are at a discount in the West. His capacity for feeling, his intuitive and aesthetic gifts, with the proper guidance, might achieve wonders. His attainments in America to date, as impressive as they are in their own right, are merely sterile compared to what they might be in the future. Robeson thereby made it clear that blacks should not glory in their gifts. Indeed he warned the American black against "further isolating himself," pointing out that it was not only useful but necessary from a social and economic standpoint for the Negro to understand Western culture and ideas. He again placed science in perspective: "Now I am not going to try to belittle the achievements of science. Only a fool would deny that the man who holds the secrets of those holds the key position in the world."

Robeson did not subscribe to the view that cultural traits are inherited in the genes. Conceding that many blacks in America had become "pure intellectuals," he questioned whether they would allow themselves to proceed all the way down "this dangerous by-way when, without sacrificing the sound base in which they have their roots, they can avail themselves of the now-materialized triumphs of science and proceed to use them while retaining the vital creative side." This creative dimension, according to Robeson, had made possible the Afro-American's artistic and spiritual achievements. His description of the causes of the cultural strengths of blacks may well be the best on record:

> Now, as to the most important part which . . . the Negro is qualified to play in the American scene, I would define it as "cultural," with emphasis upon the spiritual aspect of that culture. With the passing of the Indians, the Negroes are the most truly indigenous stock in North America. They have grown up with the country, becoming part of the soil itself. They have had a better chance than any other of the races which have come to America to identify themselves with the atmosphere of the place, if only because they have been there much longer. They have been unhappy and badly treated, but they have retained (though they have not been allowed fully to express) their best and most characteristic qualities: a deep simplicity, a sense of mystery, a capacity for religious feeling, a spontaneous and entirely individual cheerfulness; and these have found expression in the only culture which Americans can point to as truly belonging to their country.

In fact, the young philosopher observed, the whole of American culture was deriving from black culture "those qualities which appeal most directly to the intelligent European who values a depth of native tradition in art." Despite the long period of repression which the black man's "cultural actualities" and "potentialities" have survived, "they can develop only with great difficulty in a hostile environment." The uncongenial hostile American environment constituted the "new Egypt" out of which Robeson wanted to lead his people "into a new promised land." That land, as we have seen, need not be Africa, provided blacks would move en masse to gather together and build upon the foundation stones of their culture, the folk heritage which was an amalgam of African and American elements. But blacks in this country would have a better chance of finding the new ground if they cultivated those qualities in their culture which tie them to the East and to Africa. (It is especially notable that some of our leading jazz musicians have, over the past decade, turned increasingly to the East for artistic inspiration.) While the Negro "must take his technology from the West," Robeson observed, "instead of coming to the Sorbonne or Oxford, I would like to see Negro students go to Palestine and Peking." He added that he "would like to watch the flowering of their inherent qualities under sympathetic influences there."

A crucial objective of the cultural transformation would be that of a man mastering the emotional and intellectual dimensions of his personality. When he has learned "to be true to himself the Negro as much as any man" would contribute to the new cultural order. But Robeson, once again, had a special warning for blacks: "unless the African Negro (including his far-flung collaterals) bestirs himself and comes to a realization of his potentialities and obligations there will be no culture for him to contribute." In Robeson's terms, potentialities had to be developed into actualities that would tighten the bonds between blacks, especially in America. Without moving closer to nationality, to making more effective use of the attributes of a nation, they could scarcely make the leap onto the international plane to help effect the needed cultural transformation. And nations contributing to the new cultural dispensation would be answering the demands of a world-necessity which would lead in time, Robeson hoped, "to the 'family of nations' ideal."

As essential as he felt the elements of nationalism to be, Robeson realized the limitations of the nation, that the "family of nations" ideal must become the eventual reality if mankind is to survive. He wanted, in the final analysis, to see a world striving for deep spiritual and cultural values which transcend "narrow national, racial, or religious boundaries." With the right encouragement, *that* impulse, he felt, could come from blacks in America. Still, black people should share in the new world culture *as Africans*—a goal to be worked for, not willed.

A decade before the appearance of F. S. C. Northrop's important *The Meeting of East and West,* Robeson had systematized his thinking on the need for creative equilibrium between the spiritual and the material, between a life of *intuition and feeling* and one of *logical analysis.* In a word, he had called for a synthesis of the cultures of the East and West.

When Robeson turned to America he saw the worst qualities of Europe in magnified form. Having devoted years of research and reflection to identifying life styles peculiar to people on the major continents of the world, he placed white America in this broad cultural setting and found her wanting. Apart from technology (which because of its capitalistic guidance was not being used humanely), Robeson saw very little of value in white America.

> The modern white American is a member of the lowest form of civilization in the world today. My problem is not to counteract his prejudice against the Negro . . . that does not matter. What I have set myself to do is to educate my brother the Negro to believe in himself . . . We are a great race, greater in tradition and culture than the American race. Why should we copy something that is inferior.

Black liberation in such a country would not be achieved through the NAACP's emphasis on racial cooperation. Many Afro-Americans, he argued, would have to fight and die for their freedom. "Our freedom is going to cost so many lives," he remarked, "that we mustn't talk about the Scottsboro case as one of sacrifice." He continued: "When we talk of freedom we don't discuss lives." His realization that, given the objective conditions, black people might have to resort to violence before achieving their freedom was by no means the only, or even the most significant, example of his prophetic insight. With awesome precision he predicted that if Negroes persisted in efforts "to be like the white man within the next generation they will destroy themselves." Developments over the past thirty years make it eminently clear that this instance of cultural analysis and prognostication is of a very high order indeed.

Robeson said that he would, as part of his effort to convince "my poor people that their culture traces back to . . . great civilizations," make films, produce plays, sing chants, and prayers. He also expressed a desire "to play the great black emperor Mcnclik." Again reflecting on the black man's feelings of inferiority he said that he would "do anything to convince my people that they are great."

> Meanwhile in my music, my plays, my films I want to carry always this central idea: to be African. Multitudes of men have died for less worthy ideas; it is even more eminently worth living for.

This is not the place for attempting to determine precisely the extent to which Robeson helped his people realize their greatness. Yet, it is possible to draw certain conclusions on the basis of what we now know about the man during the thirties. If he had not convinced, through his incredible array of gifts, the majority of his people of the greatness of Africa, he had by 1938 shown scores of thousands of them what genius is possible for one of African ancestry. Black people could look at his example and not find another in the entire world to equal it for wide-ranging brilliance. If the race pride of some was heightened by his achievements as singer and actor in the thirties, then he brought them that much closer to believing in the possibility of the greatness of the African past, of an African return to greatness.

Had more black people read his essays and interviews of the period, his influence would have been greater still, for he would then have illumined, for them, various aspects of their culture and heritage in America and on the African continent. But since his essays and interviews contain the theoretical basis for the unity which must be built, the political implications of his scholarship, as his cultural philosophy becomes more widely known, should be perceived before long by relatively large numbers of black people.

Though we need to know more about Robeson's scholarship, we already know that his command of African linguistics, art history, folklore, and music appears to have been incomparable. Moreover, the degree to which he had, by the thirties, grasped the fundamental dynamics of world cultural groupings is especially worth pondering. This expansive knowledge, coupled with his own deep and multifaceted involvement in the arts, provided an extraordinary background for analyzing and understanding the vital components of black and white culture in America. His writings on culture, incontestably "nationalistic" in many respects, finally went beyond nationalism when he posited the preconditions for the world cultural revolution—the proper balancing of the emotional and rational, under some form of socialism, in order to avert the plunge over the precipice into the abyss of chaos and death; in order to give new, more creative life to the whole of mankind. The quest for nationality, to state the matter differently, was for Robeson a prerequisite for blacks in this country having something of truly lasting worth to offer to the world community.

On the basis of what is now known about Robeson's scholarship, it seems not unreasonable to advance the view that he has easily earned a place high on that select list of major commentators on American culture, a list which includes W. E. B. Du Bois, Sterling

Brown, Constance Rourke, F. S. C. Northrop, Ralph Ellison, and Melville Herskovits. Before long, it should not be possible to conduct a serious discussion of black culture or to relate American culture to the main value systems of the world, without giving respectful attention to the cultural philosophy of Robeson. There is much irony here, for his most enduring and profound influence, despite all of the efforts to silence the man and to blot his example from our minds, will very likely be a result of his heretofore largely unknown intellectual achievements.

CHAPTER 4

Black Nationalism and Pan-Africanism: A Social Study of African Americans Participation in United States Foreign Policy Towards Africa

James L. Conyers, Jr.

INTRODUCTION

This study seeks to examine the development of movements for self-defemination in African America and provide an analysis of various nationalistic conceptual frameworks in the disapora and on the continent. In general, the term *black nationalism* refers to an ideological repertoire, one that attempts to describe and evaluate the social, political, religious, cultural, and economic conditions of African Americans. Simultaneously, while examining multiple articulations of nationalists' schools of thought, the central aim and objective of this essay is to study methodologies, which provide an alternative analysis for examining social, economic, and political conditions of African Americans—and drawing parallels and comparisons with black life, history, and culture throughout the diaspora.

Equally important, the concept of Pan-Africanism provides a macrostructural analysis of black nationalism. Moreover, there are two basic functions of Pan-Africanism: 1) global—the focus on the unification of Africans throughout the diaspora; and 2) continental—the focus on the unification of Africans on the continent. Simply put, within this study, the structure and format lends itself to employing global Pan-Africanism, in the way of examining African Americans participation in United States and Africa foreign policy. Furthermore, this study attempts to survey the competing ideologies within the intellectual tradition of black nationalism and Pan-Africanism, in the way of raising query and seeking an alternative epistemology to study Africana history, culture, and ethos.

The focus of this essay is to examine the general concept of black nationalism and Pan-Africanism, in the organizational structure of a social study, with specific emphasis on African American participation in United States foreign policy towards Africa. Ronald Walters addresses the relativity of this issue, this way:

> Examining the force of Pan-Africanism as it exists in the African Diaspora, one understands that the African-American community has been a dynamic element in generating movement toward a world-wide African unity. With the rise of African nationalism and its driving force, ridding the continent of colonialism and establishing new nation states, an inevitable tension developed regarding the definition and function of the new Pan-Africanism. Was it meant only for those in African states? Did it extend only to Black Africans? (1993: 54)

This commentary is supported by Elliot Skinner's analysis:

> White Americans tried to frustrate any solidarity between Africans in the diaspora and those on the continent for a radical improvement of status of Afro-Americans. A number of self-proclaimed white specialists on Africans and Afro-Americans tried to reassure their fellows that there was not a real relationship between Afro-Americans and Africa. One published an article in which he wondered whether, in view of the cultural conflicts that often arose between Afro-Americans and Africans, the two groups could be said to have anything in common. He conveniently forgot that other American ethnic groups often had similar problems with people in the lands of their origin. Another writer cautioned Americans in general against taking too seriously a linkage or alliance between Africans and Afro-Americans. He asserted that the relations between Africans and Americans had always been poor and that an attempt to see a relationship between the two groups could be dangerous for all concerned—the usually discontented or disenchanted Negro, the natives [sic], and the United States. (1993: 34)

A critical query point raised in this study is: what can African Americans do, in order for the United States to establish effective foreign policy relations with Africa? One problem that hinders African American participation in the U.S./African political affairs, is the daily racism encountered by blacks on a domestic level. Nevertheless, counter to oppressive forces, African Americans have consistently agitated for enforcement, dialogue, and effective articulation of foreign policy with Africa. V. O. Key points out, "that a new group may have to fight for reorientation of the many values of old order" (Storing 1970: 149).

Moreover, the United States prior investments in South Africa, created for reaching repercussions as an international problem in the African diasporic community. This essay seeks to conduct a macrostudy examining African Americans participation and involvement concerning the United States foreign policies with African nations from a macrosociological study.

THEORY, DESIGN, AND METHODOLOGY

The theoretical paradigm employed in this study is the Ujima theory. *Ujima* is a Kiswahili term that means: collective work and responsibility. Within the context of this study, variables such as culture, ecology, and cosmology will be used to describe and evaluate African Americans participation, in United States and Africa foreign policy.

The research design employed in this study is secondary analysis, with an emphasis on content analysis, examining thematic schemes of: an historical overview of Pan-Africanist social and political thought; civil rights and Pan-Africanism; review of selected African American leadership—Andrew Young and Jesse Jackson; analysis of United States and Africa foreign policy relations; overview of African American political organizations, and concluding with offering an alternative epistemology, in fostering effective African American participation in the United States and African foreign policy relations. The methodology leads itself to using secondary sources and providing critical analysis, therefore, the methodology articulated in this study is qualitative.

HISTORICAL OVERVIEW

Historically, African Americans have illustrated a consistent pattern of demonstrating interest and participation in the United States foreign policy with Africa. During the 1800s, blacks such as Henry M. Turner and Martin Delaney were key advocates endorsing emigration to Africa. Both of these men played an important role in the establishment of the nation-state Liberia. Raymond Hall describes Liberia's sojourn to the black American experience, stating: "Established in 1822 as a colony for black repatriation and emigration by urging of the American Colonization Society in the minds of free blacks and slaves, it represented instance of black men controlling their own affairs through their own governments" (1978).

Table 1.1 provides a listing of precursors and pioneers in the development of the Black Nationalist, Africana Womanist, and Pan-Africanist school of thought.

Presently, the United States has financial investments, military bases, and political influence in Liberia. Paradoxically, the establishment of this colony presented the idea of cultural automony. Consequently, in contemporary times, this nation-state functions as a colony, in which American lobbyists are particularly concerned with protecting the economic interests of U.S. corporations.

In the 1960s, African American political and civil rights leaders became concerned and involved over African political foreign policy with America. Equally important, two men such as Malcolm X and Martin Luther King, Jr., are often not recognized for their international involvement and sensitivity towards the U.S. foreign policy with Africa. Walters discusses Malcolm X's participation and effectiveness in U.S. and African foreign policy, in the following manner:

> A factor which helped to cut through the confusion and tension produced by the "groping" to understand these intersecting histories was the clarity of Malcolm X. In the Spring of 1964, Malcolm X went to Mecca and on his way back to the United States stopped in several African countries, among them Nigeria and Ghana. His remarks at Ibadan University in Nigeria showed that Malcolm possessed an advanced conceptualization of Pan-Africanism, not only in its philosophical dimension, but in a political sense as well. (1993: 57)

As an aside, there is a consistent pattern which illustrates, that whenever African Americans rhetorically and actively express reservations about the subordination and dehumanization of African people throughout the diaspora, somehow they are labeled and scorned as being anti-American.

Table 1.1

Intellectual Tradition of Black Nationalist and Pan-Africanist School of Thought

Name DOB	IR	Commentary
Martin R. Delany 1812–1885	Black Nationalist	Mystery, first black newspaper west of the Alleghenies; also published essay titled, "The Condition, Elevation, Emigration, and Destiny of the Colored People of the United States."
Maria W. Stewart 1803–1879	African Womanist	Womens' rights activist; consistently spoke and advocated the rights of Africana people throughout the diaspora; queried the injustices that confronted black people domestically and abroad.
Henry M. Turner 1833–1915	Black Nationalist Pan-Africanist	Urged African Americans to repatriate to Africa in order to become self-sufficient and establish collective group autonomy
Alexander Crummell 1819–1898	Black Nationalist	One of the founding members of the American Negro Academy; consistently focused intellectual discussions on black cooperative advancement.
Edward W. Blyden 1832–1912	Black Nationalist	Focused on Africa American self-development; used the black church as an instrument for social change.
Mary C. Terrell 1863–1954	African Womanist	First African American woman to serve on the Washington, DC, Board of Education; founding member of tho National Association of Colored Women; and became the organization's first president in 1896.
W. E. B. Du Bois 1868–1963	Pan-Africanist	Early studies focused on integration of African Americans; later studies emphasized the need for a global Pan-Africanist perspective.
Noble Drew Ali 1886–1929	Religious Nationalist	Teachings focused on African Americans being the descendants of the Moabites from Morocco; these teachings were influential to the developmental stages of the UNIA and the Nation of Islam.

continued

Table 1.1 *(Continued)*

Name DOB	IR	Commentary
Marcus M. Garvey 1887–1940	Black Nationalist	Emphasis of teachings focused on African American development; also addressed the issue of cultural, economic, and social aspects of nationalism.
Elijah Muhammad 1897–1975	Black Nationalist	Leader of the Nation of Islam; teachings focused on economic and religious nationalism; established one of the leading African American organizations and business development enterprises in the United States.
Albert B. Cleage, Jr. 1913–	Religious Nationalist Black Nationalist Pan-Africanist	Teachings focused on Black Christian Nationalism; later teachings placed emphasis on cultural nationalism, examining issues outside the boundaries of the United States.
Malcom X Shabazz 1925–1965	Black Nationalist Pan-Africanist	Earlier teachings and message focused on using religion as a critical tool of analysis to describe and evaluate the subordination of African Americans; second resurrection teachings focused more on orthodox Islam and cultural nationalism on a global perspective.
Martin L. King, Jr. 1929–1968	Religious Nationalist International Liberal Democrat	Earlier teachings and message focused on using religion in a nationalist method, as a tool of analysis to promote social change; later teachings and philosophy focused more on the social inequality of poor people throughout the world.

Scale: DOB=Date of Birth; IR=Ideological Repertoire.
Source: Jessie Carnie Smith (1994). *Black Firsts*. Detroit, MI: Visible Ink Press.

Ironically, this political name calling is the case when we examine the final years of Malcolm X and Martin L. King's lives. Both men fervently critiqued U.S. foreign policy relations with African nations; particularly at a time when African nations were obtaining their independence. Another strategy of labeling radical black leadership is to infer that they are agitating socialism. King and Malcolm were both accused of being socialists. As an aside, during the early 1980s, this tactic was used against Congressman Ron Dellums—the rationale was because he refused to condemn the Soviet Union for shooting down a South Korean airliner. As a result, Dellums was unofficially classified as a communist.

African American leaders such as Martin Delaney, Alexander Crummell, Martin Luther King, Jr., Malcolm X, W. E. B. Du Bois, and Marcus Garvey collaborated with African political representatives, regardless of domestic pressure, to promote effective U.S. foreign policy with African nations. Perhaps, the query regarding whether or not institutional and individual racism are variables that marginalize African Americans participation in the United States foreign policy relation with African nations is relative.

Yet, Charles V. Hamilton provides a black neoconservative perspective by documenting how African Americans have made tremendous impact on domestic and international social issues, as they apply to "fairness and equality of policy implementation." Again, the concept of culture is underscored in this analysis, and greater emphasis is placed on class-bourgeoisie stratification. Hamilton's two books, *Black Power* and *The Black American Experience,* are significant contributions that critically examine African Americans participation in domestic and international politics; he demonstrates the perplexity of the systematic, subordination of blacks and how the United States conducts business with continental and diasporan Africans. He points out in *Black Power* that during the Pan-Africanist movement of the early 1920s the bond of solidarity became stronger between African Americans and continental Africans. On the other hand, Charles P. Henry, notes that too much attention has focused on African American leadership styles rather than ideology:

> Any review of the existing literature on Afro-American political thought is necessarily brief. Although the volume of material concerning Afro-American political behavior is vast, the authors of these works have generally concerned themselves with socialization, leadership, organizations, or public policy. These few devoting any attention to ideology have focused on differences between black beliefs—invariably at the elite level (e.g., Du Bois' double consciousness)—or stressed that black political thought, like black culture, is derivative from the dominant ideology. (1990: 3)

Overall, his analysis is keen; although, his conceptualization of content, addresses the issue of ideology and behavior, whereas, the variables of cosmology and epistemology, are structured and perceived through an interpretative analysis. Simply put, Henry does not address the concept of interpretative analysis with culture, but moves to discuss the formation of ideology. Paradoxically, the cultural component, through content, is critical in identifying the diversity among various cultural groups differs, regarding their axiological base to synthesize memory, ethos, history, mythology, and motif.

Of course, the presence of an estimated thirty million diasporan Africans could lead one to believe, that continental and diasporan Africans forge ties of a global Pan-Africanist perspective on social, political, and economic issues is essential. During the early 1900s, Marcus Garvey discussed the importance of the Pan-African connection in this way:

> The masses of Negroes in America, the West Indies, South and Central America are in sympathetic accord with the aspirations of the native Africans. We desire to help them build up Africa as a Negro empire, where every black man, whether he was born in Africa or the Western world, will have the opportunity to develop on his own lines under the protection of the most favorable democratic institutions. It will be useless, as before stated, for bombastic Negroes to leave America and the West Indies to go to Africa, thinking that they will have privileged positions to inflict upon the race that bastard aristocracy that they have tried to maintain in this Western world at the expense of the masses. Africa shall develop an aristocracy of its own, but it shall be based upon service and loyalty to race. Let all Negroes work toward that end. (1995: 139)

In addition, Ronald Walters states: ". . . the Pan-African analytical approach is an associated Black Studies methodology in that it recognizes the dominant influence of the racial variable within the context of domestic relations, while the Pan-African method recognizes the dominant influence of African identity, history, and culture in the transactional relations of African-origin peoples in the Disapora" (1993: 46).

CIVIL RIGHTS AND PAN-AFRICANISM

The civil rights movement witnessed a cultural connection between African Americans and continental Africans. Some contemporary

44

scholars contend this spiritual and cultural connection came about for two general reasons: 1) the global Pan-Africanist cultural consciousness awakening of African Americans, reaffirming their ancestral ties with continental Africa; and 2) the assertive posture of African nations gaining their independence, through employing nationalistic ideologies of Pan-Africanism, to promote nationhood and cultural autonomy. Walters states:

> What exacerbated the attempt of those on the continent to define Pan-Africanism in terms of the quest for *intra*continental unity based on nations was the rejuvenation of what St. Clair Drake calls "racial Pan-Africanism" in the United States and around the world through the Black Power movement. In this chapter, these developments will be discussed in order to explore relevant aspects of Pan-Africanism as they exist in a nonAfrican country and within an African-origin community. (1993: 46)

Moreover, there were political representatives who voiced a global Pan-Africanist network. Again, the independence of African nations implied that, representatives and heads-of-state, sought alternative socioeconomic philosophies, rather than submit to a dialectic of an either/or controversy and employ a free-market economy based on a capitalist structure. Unequivocally, American diplomats envisioned a pattern of political-theory flourishing throughout the continent of Africa. Skinner notes:

> The independence of Ghana did revolutionize the rethinking of the Afro-Americans about themselves and about their place in America. Ordinary Afro-Americans, seeing toga-clad Ghanaians speaking before the United Nations and being received at the White House, started to reevaluate their relationships to Africa and took great pride in its new status. Then, as more and more African states gained independence, Afro-Americans simultaneously increased their interest in Africa and fought harder for full equality in America. (1993: 33)

Simply put, the independence of African nations in the 1950s and 1960s, sparked the United States to become more pragmatic in their efforts to improve foreign policy relations toward African nations.

In 1971, Charles Diggs headed the African Committee in Congress. However, as a result of the United States supporting the Portuguese military, in the way of distributing economic aid, and extending the Axores treaty, Diggs immediately resigned from his position in Congress (Ekepebu 1980: 111). He justified his resignation by stating he would not take part in, "U.S. contributions to wars against black people" (1980: 111). Congressman Diggs' assistant was Randall Robinson. Robinson is now carrying the banner of justice, advocating a global Pan-Africanist perspective. Presently, he is a lobbyist and executive secretary of Trans-Africa (*Black Enterprise* 1981: 38). He is also an advocate for progressive United States foreign policy towards Africa. In addition, he played an important role in getting the United States government to abolish trade sanctions against Rhodesia and played a key force in the United States and Haiti foreign policy relations (1981: 38). Equally important, two selected African Americans who have played an important role in the United States and African foreign relations have been Andrew Young and Jesse Jackson.

SELECTED BLACK LEADERSHIP

Andrew Young

Andrew Young played an important role in drawing international attention to the United States foreign policy with Africa. He consistently agitated that active engagement in South Africa would have a detrimental impact on current United States foreign policy relations with Africa. Furthermore, he openly criticized American economic investments in South Africa. When Young served in the Carter administration, he sought to establish substantive political ties with African leaders: he was one of the few consistent activists on this issue within the Carter administration. Still, throughout his political career, he endorsed the proposal of African Americans establishing a black foreign constituency. Young cites the effectiveness of this constituency by stating: "The first of these has been the emergence since 1975 of a new constituency for United States and African affairs in the United States; born from a merger of civil rights organizations, young black professionals, church groups, some labor unions, college students, and groups which had opposed United States involvement in the Vietnam War" (1980–1981: 651).

Even more important he advocated that the United States government not support participation of foreign policy ties with the South African apartheid regime: he concurred that, these political, economic, and social relationships could have far reaching repercussions. Young's major contention focused on the United States' apathy towards African Americans, and their cultural linkages to Africa.

To support this idea further, he abstained on controversial issues such as the Cubans occupation in Angola. Also, Young took a position of making a comparative analysis between the rights of U.S. political prisoners and third world countries. Unfortunately, when Young met with a Palestine Liberation Organization representative, this was considered extremely controversial and queried his moral and ethical patriotism. Consequently, because of the position he took on this issue, he was labeled, ostracized, and eventually coerced from his ambassador position in the Carter administration. Haki Madhubuti notes, "there were enough power brokers in and out of the federal government crying for Andrew Young's head" (1976: 6). What is to be learned from the short but distinguished ambassadorship of Andrew Young? One could readily argue that his decline and absence in international politics created a shift, providing a contextual analysis of African Americans' participation in global politics and foreign affairs.

Jesse Jackson

The Reverend Jesse Jackson's 1984 and 1988 campaigns for the Democratic presidential nomination were pseudopragmatic steps in developing stronger ties between African Americans and continental Africans. Even so, Charles P. Henry notes, "When Jesse Jackson announced his candidacy for president in 1984, the Reverend Benjamin F. Chavis, deputy director of the Commission for Racial Justice of the United Church of Christ, immediately identified his speech as 'liberation theology'" (1994: 88). Unquestionably, he motivated African Americans to become politically conscious of: power, economics, cooperative politics, and voter registration.

Apparently, the objective of these campaigns was to advance African Americans to become politically astute and to articulate how the aforementioned variables function and operate within the political structure of the United States. In fact, Henry cites that African American turnout increased from 8.3 million in 1980 to 10.3 million in 1984 (1994:88). Hypothetically, once African Americans became politically conscious, perhaps they would develop a prism of inter- pretative analysis to address United States foreign policy relations with African nations; whereas, one moves off the domestic and inter- national periphery of political affairs to the core of world political power. Admittedly, my bias and view of Jackson's campaigns is that because of his dismissal of culture relativity and underscoring the ne- cessity of a global Pan-Africanist consciousness, his campaigns are recorded in Americana history and letters as coalition politics; how- ever, he had no alternative ideological repertoire for African Ameri- cans to maintain against the Republican conservativism of the 1980s.

Nevertheless, Rev. Jackson and the National Association for the Advancement of Colored People (NAACP) have fought legal battles denouncing the United States investments in South Africa. He has consistently advocated that the American government disband South African/U.S. economic trade relations. In particular, the NAACP has lobbyist groups in Washington, DC, protesting against the neocolo- nialist regimes in Nigeria, Burundi, Rwanda, and the Sudan (Joyce 1984: 1).

Jackson's political philosophy revolves around an idealistic Rain- bow Coalition. Unfortunately, the development of coalition politics fo- cuses on short-term goals, whereas an alliance has overlapped with coalitions and focuses on long-term strategies and objectives. Indeed, alliances provide major implications for developing an epistemologi- cal grid when interpreting effective United States and African foreign policy relations. Admittedly, Jackson has been effective with coalition politics in the way of registering large numbers of African Americans to vote in secondary and primary elections. Generally speaking, strat- egy of coalition politics adds to the political consciousness of blacks. Perhaps, this acquired consciousness could bring about African Americans taking positions in U.S./African foreign diplomacy.

Addressing the issue of coalition politics and voter registration further, Diane Pinderhughes surveyed the effectiveness of voter reg- istration seeking to examine if African Americans develop a con- stituent relationship with nations in Africa. Her findings present a context of illustration, focusing on how African Americans in the north and south benefitted from black officials elected into offices (Cotter 1979: 11). Relative to Jackson's impact and participation in global politics; a critical theme of emphasis is that black voter registration enhanced African American political activism and representation in domestic and international politics. Even more important is the commonality in the school of political thought between Jackson and Young—both men advocated the concept for the establishment of a black foreign policy constituency.

Moreover, Jesse Jackson's 1984 trip to Damascus seeking to free Lt. Robert Goodman illustrated his political impact and participation of African Americans in international politics. He described his trip to Damascus as a "moral and humanitarian mission" (Anekwe 1984: 19). Consequently, because Jackson extended his political ideas outside the United States, several of his countrymen rebuked him (Joyce 1984: B–6). Thomas Todd, former chairman of Operation Push, commented on the hideous attitude of American government officials denouncing Jackson's trip to Damascus. He states: "America has never put a premium on black life. Now they want to denigrate, they want to detract, they want to take away what Jesse has earned because he is a black man who stepped out of his place that is reserved for white people. This is the issue" (Huntington 1984: 18).

In addition, to expressing interest about United States and African foreign policy, Jackson's use of coalition politics, which were employed on a national level, and the use of global Pan-Africanist tools of analysis. In closing, Jackson's presence in the Democratic campaign shed new light on domestic and international politics (Joyce 1984:1).

AFRICAN AMERICAN POLITICAL ORGANIZATIONS

Black coalitions and political organizations such as the Congressional Black Caucus called for Americans to boycott South African multinational corporations. This strategy was employed to keep pressure on the American government, which would abolish economic ties with South Africa (Cotter 1979: 11). Nevertheless, could an effective and equitable foreign policy survive between the United States and South Africa without the United States taking an economic loss? On the other hand, the creation of a National Black Assembly could bring together African American social and political activists who are interested and concerned about the United States/African foreign policy.

Certainly, there is a need for black politics to be revitalized. Ron Daniels recalls how effective the civil rights movement and black organizations were to the overall political advancement of African Americans. He states:

> With these important and interested movements, radical activists from the NAACP, Urban league, SCLC, CORE, SNCC, and a host of nationalist, socialist organizations and independent parties, many of whom were associated with the Black Power conferences and the African congress, provided the leadership and work force that fueled the mass movement of black people in the late fifties, throughout the sixties, and early seventies. Both of these movements had a significant impact on the survival and progress of black people in America and beyond. (1979: 59)

In general, the American attitude towards African foreign policy has demonstrated a pattern of empathy and subordination for economic advancement. Dick Clark, a former U.S. Senator from Iowa, contested that friction existed between the United States and African nations. In reference to the aforementioned selected black leaders Andrew Young and Jesse Jackson, Clark's contention supports the idea of African Americans establishing a black foreign policy constituency. Furthermore, Clark implies, that in order for the United States and Africa to improve foreign relations, a transcendence would have to occur within political infrastructures within social and public policy in the United States (1978: 12). He states: "American attitudes are shaped by three negative impulses—anti-administration, anti-Sovietism, and anti-terrorism" (1978: 13).

However, if African Americans' participation in United States/ African foreign policy is to be effective, specific concessions must be addressed such as: 1) reparations; 2) indentured servitude and enslavement of Africans in the Sudan; and 3) the colonization of land and people in Africa and the Caribbean. Overall, these are pressing issues that affect Africans throughout the diaspora. Idealistically, this request could address the social inequality of continental and diasporan Africans; while simultaneously re-examining the concept of European cultural hegemony. Reparations would address the repayment to Africans, for the imposition of enslavement and free labor. Indentured servitude and enslavement in the Sudan, in contemporary times, will query the moral, ethic, and political subordination of African nations in this particular region of Africa. Colonization of land

50

and people of African decent in Africa and the Caribbean, again, is the process to query multiple articulations of race, gender, and class relative to United States and Africa foreign policy relations. Ironically, if these query were attempted to be answered, perhaps this could create effective dialog and communication to improve United States public policy with African nations throughout the so-called third world. Paradoxically, because a majority of African nations is dependent on the United States for aid in one way or another, they appear to be coerced to focus on issues in isolation of selected nation states and not in a collective broader context (1978: 14).

William Cotter also prescribes that a transformation must occur in the United States public policy with Africa, for the following reasons: "A final reason for America to increase its attention to, and links with Africa, is that we contain in the U.S. the second largest black nation in the world. Black Americans at 24 million almost equal the populations of Zaire and Ethiopia, which follow Nigeria of the largest black nation by far" (1979: 11).

CONCLUSION

There has been a moderate approach by the U.S. to actually improve foreign policy relationship with African nations. Black nationalists and Pan-Africanists have advocated the necessity for collaboration and alliances between African Americans and continental Africans. Much of this cultural nationalist ideology proscribes the relativity and commonality in ethnic and cultural identity. Consequently, Tilden Lemelle states, "American Blacks are culturally, ethically American and only American" (1981). This analysis infers somehow that blacks are hyphenated Americans, with no cultural linkage to Africa spiritually, culturally, and ethnically. The rebuttal that I present of this analysis is that a cultural migration is the ontological basis of a collective consciousness, for African Americans, to articulate a structural functionalist context of interpreting, political issues of policy, needs, and analysis in Africa.

As noted earlier, greater representation of African Americans in politically elected offices could aid diasporan and continental Africans in political affairs. On the other hand, if the American government continues to disrupt black involvement in the United States and African foreign relations, this disruption could be reflected into domestic racial tension—apropos naive nationalism festering riots. There are some variables that must be taken into account to review African Americans involvement in the United States and African foreign relations. Si Kahn states that, "historically, America has never given full citizenship and respect to people who were categorized as second-class citizens" (1970: 93). Edward Blyden discussed this issue in 1862:

> It is a sad feature in the residence of Africans in this country that it has begotten in them a forgetfulness of Africa—a want of sympathy with her in her moral and intellectual desolation, and a clinging to the land which for centuries has been the scene of their thralldom. A shrewd European observer of American society says of the Negro in this country that he makes a thousand fruitless efforts to insinuate himself among men who repulse him; he conforms to the taste of his oppressors, adopts their opinions, and hopelessly imitating them to form a part of their community. (Blyden 1862: 121)

E. U. Essien-Udom offers strategies to advance this concept further: "The nationalist leaders contend that the Negroes must become consciously aware of their identity as a group in America; they must realize their degradation and strive by individual and collective effort to redeem their communities and regain their human dignity" (1962: 3).

I contend that, in order for African Americans to increase their participation in the United States and African relations, four variables must occur: 1) African Americans must develop a line of communication with continental African leaders; 2) Neocolonialism in Africa must be marginalized and eventually abolished; 3) A restructuring of African economic dependency on foreign nations, a re-examination of the World-Bank intervention in the creation of dependency, and an advocacy of reciprocated losses from colonization and enslavement; and 4) the concept of global Pan-Africanism be advocated by Africans throughout the diaspora seeking to develop a pragmatic and functional collective consciousness registered from an Afrocentric perspective. Nzuri Sana!

Bibliography

Anderson, David (1980). "America in Africa," *Foreign Affairs* 60: 658–685.

"Africa at the United Nations," *Africa Quarterly* 19 (1980).

Anekwe, Simon (1984). "Jackson Pulls it Off," *Amsterdam News* 7 (January 7): 19.

Blyden, Edward (1862). "The Call of Providence to the Descendants of Africa in America," in Fred Lee Hord and Jonathan Scott Lee, eds., *I Am Because We Are: Readings in Black Philosophy* (1995). Amherst: University of Massachusetts Press.

Churchill, Ward (1980). "U.S. Mercenaries in Africa: The Recruiting Network," *Africa Today* 27: 2054.

Clark, Dick (1978). "U.S./African Policy at Crossroads," *Department of State Bulletin* 78: 12–16.

Cotter, William R. (1979). "The Neglected Continent," *Africa Report* 24 (March/April): 10–14.

Curtin, Phillip D. (1965). *The Images of Africa: British Ideas and Actions 1780–1850.* New York: MacMillan Press.

Daniels, Ron (1979). "Revitalizing Independent Black Politics: Toward a Strategy for 1980 and Beyond," *First World* 2: 59.

Deutsch, Richard (1981). "Building an African Policy," *Africa Report* 26 (July–August): 44–47.

Ekpebu, Lawrence (1980). "An African Perspective on U.S./U.S.S.R./China Arms Policies," *Alternatives* 6: 111.

Emerson, Ruppert (1967). *Africa and United States Policy.* Englewood Cliffs, NJ: Prentice Hall.

Gromyko, Anatoly (1980). "The USA Mainstay of Neo-Colonialism in Africa," *International Affairs* 10 (October): 21.

Hall, Raymond (1978). *Black Separatism in the United States.* Hanover, NH: University Press of New England.

Henry, Charles P. (1995). *Culture and African American Politics.* Bloomington: Indiana University Press.

Hill, Robert A., ed. (1987). "Strike for African Redemption" (August 1920 lecture), *The Marcus Garvey and UNIA Papers,* vol II, 27 August 1919–31 August 1920. Berkeley: University of California Press.

Huntington, Samuel (1984). "Jesse Mission to Damascus," *Jet* 65: 18.

Joyce, Faye S. (1984). "Jackson Candidacy is Giving New Shape to Politics," *New York Times* (April 13): 1, B–6.

Kahn, Si (1970). *How People Get Power.* New York: McGraw-Hill.

LeMelle, Tilden (1981). "American Black Constituencies and Africa a Rejoinder," in Rene Lemarch, ed., *American Policy in Southern Africa.* Washington, DC: University Press of America.

Madhubuti, Haki (1979). "Andy Young: Sacrificial Lamb, or Politics Israeli Style," *First World* 2: 6.

"New Leaders for the Eighties," *Black Enterprise* 2:8 (March 1981): 33–39.

Skinner, Elliott (1993). "The Dialectic between Diasporas and Homelands," in Joseph Harris, ed., *Global Dimensions of the African Diaspora.* Washington, DC: Howard University Press.

Storing, Herbert (1970). *What Country Have I.* New York: St. Martins Press.

Walters, Ronald W. (1993). *Pan-Africanism in the African Diaspora: An Analysis of Modern Afrocentric Political Movements.* Detroit, MI: Wayne State University Press.

Young, Andrew (1980-1981). "The United States and Africa, Victory for Democracy," *Foreign Affairs* 59: 651.

CHAPTER 5

The Afro-American's Response to U.S. Imperialism

William Loren Katz

This article is an adaptation of Mr. Katz's preface to George P. Marks III's The Black Press Views American Imperialism, 1898–1900, *to be published by Arno Press this year.*

While black leadership within the peace movement, represented by such prominent names as Dick Gregory, Rev. Ralph D. Abernathy and Coretta Scott King, is recognized and appreciated, few realize the crucial black part in the movement when it was unpopular if not dangerous to oppose the war in Vietnam. Yet in the days before Senators Eugene McCarthy and George McGovern, when the anti-war movement was hardly a viable stance for white political figures, black leaders and organizations were building its rudiments. For many years black attorney Conrad Lynn has been the nation's leading advisor and counsel to youth fighting induction into the Army. In 1965, the Mississippi Freedom Democratic party in McComb issued the first organizational opposition to President Johnson's escalation of the war, rejecting "fighting in Vietnam for the White Man's freedom" and urging black men "to not honor the draft here in Mississippi. Mothers should encourage their sons not to go." A half year later, Student Nonviolent Coordinating Committee (SNCC) became the first national organization to denounce the war. For endorsing this stand, Julian Bond, duly elected to the Georgia legislature, was denied his seat (later restored by the Supreme Court). Also in 1965, *Freedomways,* the first national magazine to denounce the war, editorially labeling it "racist" in origin and intent, became the fountainhead of a black anti-war position.

In 1966 and early 1967, black opposition to U.S. Asian policy mounted. This was dramatized by Muhammad Ali's announcing his refusal to serve in the army of a country committed to "continue the domination of white slavemasters over the dark people the world over." For his stand, Ali was stripped of his world heavyweight boxing crown. Then, in April 1967, Dr. Martin Luther King, Jr., declared his total opposition to the war, called for resistance to the draft, and named the U.S. government as "the greatest purveyor of violence in the world today." Southern Christian Leadership Conference (SCLC) joined SNCC in the vanguard of the peace movement. That spring Dr. King and Stokely Carmichael led several hundred thousand peace marchers to the UN Plaza. When Carmichael shouted "Hell no, we won't go!" to the crowd, they made it a chant. A *Newsweek* poll of Black America in 1966 showed 35 percent opposed to the war; by 1969 the figure had soared to 56 percent, and was still climbing. By then every major civil rights organization except National Association for the Advancement of Colored People (NAACP) had pronounced the American policy in Asia a reflection of racism at home.

This early and distinctive Afro-American response to intervention in Asia might indicate that a black political tradition was surfacing. And indeed it is, though one that is rarely mentioned. Black leaders and organizations through the years have repeatedly linked aspects of U.S. foreign policy with domestic racism. From 1846 when Frederick Douglass castigated this government's invasion of Mexico to W. E. B. Du Bois' and Paul Robeson's denunciations of U.S. intervention in Korea a century later, to the black anti-war voices of today, criticism of American wars against dark-skinned people abroad has been an enduring black tradition in the United States.

This book, therefore, is a revelation. Twenty years ago George P. Marks III began his investigation of the black press's response to the American invasion of the Philippines that smashed its independence movement. In 1951, he published some of his findings in a little-known, short-lived journal edited by black scholar Lorenzo J. Greene.[1] Mr. Marks has extended his research in the present volume, providing the first thorough examination of the way the black press greeted America's initial venture in imperialism. He has had to labor under formidable burdens; entire black newspapers were no longer available and few had left a complete run for the period under consideration. The work, therefore, is unfortunately fragmentary and incomplete, but it does conclusively establish a series of black attitudes that is quite distinguishable from that of whites. Further, as the ten-week "splendid little war" with Spain concluded, and the long and sordid guerrilla war in the Philippines began, black press criticism of American foreign policy mounted in fury. The newspaper comments highlighted here are no small discovery, nor are they of significance solely to scholars, for they detail a painful past that is painfully present. Indeed, this collection of clippings presents an inescapable challenge to historians who have ignored or sidestepped its information. At the same time, it reiterates the desperate need in black history for original research and fresh approaches. It will stimulate new research and provoke sharp debate on a vital but neglected topic.

That so many of the black newspapers found American interest in a "free Cuba" hypocritical is hardly surprising. During the last decade of the nineteenth century, as interest in Cuba and overseas expansion rose, black Americans lived under the yoke of a new slavery. Ninety percent lived in the south—landless and voteless peasants. Beginning in 1890, each state of the old Confederacy wrote into law, often into its constitution, provisions for the disfranchisement of its black citizens and their segregation in public schools, conveyances and facilities. In 1896, the federal stamp of approval was put on segregation when the United States Supreme Court ruled that it did not violate the Constitution of the United States (*Plessy v. Ferguson*), and Congress refused to enforce the Constitutional Amendments guaranteeing black liberty and equality.

In the south, mob action accompanied discriminatory laws and decisions. From 1889 to 1901, when overseas expansion escalated, almost two thousand black men, women, and children were lynched, often with unspeakable brutality. The Right Reverend Hugh Miller, Bishop of Mississippi, justified lynchings, saying "the laws are slow and the jails are full." In North Carolina, where a coalition of black and white voters elected some black office-holders in 1898, Colonel A. M. Waddell, representing the white opposition, said his forces would carry the next election "if we have to choke the current of Cape Fear with carcasses." Five days later he led his forces, now armed, into Wilmington to massacre black officials and terrorize black voters.

For southern blacks the American shock at "Spanish brutality" and enthusiasm for a "free Cuba" must have seemed a cruel joke. Only one week after an explosion sank the U.S. battleship *Maine* in Havana Harbor, a white mob in Lake City, South Carolina, shotgunned and fired the home and office of a duly-appointed black federal postmaster, Fraser Baker, killing him and his infant son and wounding his wife, older son and four daughters.[2] As white Americans pondered the question of war with Spain, George Henry White, the nation's lone black congressman, tried unsuccessfully to pass through Congress a resolution to provide the surviving family of Postmaster Baker with a small indemnity. He was not permitted to address Congress on the bill.

However, racist rhetoric ran rampant in the 55th and 56th Congresses that served from 1897 to 1901. On the day that Congress declared war on Spain, David A. De Armond of Missouri told his fellow congressmen that black people were "almost too ignorant to eat, scarcely wise enough to breathe, mere existing human machines." Congressman Meyer of Louisiana insisted white supremacy was necessary to save "us from the forces of ignorance, lawlessness, vice and irresponsibility." Senator "Pitchfork" Ben Tillman of South Carolina explained how his state saved itself from "black domination": "We have done our level best; we have scratched our heads to find out how we could eliminate the last one of them. We stuffed ballot boxes. We shot them. We are not ashamed of it."[3]

In ten weeks, United States armed might crushed Spanish power from Puerto Rico to the Philippines. But it would take three long years to smash the Philippine independence movement led by young Emilio Aguinaldo. In words reminiscent of the southern congressmen, the Republican San Francisco *Argonaut* made this suggestion in "grim earnest":

> . . . In pursuance of our imperialist plans, it would be well to hire some of the insurgent lieutenants to betray Aguinaldo and other chieftans into our clutches. A little bribery, a little treachery and a little ambuscading, and we could trap Aguinaldo and his chieftans. Then, instead of putting them to death in the ordinary way, it might be well to torture them. The Spaniards have left behind them some means to that end in the dungeons of Manila. The rack, the thumbscrew, the trial by fire, the trial by molten lead, boiling insurgents alive, crushing their bones in ingenius mechanisms of torture— these are some of the methods that would impress the Malay mind.[4]

While the white press and congressmen were denouncing Aguinaldo, the black press viewed him as a dark-skinned liberator, fighting for independence by expelling a foreign oppressor. Salt Lake City's *Broad Ax* lashed out at U.S. "robbers, murderers and unscrupulous monopolists, who are ever crying for more blood." This black paper explained the fierce guerrilla resistance by noting that "maybe the Filipinos have caught wind of the way Indians and Negroes have been Christianized and civilized" in the United States.[5] In the month that Representative White left Congress, North Carolina state law prohibiting him from ever returning, Aguinaldo was captured by American treachery. Until 1946, American authorities kept Filipinos from choosing their own government; white rule in the south still prevents the election of black men to Congress.

Painful ironies run through this era of racism at home and abroad. Black anti-expansionists thrashed about looking for a political home. William Jennings Bryan and the Democrats opposed imperialism abroad while enforcing white supremacy at home. Bryan, three times the Democratic presidential candidate, announced: "Anyone who will look at the subject without prejudice will know that white supremacy promotes the highest welfare of both races." The Republicans, supported by most blacks, had become the party of imperialism. The best President McKinley could offer black southerners was this advice: "Be patient, be progressive, be determined, be honest, be God-fearing, and you will win. For no effort fails that has a stout, earnest heart behind it."[6]

In the U.S. Senate, South Carolina's Ben Tillman denounced the hypocrisy of his Republican colleagues who insisted the Filipinos were unfit for self-government and required American control. "In the name of common sense and honest dealing," he said, "if the Philippines are unfit, why are the negroes fit?" He drew another parallel:

> . . . No Republican leader, not even Governor [Theodore] Roosevelt, will now dare to wave the bloody shirt and preach a crusade against the South's treatment of the negro. The North has a bloody shirt of its own. Many thousands of them have been made into shrouds for murdered Filipinos, done to death because they were fighting for liberty.[7]

But the white community remained deeply split over imperialism. Less than two months after Congress declared war on Spain an Anti-Imperialist League was formed by prominent Americans ranging from Mark Twain to Grover Cleveland. By the election of 1900, the Democrats had elevated expansion to a major campaign issue. The division among whites further emboldened the black press's attacks. They undoubtedly benefited from this extra strength when facing either entrenched beliefs or implacable foreign policy, the black editors had to flaunt the public views of Afro-America's leading spokesman, Booker T. Washington. He had urged his people to sacrifice their battle for equal rights and accommodate themselves to the white South—and this during an age of mounting mob violence and disfranchisement. An intimate of leading industrialists, who provided him with funds, and a consultant to Republican Presidents, who sought his advice on southern Federal appointments, Washington would soon launch his successful drive to bend much of the black press to his way of thinking.

To emphasize their strong disagreement with the Republican president and administration, the black press forcefully challenged or established black political tradition—unswerving loyalty to the party of Lincoln. One paper printed the advice of Stanley Ruffin of Boston, "a leading Afro-American," who urged black clergymen and editors to declare: "We shall neither fight for such a country or with such an army." Though others never went that far, few failed to express some hostility or suspicion of the administration. In 1898 the Washington *Bee* claimed: "A majority of the Negroes in this country are opposed to expansion." Its opinion, "expansion is a fraud," may well have been the majority view held by articulate blacks.[8]

By 1900, the spokesmen for expansion had become more outspoken and arrogant. On January 9th Senator Albert J. Beveridge, a leading advocate of imperialism, announced: "God . . . has made us the master organizers of the world to establish system where chaos reigns. . . . He has made us adept in government that we may administer government among savages and senile people." Paradoxically, eleven days later, Congressman White, in a dramatic move to halt U.S. barbarity at home, introduced the nation's first anti-lynching bill to Congress. To halt this widespread and escalating crime, his bill provided the death penalty for convicted lynchers, but it died in committee.

By this time black opposition to imperialism was mounting. Early in October a black paper quoted Howard University professor and black essayist Kelly Miller, saying: "To be plain about the matter, I don't think there is a single colored man, out of office and out of the insane asylum, who favors the so-called expansion policy."[9] Later that month, in an article, "The Effect of Imperialism Upon the Negro Race," Professor Miller concluded: "Acquiescence on the part of the Negro in the political rape upon the Filipino would give ground of justification to the assaults upon his rights at home."

In 1966, during a scholars' conference on black thought at the turn of the century, the editor mentioned black anti-imperialist sentiments and cited the Kelly Miller article. The only response came from a noted white scholar, prominent in historical associations and widely-known for his early work in black history and thought. He insisted "there was no Negro opposition to our foreign policy then," and said he had "been all through the Booker T. Washington papers at the Library of Congress, including his extensive collection of news clippings, and found nothing of the sort." He concluded: "Why mention the Kelly Miller article when the one following it by Frederick McGhee refuted it?"

While this historian may have been correct about the material in the Booker T. Washington papers, he was incorrect in his generalization. And, although the article he cited by Frederick McGhee did follow the Miller article in *Howard's American Magazine* that October, he had either misread or misrepresented its contents. Far from disputing Miller, McGhee, a leading Catholic layman and a prominent black Minnesota lawyer, carried his argument much further. He insisted "the murder and assassination going on in the Philippine Islands under the guise of war with the insurgents" was the cause for "the spirit of mob rule, the prevalence of lynch law, in all parts of our country." In a passage particularly relevant today, McGhee continued:

> . . . Our soldiers wrote home of what fun it was to shoot the "niggers" and see them keel over and die. Then came the famous order, "Take no prisoners," followed by the shameful account of the fiendish slaughter of forty-six Tagals, because one had killed an American soldier. Of the number of women and children killed in attacks upon villages defended by men armed with bamboo spears, this with the profoundly and oft-repeated assertion, of late so prevalent, that the proud Anglo-Saxon, the Republican party, by divine foreordination, is destined to rule earth's inferior races, and if they object make war upon them, furnishes an all-sufficient cause. Is it to be wondered then that so little value is placed upon the life, liberty, freedom, and the rights of the American Negro?[10]

To misread this clear denunciation of U.S. foreign policy required a formidable bias, one our respected scholar shared with many others, despite their training in objective analysis of historical evidence. This volume, then, cannot help but ruffle a few academic feathers. And well it should. Neither complacency nor bias ever produced accurate history. But more important, these laymen who wonder why some black spokesmen today insist on drawing parallels between the shooting of blacks in Orangeburg, South Carolina; Jackson State College, Mississippi; Newark and Detroit, and the massacre at Songmy, Vietnam, should find this volume enlightening.

Notes

1. See George P. Marks III, "Opposition of Negro Newspapers to American Philippine Policy, 1899-1900," *Midwest Journal* IV (Winter, 1951–1952). Another contributor to the journal, August Meier, wrote the definitive *Negro Thought in America, 1880–1915* (Ann Arbor 1963), which does not mention a single black criticism of U.S. imperialism. However, this staggering omission is more typical and traditional than exceptional for historians.
2. As the clippings in this collection demonstrate, the murder of Postmaster Baker drew heavy fire from the black press. It so impressed novelist Sutton E. Griggs that he used it in his revolutionary, if not seditious, book, *Imperium in Imperio,* which he published in 1899 (reprinted in 1969 by Arno Press and *The New York Times*). In the novel, the Baker assassination leads to a meeting of a secret black congress that considers the seizure, with the aid of some foreign powers, of Texas and Louisiana during the Spanish-American War. As a reward for their assistance in this coup, the allies are to keep Louisiana, and Texas is to become a black republic.
3. See *Congressional Record,* 55th Congress, Second Session, Appendix pp. 362-363, 620; Third Session, p. 342; 56th Congress, First Session, pp. 2242, 2245.
4. See H. Aptheker, "American Imperialism and White Chauvinism," reprinted in *Toward Negro Freedom* (New York 1956), p. 93.
5. See Marks, *Op. Cit.,* p. 24.
6. See William Loren Katz, *Eyewitness: The Negro in American History* (New York 1970, revised edition), pp. 372-373.
7. *Ibid.*
8. See Marks, *Op. Cit.*
9. *Ibid.*
10. Kelly Miller, "The Effect of Imperialism Upon the Negro Race," and Frederick L. McGhee, "Another View," in *Howard's American Magazine* V (October 1900): 87-96. After both articles, publisher James H. W. Howard added this comment: "People who try to cover the cloven hoof of empire with the petticoats of 'Expansion' are as careless of the dictionary as of the constitution. . . . What is proposed to do with [the Philippines] is no more like expansion than the present administration is like Lincoln's."

CHAPTER 6

African American Women Preachers: Fulfilling a Mandate and a Calling

Venita Kelley

BLACK WOMEN PREACHERS AND RHETORICAL FOUNDATIONS

African American women have been preaching and ministering to people, "flocks," and congregations for hundreds of years. If you subscribe to the belief that Jesus, with woolly hair and skin like burnished copper, was an African man, then it was Jesus himself who commanded Mary to go forth and spread the word of his resurrection. Thus, African and African American women have been given a mandate by God to speak the Word and to spread the Gospel for over two thousand years. Myriad numbers of them do. In the book, *Those Preaching Women: Nineteen Sermons by Black Women Preachers,* Dr. Ella Pearson Mitchell compiles stirring sermons that demonstrate the rhetorical skill and strong faith of the preachers "chosen." The statement is important because, according to African American rhetorical tradition, a person who seeks the attention of an audience must be able to intellectually captivate the audience while simultaneously engaging the emotions. The ideas must be strong, the speech must have "soul" (have the aura of being in direct connection with the universal source/origin/foundation of the rhetoric).

The African American rhetorical tradition lends itself easily to preaching. According to Molefi Kete Asante, *The Afrocentric Idea,* African American rhetorical traditions have four basic parts: 1) frame of mind; 2) scope of context; 3) structure of code; and 4) delivery of the message. Vernon Dixon and Badi Foster describe essential characteristics of the African American audience, which have: 1) the value of humanism; 2) the value of communalism; 3) the attributes of oppression/paranoia; 4) the value of empathetic understanding; 5) the value of rhythm; and 6) the principle of limited reward. Asante adds a seventh, the principle of styling.

"Frame of mind" means that "certain social, creative, and psychological factors contribute to a total view of language." There is no rigid line or demarcation from which the speaker is bound to choose his rhetoric: everything is used as a resource for the speaking occasion. All that is appropriate is used in order to make a point and to have the audience identify with the speaker.

A speaker demonstrates her frame of mind through her own rhythm and style. For a speaker to be successful with an African American audience, the proper use of rhythm and style has to be achieved. Yet, this rhythm and style is usually highly individualistic. A speaker has to be, and appear, comfortable within her own style in order to be accepted by an African American audience. The rhythm— the regulated flow of words and pauses that a speaker establishes— creates an intimacy and fellowship with the audience. The flow of words, or even sounds from the speaker gives a "call" to establish community, and relationship with the speaker and among members of the audience. The speaker's rhythm demonstrates the *act* of unity that the audience emulates and "takes up."

The discourse of the speaker must also *sound* good as well as *say* something good. To "say" something good the speaker must address the audience's individual and group experience. The speaker must be able to relate to the difficulties and triumphs of the audience. The speaker must be able to articulate what are often the interior thoughts of the audience because the audience is the regulating agent, they tell the speaker whether or not he or she is being effective through how well the speaker "extracts" their hidden and intellectualized thoughts. They define the boundaries of communication. They respond to the speaker verbally and nonverbally, voicing approval or disapproval. The speaker is expected to respond to the audience as well as the audience to the speaker, thus, a mutuality of existence is established and drawn upon as further resource for the speaker to access. As this "call and response" is exchanged, the interactive force reaffirms the humanity of all involved. The community is built and/or reaffirmed and understanding or acceptance of self and others is the result.

In her sermon, "On Remembering Who We Are" (1985), Katie G. Cannon makes her point through using the text of Sarah and Hagar. Although the Lord has told Sarah she will have a child by Abraham,

Sarah doubts and sends for Hagar and gives her to Abraham. They conceive a child. Later, Sarah too conceives and becomes jealous of Hagar and "her" son and has Abraham send them into the wilderness. Hagar, upset and traumatized, calls upon God and is assured by the Deity that she will be blessed and protected and that God has heard her cry. After she reads and summarizes the text, Cannon moves to her points which are:

1. "We have a tendency to overstep our boundaries as human beings." By this statement, she means that Sarah took it upon herself to "help God" by giving Abraham Hagar rather than wait for God to "move."

2. People tend to become people pleasers rather than God pleasers. Here, she calls the phenomenon "the Abraham syndrome" because Abraham knew that he should not have fathered a child with Hagar, but to appease Sarah, did so. Her subsidiary points are that "we" spin our wheels and indulge in self-pity trying to change the things that we cannot change and therefore do not work on the things that we can (1985: 46). And, that "we" try to become false gods to ourselves and to others by controlling too much the Spirit that moves within us.

Cannon's sermon is moving and thought provoking. She creates a shared feeling of community through her use of "we" and "I" phrases. She specifically delineates:

> We too as grandmothers and mothers, as sisters and daughters, as aunts and nieces, receive as part of our socialization as Black females growing up in a racist white society the notion that we are supposed to take care of everybody except ourselves. . . . [M]any of us mess ourselves up over and over again by giving in to the pressures around us to do what we know in our heart of hearts to be wrong . . . we forget who we are. . . . [W]henever we get caught in the Sarah syndrome, we snatch back our lives and our wills from God and we try by hook or crook to make people do what we want them to do. . . . [W]e pray that our will be done instead of humbly surrendering ourselves before God and asking that God's will be done in our own lives. . . .(1985: 46)

Cannon continues by bringing into focus the worldly ills that result from the spiritual decline among those with the Abraham and Sarah syndromes:

> More Black women than ever are dying from strokes, high-blood pressure diseases, and heart attacks. More than ever we are victims of chronic depression, nervous break downs, and schizophrenic behavior. The number of Black women suffering from alcoholism, drug abuse, and compulsive substance consumption has reached an all-time high. Too many sisters are dying with broken hearts, broken minds, and broken spirits, not knowing who they truly are. (1985: 47)

After presenting the effects of turning away from God, and detailing the maladies that accompany that practice, Cannon offers a threefold avenue to renewed spirituality and salvation. She encapsulates her counsel in the acronym, WHO. "W" is for *willingness* to find one's own oneness/relationship with God. "H" is for *humility,* or a humbling of self before God. She importantly notes that this humility is not one of subservience, but is of a kind:

> ... that strengthens us for the struggles before us ... not the dramatic put-down of ourselves wherein we exaggerate all the mistakes and sins of our past ... does not mean being completely submissive, wallowing and shuffling, putting everyone else on a pedestal, and accepting everything that comes our way. (1985: 48)

She continues to reframe the concept by reiterating that people need to be able to gauge where and what kind of relationship they have with God, by saying that pains and delusions need to be "let go," and by urging the congregation to reach toward the Power that frees them from their finite selves. The "O" stands for *open-mindedness* that requires "us" to "seek to understand others rather than always trying to be understood" (1985: 49). Open-mindedness, states Cannon, allows us to be nonjudgmental of each other, and to "develop a receptive attitude that allows us to listen, to learn, and to love" (1985: 49). Thus, people grow and develop a mature faith in God.

Cannon's sermon is an amazing one. Her frame of mind is one that recognizes the pressures that cause her audience to indulge themselves and judge each other. Yet, she calls for them to re-establish and strengthen a community of caring. Since the sermon is taken from printed text, pinpointing the rhythm she presented while speaking is difficult. Assumptions can be made though, from her use of "stacking"—grandmothers, mothers, sisters, daughters, aunts, nieces—that her intonation was staccato, and her pauses caught the attention of the audience and established, as well as built upon, their expectations of what was to come. As a sidenote, Cannon honors a cultural tradition of naming the matrilineal line, and that she begins with the elder and "originator of the line" and traces the relationships by recognition factors: griot-style.

Cannon's sermon is excellent because she *says* something good. She is perfectly within her rights as a speaker to critique the behaviors of those listening. As a matter of fact, she establishes her credibility by *knowing* what she should or should not critique. She shows by her ability to "witness" to the audience their pain, thus their mindsets and their reactions to their pain, that she deeply understands their lives. She is able, then, to move them from a discussion of the negatives that they perpetuate and suffer from to an affirmation of their better qualities and ways of being; she interprets for the audience the experiences that place them in peril and offers them an avenue by which they can reclaim their true selves. By discussing the audiences collective ailments, and by addressing their individual negative responses and abilities to reject the negative and affirm a positive that will contribute to the health of the community, Cannon validates the personhood of all involved and moves them towards accepting and recognizing themselves.

African American rhetoric incorporates style, a criteria that can be visual, auditory, or both. Visually, a speaker may gesture or affect a mannerism that is symbolic of their skill and comfort with a topic, or they may "draw a picture" so the audience can identify more readily with the point to be made. Aurally, a speaker's tone, deliberate variations of pronunciation, vocal cues, and intercalations or filler phrases, give "life" to a speech. A speaker may use repetition to emphasize points, or rhyming schemes, or any number of "everyday" language forms (sarcasm, plays on words, reversal of word order, witticisms, "testifying" or "signifying") to engage and entice the audience into participating. The speaker's style helps give the audience "permission" to respond or participate in the event (of the speech/rhetoric/sermon); the speaker establishes the environment within which the audience can be creative, active, and responsive, too. It is a requirement of the African American speaker who wishes to be successful, that is understood and accepted, with (by) the African American audience. "Amen's" (even in secular speeches), "tell it's," "go on's", "tell the story's," even an occasional "hush your mouth" or "shutup!" (when the speaker is speaking a particularly valid truth), are some examples of responses from African American audiences when they appreciate and encourage the words of the speaker. In all, the rhetorical tradition of African Americans is one that seeks to create harmony through the word, and the action and deeds that "accompany" the words. (In African American rhetorical tradition, action and words are not strictly distinct from each other—they reflect and embody each other, thus, words, to a certain extent, *become* action.) Everyone is elevated or made to feel a part of a cohesive, mutually dependent whole; the tradition is holistic by nature and by practice.

The sermon by Sharon E. Williams, "Studying War Some More" (1985), is another excellent example of the ministry of women. The reader may be familiar with a speech by Martin Luther King, Jr., wherein he asserts that he is not going to study war anymore. His speech was a response to America's involvement in the Vietnam War, and he advocated the day when nations would "study war no more" so that the world would "get on" with the business of acknowledging and preserving God in all of our lives.

Williams, implicitly responding to King's sermon, assuming all to be familiar with it because of its fame, begins by denouncing war, saying that it does not "suit the Christian personality" (1985: 77). She notes, though, that God's kingdom does suffer violence from without. That "our peace with God" is threatened and "taken from us by violence" (1985: 78). She moves into a discussion of whether or not it is fair that a peaceful and loving people are beset by violence and whether or not it is "okay" for these people to arm themselves against such violence.

She then quotes a scripture that states the war is not a worldly war, and that the weapons to be used are those that "destroy strongholds . . . destroy arguments and every proud obstacle to the knowledge of God, and take every thought captive to obey Christ. . . ." She quotes another scripture that blesses the peacemakers but (from Jesus' lips) says that he brings a sword. She says that "Jesus sent us to war, but not against one another" (1985: 79). The war, she says, is against the evil that attacks and diminishes God's kingdom. This evil may be *in* other people she says, but the war is still not against them as people but against the "darkness and spiritual wickedness *within*" (1985: 79). She furthers her premise by saying that it is God who gives people their weapons by which to fight this war.

Williams's sermon is a visual one in that she "puts on God's armor" (1985: 81) in order to resist "the wickedness and evil" of the

world. Her weapons are spiritual. She says that the battle is dangerous but that people must know there is a "guarantee of victory" (1985:
80). Jesus "girds your loins . . . with the . . . truth," and issues a "regu-
lation breastplate of righteousness" to avoid a person being "pierced
with corruption" (1985: 81). There are new shoes for the soldier's feet,
the "marching boots" of the "gospel of Peace." There is a shield of
Faith, that puts out the "darts of fire with which the wicked surround
us and threaten us" (1985: 82). And, there is a helmet that Jesus has
fashioned:

> It took him three whole days to make it up just for me. He began forging
> the metal one Friday in the scorching noonday sun. And he didn't finish it
> until Sunday morning in the cool darkness of a rich man's tomb. When the
> stone was rolled away, out came Jesus, carrying my helmet of salva-
> tion . . . I just can't go out into battle with my head uncovered. Since 95
> percent of a person's body heat goes out through an uncovered head. I'm
> going into battle with my head covered with salvation. (1985: 82)

She says Jesus also fashioned a Sword "called the Holy Ghost" (1985:
82). And, finally she goes into battle with the Word—her Bible, so as
to "wage war." She ends the speech by using anaphora (repetition of
key phrases) in order to drive her final points home and to instruct the
audience as to how to fight the war:

> I'm waging war by forgiving all enemies.
> I'm waging war by practicing gentleness.
> I'm waging war by giving up jealousy and backbiting.
> I'm waging war by walking in a meek and lowly way.
> I'm waging war by telling the truth, even when I am threatened by
>   violent liars.
> I'm waging war by bringing peace.
> I'm waging war by feeding the hungry.
> I'm waging war by supplying the poor with what they need.
> I'm waging war by healing the sick.
> I'm waging war by having patience and reconciliation.
> I'm waging war by having a contrite and broken spirit.
> I'm waging war by a will surrendered to God.
> I'm waging war.

The auditory style of Williams probably moved her audience the
most. By assumption, her voice and tone were probably strident and
confident. She would have been teasing the audience, establishing

suspense when she told them that she was going to arm her self for battle. She quickly resolves their curiosity by telling them what kind of battle she will wage: a spiritual one. She resolves the inherent conflict she has established with King, by echoing his position with words and visualizations of her own, thus linking the two sermons and strengthening the message of them both.

Her technique is brilliant; she implicitly brings the civil rights and Black Power struggle of the 1960s into the 1980s and never says a direct word about it. She operates from a foundation of understood conditions and struggles of African American people. Knowing that people still revere and admire King, and that they still consider his articulation of the problems of America and of African American ways to combat it, she renews their commitment towards the war against the wickedness that afflicts them. Her visualization and putting on of the armor creates a vivid picture *and* serves as a model for her audience. It truly puts *her* stamp on the sermon, thus making it an African American woman's response to her own oppression. Because surely as much affliction that she suffers from those who are not a part of her basic community, there are afflictions that she suffers as a woman from that same community, thus, her sermon does not indict a particular community—it is *all* those that are "wicked" that she indicts. Her major purpose though is to create a climate of shared struggle. She uses the "our" and "we," the "they" and "their" of group consciousness and loyalty building to maintain an environment of trust and strength, and to keep the focus on what God would do for them all: *if* they put on the armor.

The traditions of African American rhetoric cannot be separated from the African American approach to life and issues. African Americans, as with all people are reflections of their group mores and values. To define African Americans as one particular group *is* difficult. The felt needs, attitudes, and opinions are exceedingly diverse. But, there is a common foundation that is shared, and from which similarities can be drawn, to describe the needs and wants of African Americans and their communities. There is enough so that it is predictable what African Americans require of those who would profess to be in communication and relationship with them.

African Americans value harmony, humanity, fairness, strength of character, and so on (as do many peoples). But, two values, one of which is so strong that it developed into a mental practice among them, are of utmost importance to understand. The first is "nommo," the power of the spoken word. Nommo is what has been described earlier—the creative, generative, strength of the word that can call/cause something to be *into existence* (words become action). The second value is that of meaning of the word/Word. For African Americans, words themselves are tools. Words can be indicative of, contradictory to, or in irony with, the true *meaning* that is being established or presented as the words are spoken. This is how Reverend Williams can talk about studying war some more, and evoke myriad associations of the struggles that African Americans go through, as well as memories of Martin Luther King, Jr.

The meaning then, in tandem with the word, (nommo) *must* invoke harmony, that is, *connection* among the listeners. Unless harmony of word and (actual) deed are established, the rhetor and his or her rhetoric are rejected in voice or by actions of the audience. Briefly, "harmony of meaning" can be better understood if it is remembered how language has been used by African Americans historically. The culture is an oral one. The orality of the people demands that they be able to listen and establish the meaning of what is said simultaneously; what is said must be quickly interpreted and assigned perceptual category so that a consequent behavior can be chosen.

The conditions of African American physical slavery in America's history have also been one within which subterfuge in discourse has been the (forced) rule. Indeed, African Americans who do not speak in code are often destroyed. The assassinations of Martin Luther King, Jr., and Malcolm X are testimonies to this historical practice applied to African Americans, and King and Malcolm X are only among the most famous rhetoricians and ministers. From the slave spirituals wherein a slave would walk through the fields singing "Steal Away to Jesus" or "Swing Low Sweet Chariot," the *words* used, conveyed a *meaning* different than would typically be assumed. A slave might sing what was thought to be an innocuous time filler but would be giving a message to other slaves that he or she was going to run away from the plantation. To make the example more current, from the turn of the century to about the early seventies, the phrases "Mister Charlie" and "Miss Ann," while purporting to be the formal, respectful address towards European Americans, were negative, disdainful terms. Again, the words were not indicative of the meaning. No matter how many times slaves called someone master or mistress they did not believe that that person was a master over or superior to them. Jacquelyn Grant in *White Women's Christ, Black Women's Jesus* (1989) cites a slave woman's prayer to demonstrate the point:

> "Dear Massa Jesus, we all uns beg Ooner (you) come make us a call dis yere day. We is nutting but poor Etiopian women and people ain't tink much 'bout we. We ain't trust any of dem great high people for come to we church, but do' you is de one great Massa, great too much dan massa Linkum, you ain't shame to care for we African people." (1989: 213)

"Massa" becomes a word, a form of address, rather than an acknowledgment of innate superiority. To be sure, since this word was used as a tool of subjugation, it had real effects on African Americans' psychological make-up and belief systems. Yet, there *was* strong resistance to this inflicted damage. People *did* have to use the words meant to ensure their bondage, but there was rebellion even in their use of the words. What if Mr. Linkum had been present during the slave woman's prayer? The boundaries of his culture and religious belief system would probably have kept him from intruding or reacting physically to censure her. Historical knowledge tells us that he probably would have found a way to punish her, but in her own context of praying in church she had protested her condition and thus advanced her cause.

So, as a part of the culture, through the natural practice in orality and the need to be protective of true thoughts, African Americans were and are adept at finding, analysing, and discerning the meaning behind the words used: the explicit and implicit messages have both an impact on each other and do not reflect each other at all. This fact explains how Reverend Williams can reference King's entire speech through a brief "antistance" to his position, and how Katie G. Cannon can simultaneously denounce the failings of her African American listeners while encouraging them to change and alter their responses to the world. African American women preachers use this technique to fulfill their mandate from God: they do what they say they are going to do, and they do not say what they are going to do; they say what they mean and they do not say what they mean.

As for African American women preaching, there are ideas and opinions that they voice that cover areas pertinent to their experience, thus they validate the experiences of African American women *in concert* with those of African American men. The integrative nature

72

of their rhetoric is that which merges the real world with the spiritual world, thus, the ministry of these preachers contributes to the strengthening of whole communities, male and female, young and old. Yet, there are still problems that they face in being accepted in the *profession* of the ministry.

THEIR TRIALS AND TRIBULATIONS

As profound and proficient as they are in the rhetorical tradition of their people, African American women preachers have had difficulty being accepted by their own communities. There is a struggle to keep them from being ordained, from being assigned to ministers at large and, "more important," to churches, and from being accepted as having "legitimate calls" to preach and serve. In short, they are the victims of oppression, often manifested as sexism from male ministers, within their own community. Some African American women preachers (and lay women) fight and "talk against" these ministers, but largely it *is* African American men who keep the door of opportunity closed.

In the African American community the church is the oldest, strongest and most powerful institution. The church has been the safest haven and a legitimate bastion of power by which African American men could exercise their thoughts and opinions. By which they could *be* with little threat from outside or mainstream society. African American men have been reticent to share that power and protected place with African American women. They have used their positions of "collective voice" and "articulators of African American policy" to deny women's claims to the pulpit, and to subjugate women's call to preach the Word to their own interests. In doing this they have done the same thing as their European American male counterparts have done to European American women ministers and aspirers to the pulpit.

James Cone (1984b), an African American theologian, states that African American male preachers have *got* to address the dualism that they confer upon African American women. Since women make up over seventy percent of the black church, they are the "glue" (Pauli Murray) that hold the church together. As women are the backbone of the church (Theressa Hoover), men are reluctant to let them *lead* the church as well. Cone says that this resistance is categorically wrong. He asserts that it is sexist, which he equates with the most virulent racism, and that men cannot remain faithful to the Gospel or their own ministry if they continue this stance. He encourages a return to African and African American spiritual traditions, a renewal of faith, a reconciliation of the male ministers' duality, and a moving forward into a ministry of affirmation and inclusion. Women who minister have problems to overcome, to be sure. Even when writing this paper a male colleague, a minister, who was extremely helpful in suggesting sources and women preachers to investigate, and who praised women preachers highly, said that he still believed that preaching was meant for men.

Of course, there are African American (and European American) male ministers who fight this oppression of women. James Cone has taken a stance against it since the early days of black theology (he is one of the originators of this current form of the theology). Other male preachers have suffered exclusion from national conventions and meetings because the ruling bodies would not honor their demands for women to be included. There is a struggle, even amongst the men, about this oppression of women. It is sure to continue.

At the same time, African American women voice their own opposition to this condition—at times, even from the pulpit. Suzan D. Johnson, in her sermon "God's Woman" (1985), criticizes male ministers' stance and male sexism, interestingly, through scripture about a woman. She begins her sermon by admonishing those preachers who only speak of women on Women's Day in the church (once a year).

She then moves into a story about Queen Esther, a Jewish slave who was chosen to be the Queen of Persia (the king not knowing she was a Jew). It came to pass that a decree was made to kill all the Jews, and her cousin Mordecai (who was the only one who knew she was a Jew) asked her to intervene. Esther's predicament is that she has to ask the king for something she is not supposed to care about. Johnson states she turns to God to get guidance about what to do and therein turns to the correct "Source of power." The point is that the power that she needs is not within man's grasp to give, it is through God that she will receive what she and others deserve. The king, (men) or the material holder(s) of power, is (are) not important. It is the faithfulness by which Esther (women) establish(es) a relationship

74

with God, thus bring(s) on God's favor and faithfulness that will ensure victory over an oppressive condition.

While in the midst of her story of Esther, Johnson continues her critique of oppressive male ministers and includes a critique about those who turn against themselves because of their oppression:

> . . . some of us Black women and men want to do right. Yet, our very existence is threatened for something completely out of our control. We've been so scattered and dispersed for much of our lives that sometimes we feel that we have to disguise who we are and live a schizophrenic existence. It seems we can't tell folks who we really are . . . we can use many disguises . . . many of us feel that we can't even tell folks we're Christian . . . we can be so *cool* on God sometimes. We act cool when we don't say "Amen," and know the Spirit has hit us, or when we don't shout even though the Spirit says to shout . . . there's always a risk involved when you reveal who you are. And many of us, like Esther, do not find people around to support us: no friends and few family members. But, God always places someone around us who will remind us of who we are. . . . There's always someone around whom God will touch to reveal the responsibility that's attached to a position, whether it's that of queen, or a deacon, or an usher. (1985: 123)

Johnson may as well have said, "or that of an African American male preacher." But, then again, in her use of subtext she already had. African American women bring a fundamental spirituality to the profession and practice of preaching. Their stories of conversion or being "called" to preach usually involve some personal experience, conversation with, or sighting of Jesus or God. The Reverend Jarena Lee (1850s) described her experiences with the Deity, as well as those with the devil. She saw God in body, and listened as God told her she must preach. There were times she was "low in spirit" and doubted that God cared for and stood by her (she doubted her own worthiness) and she would literally see the devil manifest in the body of a great black dog. Her commitment to her calling became even stronger because of her personal experiences. With Reverend Lee as a strong example of the types of rewards and crises that are indicative of an African American woman's call to preach, it is no wonder that so many of them fight their oppression from the male ministers.

Frankly, it is anathema that so many African American men (and women) object to and fight against African American women being included in the ministry, and that they resist female ordinations. According to Cheikh Anta Diop, and other scholars, women were the bases of African society. Family lines were traced through the mother, and women were honored as being the "bearers of life." They were acknowledged to be wise, intelligent, and worthy of being adored. Wisdom was said to be within their very genes. Various invasions into the exterior and interior of Africa brought different religions and different ways of treating women into traditional African society. Africans, being a humanistic people, took on some of the characteristics of those that they came into contact with. Thus, African culture became "integrated" with notions of women's inferiority, and that women had a "particular place" to adjourn to in society. That mindset, in varying degrees, traveled the waters with the Africans, and found even stronger ideas of women's subjugation on the shores of America. Influenced twice by "outside ways," some African Americans have forgotten and foregone their once unbreakable bond to the majesty and intrinsic significance of the woman's voice to their lives. In doing so they have lost, and sometimes do not miss, the essence of themselves.

Ayi Kwei Armah's *Two Thousand Seasons* (1979) is an allegorical historical tale that draws from anthropological, sociological, psychological, and theological disciplines. He details the story of a "black skinned people's" descent into degradation and loss of sense of self. A prophecy is made by a woman in the tale that these people would be for two thousand seasons wandering from home and from themselves—one thousand seasons into the abyss, and one thousand seasons climbing out. The proclamation is necessitated by the people's forgetting of the Way, that is that *reciprocity* offering it and receiving it, is the manner by which longevity of existence and favor of the Deity is to be regained and retained. That the people have neglected to ask for "repayment" of their generosity from those who they know have been stealing from them, and who take what is offered with no offer of returning what they have received, they bring disfavor upon themselves. There is much more to this tale, but what is pertinent to this point is that the long years and seasons it took to bring such great disfavor upon the people began with some simple actions by the two genders.

Recorded by Armah, these dark skinned people were peaceful hunters and gatherers. Their society was stable. They had elders. Their children were well taken care of and well schooled in the ways that they should go. The roles of the women and men were defined such that the women farmed and the men gathered the meat. It seems though that getting meat was not a full time endeavor for the men, unlike farming for the women. Because the roles for providing for the society were so firmly entrenched, the men did not offer to help with the farming anymore. Armah writes that they become fat and lazy, sitting up under trees to shade themselves and asking the women to wait upon them when they needed refreshment. Armah says that this was the beginning of the people losing their knowledge of the Way. It was a travesty, he states, that the men so freely chose to become sycophants of the women, and began practicing the subjugation of the women to themselves. But, he also suggests that there was equal tragedy perpetuated in the fact that *the women allowed them to do so.* They acted as if they did not have a say, or could not require the men to contribute equally to the preservation of and provisions for the society. They freely gave away their voice and their resistant actions to the wrong that was done to them.

But, the descent into the abyss, remember, was to take only a thousand seasons, and there was to be a climbing back into favor of another thousand seasons. Though these seasons cannot be said with finality to equate to years, it was some two thousand years ago that Jesus died on the cross to atone for our sins. African and African American people have been through terrible seasons of degradation, and though some women have always spoken the gospel and have interpreted the Bible's significance to African American lives, only now are they making their voices heard loudly and firmly against any kind of oppression that they receive at the hand of others. Perhaps, it is Divine justice that they are fighting against one type of oppression that rises in the ranks of their own race and culture, *and* that they are fighting an oppression that they may have contributed to themselves: freedom must now come by their own hands.

Bibliography

Andrews, William L., ed. (1986). *Sisters of the Spirit: Three Black Women's Autobiographies of the Nineteenth Century.* Bloomington: Indiana University Press.

Armah, Ayi Kwei (1979). *Two Thousand Seasons.* Chicago: Third World Press.

Asante, Molefi Kete (1987). *The Afrocentric Idea.* Philadelphia, PA: Temple University Press.

Beale, Francis (1979). "Double Jeopardy: To be Black and Female," in Gayraud S. Wilmore and James H. Cone, eds., *Black Theology: A Documentary History, 1966–1979*. New York: Orbis Books.

Bruce, Calvin E., and William K. Jones (1978). *Black Theology II*. New York: Associated University Presses.

Cannon, Katie G. (1985). "On Remembering Who We Are," in Ella Pearson Mitchell, ed., *Those Preachin' Women*. Valley Forge, PA: Judson Press.

Cone, James H. (1986). *A Black Theology of Liberation*. New York: Orbis Books.

———. (1984a). *For My People: Black Theology and the Black Church*. New York: Orbis Books.

———. (1984b). "New Roles in the Ministry," in Gayraud S. Wilmore and James H. Cone, eds., *Black Theology: A Documentary History, 1966–1979*. New York: Orbis Books.

Cooper-Lewter, Nicholas C., and Henry H. Mitchell (1986). *Soul Theology*. San Francisco, CA: Harper & Row.

Davis, Gerald L. (1985). *I Got the Word in Me and I Can Sing It, You Know: A Study of the Performed African-American Sermon*. Philadelphia, PA: University of Pennsylvania Press.

Etuk, Emma S. (1989). *Destiny is not a Matter of Chance*. New York: Peter Lang.

Gibson, Elsie (1970). *When the Minister is a Woman*. New York: Holt, Rinehart and Winston.

Grant, Jacquelyn (1989). *White Women's Christ and Black Women's Jesus*. Atlanta, GA: Scholars Press.

———. (1979). "Black Theology and the Black Woman," in Gayraud S. Wilmore and James H. Cone, eds., *Black Theology: A Documentary History, 1966–1979*. New York: Orbis Books.

Grier, William H., and Price M. Cobbs (1971). *The Jesus Bag*. New York: McGraw-Hill.

Hoover, Theressa (1979). "Black Women and the Church: Triple Jeopardy," in Gayraud S. Wilmore and James H. Cone, eds., *Black Theology: A Documentary History, 1966–1979*. New York: Orbis Books.

Ice, Martha Long (1987). *Clergywomen and Their World Views: Calling for a New Age*. New York: Praeger Press.

Johnson, Suzan D. (1985). "God's Woman," in Ella Pearson Mitchell, ed., *Those Preachin' Women*. Valley Forge, PA: Judson Press.

Lincoln, C. Eric, ed. (1974). *The Black Experience in Religion*. New York: Anchor Books.

Mitchell, Ella Pearson, ed. (1975). *Those Preachin' Women: Nineteen Sermons by Black Women Preachers*. Valley Forge, PA: Judson Press.

Mitchell, Henry H. (1975). *Black Belief: Folk Beliefs of Blacks in America and West Africa*. New York: Harper & Row.

Murray, Pauli. (1979). "Black Theology and Feminist Theology: A Comparative View," in Gayraud S. Wilmore and James H. Cone, eds., *Black Theology: A Documentary History, 1966–1979*. New York: Orbis Books.

Proctor, Samuel D., and William D. Watley (1984). *Sermons from the Black Pulpit.* Valley Forge, PA: Judson Press.

Thistlethwaite, Susan Brooks (1989). *Sex, Race and God: Christian Feminism in Black and White.* New York: Crossroad Publishing.

Walker, Alice (1979). "In Search of our Mother's Gardens," in Gayraud S. Wilmore and James H. Cone, eds., *Black Theology: A Documentary History, 1966–1979.* New York: Orbis Books.

West, Cornel (1982). *Prophesy Deliverance: An Afro-American Revolutionary Christianity.* Philadelphia, PA: The Westminister Press.

Williams, Sharon E. (1985). "Studying War Some More," in Ella Pearson Mitchell, ed., *Those Preachin' Women.* Valley Forge, PA: Judson Press.

Wilmore, Gayraud S., and James H. Cone (1979). *Black Theology: A Documentary History, 1966–1979.* New York: Orbis Books.

Witvliet, Theo (1987). *The Black Messiah.* Oak Park, IL: Meyer-Stone Books.

Young, Henry J., ed. (1976). *Preaching the Gospel.* Philadelphia, PA: Fortress Press.

PART II

Social Welfare and Critical Analysis

CHAPTER 7

The Ethics of Futility in Healthcare Theological, Psychological, Medical, Social Implications

Juanita Fletcher-Cone
Cecil Cone

CASE HISTORY

H. Tubman is an eighty-four-year-old African American female with a history of insulin dependent diabetes mellitus, coronary heart disease, hypertension, and congestive heart failure. She is on multiple medications, including thirty units of insulin every morning, transderm nitro-5 heart patch once every twenty-four hours, procardia XL-60 daily, and lasix eighty mg daily. At the recommendation of her physician she is trying to maintain a low salt diabetic diet, but more often than not, she finds herself eating foods that are high in sugar, fat, and salt. She is married and resides with her eighty-six-year-old husband in their own home. They have three adult children; one lives in the same city, the other two live from five hundred to eight hundred miles away. Up to this point, Ms. Tubman and her husband have been able to take care of themselves reasonably well, except memory deficits (resulting from old age) sometimes cause her to forget to take her medications. At other times she does not take her medications because she cannot afford to purchase them. She likes to see the doctor and keep a close check on her heart and blood sugar, however, she will not keep her appointment if she does not have the money or transportation. She also feels that her visits to the doctor are supportive and helpful, but unfortunately there is never time for discussions regarding the home situation, advanced directives, living wills, or medication compliance.

Ms. Tubman is doing reasonably well until December 19, 1995, when she starts to develop fullness in her midchest area, brought on by exertion and associated with a shortness of breath. Over the next few days, the chest discomfort limits her ability to perform household chores. She also notices swelling in her legs and feet.

On December 22 around three in the morning, Ms. Tubman awakens with the feeling she is suffocating. Her husband (who is not well himself) recognizes that she is in distress and that she is cold, clammy, and foaming at the mouth. He calls 911 and, in about fifteen minutes, Rescue is at their home. By the time Rescue arrives, her respirations have become very labored and, of course, after applying appropriate care in the home setting, she is immediately transferred to AMEC Medical Center.

With no advanced directives regarding how to proceed with this elderly woman, the emergency room physician observes that she is in acute respiratory distress and that she needs to be placed on a respirator until her capacity to breathe for herself is returned. As a result of the tests that are completed in the emergency room, it is discovered that the buildup of fluid in her lungs is a result of a heart attack. In addition, the lack of oxygen deprivation may lead to a stroke.

Laboratory tests reveal that her liver is damaged and requires further investigation and treatment. Also, her blood sugar is out of control. After rendering acute treatment, the patient stabilizes and is admitted to the intensive care unit by her primary care physician, a board certified internist Dr. J. Cone. To ensure appropriate care, Dr. Cone consults a pulmonary specialist to manage the patient on the ventilator; a cardiologist to assist with the patient's heart attack; a neurologist to evaluate the patient's stroke condition; and a gastroenterologist to case for the patient's damaged liver. The patient's extremely high blood sugar is monitored and carefully treated by Dr. Cone and, of course, Dr. Cone has the responsibility of directing and making sure all medical efforts are coordinated to the best interest of the patient.

It is clear that an eighty-four-year-old lady who has major medical problems prior to developing an acute emergency, would be slow to recover. The husband and family members present at the time the patient is seen in the emergency room, are hysterical and want "everything that can be done" available to their loved one. Obviously, they need lots of emotional support, but, unfortunately, the physician is unable to provide such necessary help and comfort. The family pastor is not available, and the family has a hard time relating to the hospital chaplain. The hospital social worker is mainly there to help with discharge planning and her ability to provide emotional support is limited.

The patient remains on the respirator, in a comatose state, in the intensive care until she passes away twenty-three days later. During this time, multiple complications ensue, including the need for surgical procedures and multiple blood transfusions. Her frail body compromises her kidneys and dialysis becomes an added necessity. Her heart stops three times, but with all of the highly technological equipment and medicines, a normal heart rhythm is restored each time. There is the concern of whether or not she has functioning "brain activity." The neurologist performs brain wave tests (electroencephalograms) that always indicate some degree of brain activity. Although some physicians express that it is unethical to continue technological support for an eighty-four-year-old lady who appears to have only minimal brain activity with virtually no likelihood of recovery, there are others who feel they are obligated to move forward.

The family is questioned repeatedly about their feelings on whether or not to resuscitate and, with emotions running high and plagued by the lack of sleep or rest, their answer is always "yes, do everything." Unfortunately, Mr. Tubman's health breaks down during this time and the major stroke that ensues causes him to end up in the AMEC Medical Center in a near similar condition.

By the twenty-second day, the physician in charge is fed up, frustrated, and senses the futility of everything that is being attempted. She consults the chairman of the Hospital Medical Ethics Committee, who calls a special meeting to discuss the case. The committee members present consist of the hospital chaplain, the social worker, the medical director, and the chairman of the Hospital Medical Ethics Committee. There are other lay members on the committee but they cannot be present, nor can any of the doctors involved in the case. The patient and her husband have been members of the Morris African Methodist Episcopal Church for forty-eight years and, although the pastor comes to see her from time to time in the hospital, he does not play an active role in her medical care or decision-making process. When the meeting is concluded, all efforts to cure the patient are unanimously decided futile, and the recommendation to terminally wean the patient from the respirator is made. The family agrees with the decision. However, before the weaning from the respirator is initiated, the patient's heart stops again. This time no attempt is made to resuscitate the patient. She is pronounced dead at 3 A.M. on January 14, 1996.

The presented case history could represent many patients seen by physicians in hospitals everyday. Most individuals who read this essay will be reminded of similar situations they have known. But if you are one who has not yet experienced this life challenge, just keep living. Currently, those over the age of sixty-five comprise 12 percent of America's population; this figure will rise to 20 percent by the year 2020. Advances in medical science and technology have extended the life process and we are sure to be confronted with many, many more experiences similar to this case history.

Great wisdom is hidden in the depths of a situation like this, but our ability to receive the insight that it brings is usually determined by our perceptions and our emotions. As you read the case history you will recognize that there are multiple issues needing to be addressed. These include the limited social and financial resources available for our senior citizens, improving the physician-patient relationship, the usefulness of advanced life support technologies, an appreciation for the dying process, the pastor's role in health care delivery, and finally the issue of futility in health care.

Although all of these issues are significant, interrelated, interdependent, and play a vital role in determining how health care is delivered individually and collectively, the primary purpose here is for the reader to develop a better understanding about ethics and how it relates to futility in health care.

As far back as history can record, the goals of medicine have always been "to cure sometimes," "to relieve often," and "to comfort always." Therefore, the statement could be made that futility does not really have a place in the delivery of health care because beneficence is possible at every level of caring. However, when futile medical care is defined as it is viewed in the health arena, sometimes it is seen as that point where treatment is considered of zero benefit (the point in the life of a patient when everything we do to better the patient's health fails); other times, futile medical care means treatment that is highly unlikely to be efficacious (treatment that is virtually certain to produce a low-grade effect). The sophisticated technologies that have been designed for the care of patients often leads to a crisis in the souls of all individuals involved in a particular case. Our ability to face this issue with clarity and purpose will help us to systematically evaluate every situation and be better able to determine that which is right and wrong; good and evil. This ability is the basis of ethics and its origin is deeply rooted in religion, although it is not generally presented in medical ethics this way.

Without doubt, we are always focusing on ways to sustain life, because the fear of death creates in us an intense desire to live forever. As human beings, we struggle continuously with certain givens and ultimate concerns of existence. Among these ultimate concerns are isolation, freedom, meaninglessness, and death. Emotional anxiety erupts from basic conflicts in each of these areas: our deepest need is to be at one with someone and have someone be at one with us, while we experience an unbridgeable gap between self and others; we long for structure, stability, and something solid beneath our feet, while each day we are confronted with an unstable sense of existence; we seek meaning every day we live, while the world appears to have no meaning; we wish to continue to be, while we are aware of our own inevitable death. The desire for longevity, together with the desire to find meaningful existence, keeps scientists researching, experimenting, and developing even more advanced medical technologies.

The development of a higher level of technology created a new discipline in medicine known as the field of modern American bioethics. It originated in 1962 when dialysis was made available for patients with kidney failure who would have otherwise died. At that time, there were many more patients than dialysis machines, and the University of Washington where the procedure was being instituted had to form a committee to literally decide who would receive dialysis and live, and who would not and die. This committee could be considered America's first medical ethics committee at work. Thirty-four years have passed since that time, and, with an overabundance of technological advances, an aging population, and managed health care, bioethical issues that deal with medical decisions at the end of life are placing great challenges on our total society.

A case that involves medical futility always creates emotional turmoil for everyone involved, including the patient (who may or may not be physically aware), the physician, family, nurses, social workers, pastor, and therapist, as well as hospital administrators. The physician, whether he or she admits it, has a difficult time dealing with their inability to save the patient, or, unfortunately, may be motivated by financial greed or the possibility of a malpractice suit. Clearly, the proper use of end of life decisions should always be guided by the primary motive of helping people—to do no harm.

As a part of denial seen in the dying process, families may request nonbeneficial care against the doctor's medical judgment. And doctors can and have actually refused futile care which neither treats or palliates. In either of these situations, the hospital ethics committee could be most helpful in coming up with the best possible decision for the patient. These difficult situations are best handled by the family, pastor, and designated hospital staff, but often times it has been the courts that have decided on such issues as to continue or not to continue ventilator support in a particular patient.

When hospital administrators are confronted with long term ICU patients like Ms. Tubman, they are on pins and needles because of the tremendous bills that are continuously mounting up. Although it would never be ethically right for the administrator to say anything to the physician or family regarding their feelings, physicians know that they are up against a monster called economic credentialing—being able to provide quality care in the most reasonable period of time with the least amount of money necessary. Realizing that you might be deselected from hospital staffs, or managed care programs because you spend too much of the hospital or managed care budget taking care of your patients, you just might move to the conclusion of futility quicker than deemed appropriate for some of your patients. Allowing financial incentives to be the driving force in health care delivery is unethical.

Since managed care (the application of standard business practices into medical health care) is clearly the way our country is headed, we must make certain that, in our quest for containment of cost and promotion of the profit-making status, our care of the patient not be jeopardized. Envisioning medical care as a commodity that can be sold in the market place is difficult, but whatever the case, health care must always be just, virtuous, autonomous, beneficent, and nonmaleficent.

In the case history presented, an advanced directive would have better benefited Ms. Tubman before her becoming acutely ill. An Ethics Committee would not have been called in to act on her behalf. An advanced directive, also referred to as a Living Will, is a legal document that signals patient self determination. It comes out of a bioethical principal that states that all competent persons are believed to have a fundamental right to control decisions relating to their medical care. It empowers the patient with control over his or her body, even for decisions against medical advice. When patients become seriously ill, they may become confused, delirious, or comatose, and therefore incapable of making decisions regarding their treatment. Knowing their wishes is important, since some treatment options may only prolong the dying process while offering little or no reasonable chance of recovery.

The majority of Americans are fearful of this available option and have not executed such a document. Federal legislation that went into effect in December 1991, mandates all hospitals to inform patients of advanced directive statutes when they are admitted to the hospital. Being confronted with this question at the time of admission to the hospital often creates apprehension about medical care. There are even instances in which patients who are already on ventilators, because of their condition (e.g., end-stage emphysema) are asked if they would like to be taken off, with the full understanding that this could mean the end of their life.

Effective educational strategy should be developed that would help individuals gain a deeper understanding of the value of advanced directives and allow them to make an intelligent decision in an appropriate setting. The African American is even more distrustful of the health care system and will more readily shy away from Living Wills. The education directed towards the African American must be culturally sensitive and religion oriented.

There is no better vehicle to keep health care ethical and make sure managed care is just, than through churches. A trillion dollars is spent on health care annually in the United States, yet the uninsured, under insured, poverty stricken, uneducated, and even some middle-class persons do not benefit fairly. And most times these persons represent the unhealthiest part of our society. The pastor and the physician must become a team working cooperatively to meet the physical and spiritual needs of the patient. People need to intensify their relationship with their minister when they are sick. Church has always been the center of the life process for the African American and it needs to become the center of the dying process.

The following recommendations are submitted to the General Conference for consideration, with the anticipation that they will enhance our health focus and strengthen our individual and collective service to God:

- Appointment of a Board of Health within the African Methodist Episcopal Church (AMEC), headed by a Director of Health, whose primary purpose is not only to actively find means to improve the health of our church body, but to focus in on those who are uninsured, under insured, and unhealthy; and make certain that the government and even big businesses that insure employees are providing just health coverage. The recommendations of the Board of Health should be carried out on the local level and include such items as doing periodic health screenings and regularly scheduled workshops on preventive health, behavior modification, advanced directives, health insurance, and managed care.
- The AMEC should form a consortium with community hospitals and health centers in order to make pastoral involvement with members who are acutely ill more official. For example, the patient's pastor should be automatically consulted when a patient, who is critically or terminally ill, is admitted to the hospital. The pastor should be called to serve on the Hospital Ethics Committee when one of his or her parishioner's medical situation requires their attention.
- The AMEC should form a consortium with a community hospital or a medical college in its area for the specific purpose of forming clinics in the church that can screen for heart disease, cancer, hypertension, and strokes, and any other appropriate screening that can educate, motivate, and demonstrate on health nutrition, smoking cessation, and the value of exercise.
- The AMEC should make issues related to death and dying a part of the minister's four-year conference course of study;

continuing education on death and dying should also be made available to all pastors.

Our health care system is changing and since African Americans experience a disproportionate rate of medical diseases, there seems to be a pressing need for the church to become more actively involved in the health care of its people.

•••••••••••••••••

CHAPTER 8

Contributions of Black Theology

Dorraine A. Hooks

Among black people, cultural sharing transcends religious affiliation. One would think, theoretically, that a black religion in relation to the Bible would include a number of blacks who are religious but who are not Christians. There however, is a shared, transcendent cultural reality experienced by black Christians and nonChristians alike: black suffering. Black suffering shares the suffering that is common to all human beings; sickness, broken homes, tragedies of death, accidents, wars, and so on. On the other hand, that suffering has been compounded by slavery, discrimination, and racism. The sociological grid of blacks provides a solidarity that transcends even membership in the Christian religion (Felder 1991: 25).

European slave masters used the Bible to humble the African by teaching submission as a basis for Christian guidelines. As slaves learned more about the Bible, they interpreted the book differently than their masters; they related themselves to the story about the Hebrew slaves who received freedom through the hands of God. African Americans believed Christ's time on earth demonstrates the Lord's desire to guide and help all mankind and not a certain group or culture of people. While slave masters used the Bible to justify slavery, African Americans found their actions contradictory. Still, many of them accepted biblical teachings and embraced Christianity (1991: 28).

In the field of theology, students attempt to assess words and elements of beliefs that are implicitly or explicitly contained in faith (Encarta 1997). For the African American theology student, the problem of interpretation compounds itself through living, growing, learning, and functioning in an oppressive society. African Americans must ascertain what Christian faith means for them; due to their conditioning and socialization, this process often proves difficult. In his piece on "The Mis-Education of the Negro," Carter G. Woodson states:

> In schools of theology, Negroes are taught the interpretation of the Bible worked out by those who have justified segregation and winked at the economic debasement of the Negro sometimes almost to the point of starvation. Deriving their sense of right from this teaching, graduates of such schools can have no message to grip the people whom they have been ill trained to serve. Most of such mis-educated ministers, therefore, preach to benches while illiterate Negro preachers do the best they can in supplying the spiritual needs of the masses. (1990: 4–5)

Once Africans came to America and learned of the white man's Bible, they believed in the book's power. While slave masters used Scripture to hold slaves to their rules, the African saw and developed different biblical interpretation. In all probability, this interpretation fueled the determination, faith, belief, and birth of two different realities. Woodson demonstrates how these realities present themselves in almost every discipline. The most recent and blatant reminder of these different viewpoints can be seen in the reactions to the infamous O.J. Simpson trial.

History describes America as a biblical nation; therefore, in all probability, slaves began their hegemonic education through the learning of the Scripture. This successful use of the Bible necessitates the need to address theology from a black standpoint in hopes of obtaining purposes for life, releasing mental bondages, understanding God's will, and ultimately gaining liberation.

Given the multitude of inferences to the inferiority of African Americans, the first task involves securing and comprehending life's purpose. One begins this process by acknowledging, "I am here for a reason." Upon this acknowledgment, the African American then considers the environment and his or her status. This step proves important since the choice involves either assimilation or a desire to function from a cultural standpoint. Either choice involves finding a purpose for being and basing one's life on that purpose. The bombardment of majority stimuli makes choosing assimilation an easier effort, but choosing to live culturally requires work.

Establishing a purpose becomes essential when considering the popular western theological notion of dark peoples as cursed. In *Stony the Road we Trod* (1991), Cain Hope Felder reviews the story of Ham's curse. The Bible illustrates how Ham sees his father Noah as nude, and fails to cover him (as was the custom of the time). When Noah wakes up, he curses his son for his disrespect. After researching the scripture,

Felder explains the different Bible interpretations, connotations, and inconsistencies surrounding the incident. Felder concludes, "In my view, it is this development that clearly attests to the process of sacralization where cultural and historical phenomena are recast as theological truths with vested interests for particular groups" (1991: 130).

By rejecting Ham's curse, African Americans can then reject views of inferiority placed upon them by some higher power. The biblical inconsistencies clearly show how different cultures have used the Scripture to enhance their purpose. Dark-skinned peoples who observe the patterns of society and determine their race do indeed appear cursed, can find solace throughout the Bible with Scripture stating all can freely worship. The scripture repeatedly states how all peoples can worship and share in God's salvation. The example of Ham's curse demonstrates how most cultures tend to present information and values in favor of their best interests. Developing a purpose provides a reason for existence, and affirming existence enforces the ability to understand oneself as human. As involuntary immigrants, African Americans suffered humiliation without regard to the concept of their humanity. The suggestion of slaves not constituting a whole person justified their mistreatment and invited intricate and consistent inferiority models espoused in academic disciplines. Woodson demonstrates these processes by detailing the derogatory education African Americans receive.

Na'im Akbar states that:

> One of the persisting difficulties facing African American people is the difficulty to think independently. We are constrained by the perception that thinking and ideas are the exclusive privilege of those who are similar to the image of divinity. Our scholars are limited to imitating the scholarship of independent Caucasian thinkers. We analyze our situation and the nature of the world in general, exclusively from the frame of reference of Euro Americans. (1984: 63)

Akbar's contention demonstrates the danger of functioning in hegemony. "The traditional Western separation of the physical and the spiritual, the sacred and the secular is foreign to the Afro-American sensibility" (Evans 1987: 2). This statement espouses the concept of cycles and their rhythmic impact they play in life. Just as the universe is formulated and functions cyclically, humans so do (Dewey

94

1971: 4). As a result of their involuntary immigrant status, African Americans often find themselves functioning under the alien cycle of majority culture. By rejecting the majority cycle, African Americans can cultivate definitions for existence and release mental bondages.

Once establishing purpose, African Americans can remove mental bondages. This suggestion means exchanging the current hegemonic paradigm for a culturally aware mind-set. In theology circles, this process involves obtaining a revelation of God's purpose. It also places the supposedly orthodox teachings into question. Even black theorists and writers who lack a strong religious background present the need to operate in the sacred as opposed to the secular. With an emphasis on spirituality, the role of the theologian increases along with the responsibilities of the black church.

"In the midst of slavery, Jim Crow laws, and overt racism, the black church was interpreting scripture and experience to enhance the self-esteem of children and adults who were being dehumanized by laws and customs" (Harris 1991: 115). Black Christian churches vigorously preach for African Americans to enhance their lives and the basic teaching suggests this process must occur spiritually. A crucial goal of the black church involves elevating self-esteem and rejecting negative images, stereotypes, and myths so generously provided to African Americans by the majority culture. James E. Harris, discussing self-esteem, states:

> Poor self-esteem manifests itself in a lingering torpor that is both frightening and sad. In observing the behavior of some in the black community, I often see and hear about insecurity, insensitivity, anger, and violence directed against each other rather than against the "world rulers, principalities, and powers" (cf. Ephesians 6:12) that are responsible for the oppression. (1991: 117)

Harris sees low self-esteem as prevalent in the African American community, and he explains how these dysfunctional phenomena result from oppression. The impact self-perception has on other areas of an individual's life endorses the need to create a strong positive self-image. This process begins within. The black church helps elevate this process with prayer, faith, giving, growing, and establishing oneself. Harris warns pastors of black churches not to take their roles lightly. Their vast responsibilities extend far beyond preaching at the pulpit on Sundays. They must establish themselves as leaders and promoters of the total process of evolving out of oppression (1991: 123).

Black theology also involves an applied study of scripture in order to assist the black church in its role. Presently, unity does not exist between the black church and black theologians. The division results from different objectives—the role of the church involves uplifting its members and community with knowledge and faith of God's power, while theology focuses on biblical interpretation and analysis. Harris explains how these problems often present themselves in most disciplines when attempting to merge theory with practice (1991: 58). Black theology strives to answer questions and present holistic models of concreteness for complete religious practice; therefore, unity between the black church and black theologians can assist in progressing conditions in the African American community. This unity suggests the merging of church and theology has the ability to confront, dispel, or change negative and unproductive stimuli and behavior in the African American community and move them out of mental bondage.

With the removal of mental bondages, African Americans can enlighten themselves by fulfilling God's will. In Christianity, the essence of spirituality encompasses a strong relationship with the Supreme being. Lacking purpose and holding on to mental bondages makes fulfilling God's will difficult. Both the church and theology see the significance of this, so any congruence of the two should probably begin here.

Theology extensively studies the impact of the historical and the kerygma Jesus while the church attempts to enhance through faith, a belief and desire to emulate Christ. Cone writes of Jesus' purpose and how he exemplifies a crusader for the oppressed:

> Jesus' teaching about the kingdom is the most radical, revolutionary aspect of his message. It involves the totality of a person's existence in the world and what that means in an oppressive society. To repent is to affirm the reality of the kingdom by refusing to live on the basis of any definition except according to the kingdom. Nothing else matters! The kingdom, then, is the rule of God breaking in like a ray of light, usurping the powers that enslave human lives. (1990: 116)

The different interpretations and inconsistencies within the Bible explain the multitude of approaches and models of belief extending from it. Still, the Scripture provides indisputable instruction and concrete information in many areas. Many of its stringent guidelines demand an existence totally geared towards living God's will. African American Christians must find their place within this ideology in order to live God's will. In order to achieve this ideology, they must find identity in a religion they learned from white culture. Muslims and others who reject Christianity often marvel at how African Americans worship a god who, as Dr. John Henrik Clarke states in a video documentary "African People Facing the 21st Century" (1991), was assigned to them. The worship includes a total acceptance of functioning for God and embracing his doctrine as a blueprint for life. Cone presents a theology model where African Americans can identify with their Savior by connecting to an oppressed historical black Christ. He believes this identification proves necessary for African Americans to relate to Christ. If African Americans cannot identify with Christ, then he sees no reason for Christian worship (Cone 1990).

Cone further defines black theology and, as crucial to liberation just as Harris also expresses, a need for the black church to participate in black liberation. While theology attempts to find answers to various gray areas in the Scripture, the church tries to help its members liberate themselves. The effort involves initially striving towards liberation on an individual level before moving towards a collective effort. The quest for black liberation must reject integration and assimilation because these efforts disregard the significance of African heritage and assumes little value about the dark continent.

American history paints a derogatory view of African culture, and African American academe must make efforts to balance this distorted picture. "As long as blacks let whiteness define the limits of their being, blacks are dead" (1990: 12). In order to gain insight about the degree in lost culture, a knowledge of African American history and culture must begin before the slavery time frame. By understanding Africa before the slave trade, African Americans can take control over and cultivate their culture, based on principles consistent with their psyche. Failure to achieve this understanding keeps hegemony alive since many customs, mores, and values of majority culture differ.

In his "Message to the Grassroots" (1964), Malcolm X discusses the force behind black nationalism. By examining other historical events, he explains the ideology of revolution and its implications, and how liberation cannot be obtained peacefully. Cone agrees with Malcolm's assessment concerning the need for a revolution in order to achieve liberation:

> Blacks know that there is only one possible authentic existence in this society, and that is to force a radical revolutionary confrontation with the structures of white power by saying yes to the essence of their blackness. The role of black theology is to tell blacks to focus on their own self-determination as a community by preparing to do anything the community believes necessary for its existence. (1990: 15)

As evidenced through the response to the black power movement, the majority culture rejects the idea of African Americans defining themselves. They believe the movement clashes with democracy. The arrogant assumption of civilizing a primitive culture and providing it with Christian principles and morals supersedes attempts at comprehending the magnitude of their actions. African Americans lack the luxury to ignore negative views and actions placed upon them; therefore, this unrest and tension made both Malcolm X and Cone conclude a revolution must result.

Liberation involves building a power base, cultivating a culture, and establishing collective consciousness. For these things to manifest, the risk involves stepping on the toes of the majority culture and exposing their inconsistencies. In all probability, this revolution will be met with neither kindness nor appreciation for establishing a balanced and real presentation of the past and present. Even though not all theorists and academic scholars agree with the need for a revolution, no one can discount this possibility.

For Christians, black theology provides focus and legitimacy to the worship and process of serving God. The need for this discipline derives from the introduction of Christianity through the slave trade. As Felder points out, this task proves no different from efforts of other cultures. The black church evolved early in order to assist slaves with their faith and meaning for existence. The cumulative nature of racism and discrimination can be seen in consistent patterns within the African American community. Unique and sacred steps provide keys to unleashing this dilemma. Black theology attempts to give purpose to being, and this purpose assists in efforts of unleashing mental bondages resulting from slavery. Since the Bible proclaims the reason for existence involves doing the will of God, complicated issues surrounding purpose and mental bondage must be overcome. Once African Americans strive towards dealing with these issues, they have the tools necessary to begin building towards liberation.

Bibliography

Akbar, Na'im (1984). "Africentric Social Sciences for Human Liberation," *Journal of Black Studies* 14:4 (June): 395–414.

Clarke, John Henrik (1991). Video lecture, "African People Facing the 21st Century," New York City.

Cone, James H. (1991). *A Black Theology of Liberation*, 2d ed. Maryknoll, NY: Orbis Books.

Conyers, James L., Jr. (1995). *The Evolution of African American Studies: A Descriptive and Evaluative Analysis of Selected African American Studies Departments and Programs.* New York: University Press of America.

Dewey, Edward R. (1971). *Cycles: The Mysterious Forces that Trigger Events.* New York: Hawthorn Books.

Encarta (1997). PC, Microsoft Home, Tech Data, Germantown, WI, c. 1996.

Evans, James H., Jr. (1987). *Black Theology: A Critical Assessment and Annotated Bibliography.* New York: Greenwood Press.

Felder, Cain Hope (1991). *Stony the Road We Trod.* Minneapolis, MN: Fortress Press.

Harris, James H. (1991). *Pastoral Theology.* Minneapolis, MN: Fortress Press.

Woodson, Carter, G. (1933, reprint 1990). *The Mis-Education of the Negro.* Trenton, NJ: Africa World Press.

CHAPTER 9

Social Work: A Cultural Perspective

Audreye Johnson

Social work and social welfare are intended to help people attain the basic necessities of life—food, clothing, and shelter—as well as to aid them in developing their human potential. Throughout the twentieth century such efforts have often, though not always, been carried out in conjunction with programs for social reform. Although social welfare activity initially was the preserve of private services and organizations, over the years government has come to play an increasingly active role. The history of U.S. social work, its relationship to social activism, and its growing importance within government distribution of services have had important implications for the quality of life of African Americans as individuals and as a community.

Long before social work emerged as a professional field, African Americans had carried out a wide range of cooperative self-help and mutual-aid programs in order to better their lives and their communities. Throughout the eighteenth and nineteenth centuries, free black women and men in the north organized benevolent societies; among the earliest was the Free African Society of Philadelphia, formed in 1787 to provide cradle-to-grave counseling and other assistance, including burial aid. Other groups raised money for educational programs or relief to widows and orphans. Northern blacks not only helped themselves, they extended aid to fugitive slaves and linked their work to a larger effort to improve the standing of African Americans in society.

Following the Civil War, the Freedmen's Bureau, a federal agency, initiated a series of social welfare policies designed to help newly freed black people in their struggle to survive; during Reconstruction many southern states promoted similar relief efforts. But in the context of emancipation, such economic, educational, and other assistance not only improved the lives of individual African Americans, it posed a challenge to the system of racial inequality itself. After Reconstruction, therefore, most states of the former Confederacy resisted adoption of programs that would alter the status quo; when local and state government did intervene on behalf of the aged, infirm, and others in needs, it did so on a segregated basis.

Largely excluded from such services, African Americans in the north and the south continued to practice the kind of "social work" that had served them for centuries. Black women were often at the forefront of these efforts, pooling resources and playing a leadership role in establishing orphanages, homes for the poor and aged, educational and health-care services, and kindergartens. The abolitionist Harriet Tubman turned her residence in Auburn, New York, into the Home for Indigent and Aged Negroes, one of perhaps a hundred such facilities by 1915. In urban centers, black women organized to aid newly arriving migrant women in finding lodging and employment; among the most prominent of these efforts was New York's White Rose Working Girls Home, founded by Victoria Earle Matthews in 1897.

Professional social work emerged around the turn of the twentieth century in response to conditions generated by the processes of industrialization, urbanization, European immigration, and southern migration. Charitable organizations, such as the National Conference of Charities and Corrections, sought to coordinate and professionalize their work, but they continued to emphasize personal misfortune or moral failing instead of larger institutional explanations for the pervasive poverty in urban industrial centers. Before the massive exodus of black people from the south to north, most charity workers paid scant attention to the problems of African Americans. With the Great Migration, some charitable reformers came to view black people as another immigrant group needing "Americanization," and they found ample support for their moralistic emphasis on thrift and industry from Booker T. Washington's philosophy of individual uplift. Other philanthropists insisted that black people were meant to occupy an inferior station in life and urged that they acquire industrial training suited to their "natural" limitations.

In contrast, settlement workers, mostly college-educated white women, sought to learn from immigrants and migrants themselves instead of imposing their own values and assumptions. They proposed to live in impoverished communities, providing services that would help newcomers adjust to urban industrial life without giving up their own beliefs and cultural traditions. Though settlement workers could not always mask their middle-class backgrounds, they did establish job-training and placement programs, health care services, kindergartens, and recreation facilities. Perhaps the best-known settlement was Chicago's Hull House, founded by Jane Addams and Ellen Gates Starr in 1889.

Unlike charity workers, white activists in the settlement movement were often quicker to recognize that poor housing, educational, and job opportunities in the burgeoning black communities of the urban north were the direct result of segregation and racial discrimination. Using scientific methods to identify and analyze social problems, settlement workers pressed for government reforms in such areas as factory and tenement conditions, juvenile justice, child labor, and public sanitation. Their efforts to fuse social work with social reform also extended to race relations; one-third of the signatories of the 1909 "call" that led to the formation of the NAACP either were or had been settlement workers.

Advocating racial tolerance and an end to discrimination, however, was not the same as calling for social equality. Many social service agencies in Chicago, New York, and elsewhere either refused help to African Americans outright or offered poor quality assistance on a segregated basis; this fact was especially true for organizations providing lodging, board, and medical care. The settlement houses were no exception. Many were located in white immigrant communities, but a number of settlements that were easily accessible from black neighborhoods still did not serve the African American population. Some white reformers pursued alliances with black community leaders in establishing "interracial" settlements; one notable example was Frederick Douglass Center, founded in Chicago in 1904. However, the center disdained "slum work" among the black poor, so its leaders, including white minister Celia Parker Wooley and black club woman Fannie Barrier Williams, sought to bring together the educated elite, black and white, for lectures, concerts, and other cultural activities.

Often, African Americans themselves were the ones who, seeking to remedy the inequalities in social service provision, seized the initiative in addressing individual and social problems in the black community. But such activists were faced with a stark dilemma. Without the assistance of white philanthropists, they could not hope to match "white" agencies in staffing and programming; indeed, their facilities rarely survived. Between 1900 and 1916, at least nine settlements were established in Chicago's black neighborhoods; by 1919 only one remained. In 1910 renowned anti-lynching agitator Ida B. Wells-Barnett formed the Negro Fellowship League, which offered recreational services for black men and boys, an employment agency, and later, lodging. But she was forced to disband it for lack of funds.

The alternative—support from white people—usually meant control by white people. Chicago's Wendell Phillips Center, for example, was initiated in 1907 by a group of twenty black activists, and its staff was mostly black; its board, however, was overwhelmingly dominated by whites. Thus, white reformers were able to limit the autonomy of black community leaders. In so doing, they often contributed to the preservation of the racial status quo. Even so, they helped shape the kinds of programs that were available; services for black girls, for instance, were more likely to win financial support if they emphasized morality and offered training in domestic work. However, the very involvement of whites in the creation of services "for blacks" often reflected their desire to maintain segregation in social services.

Even when forced to rely on the resources of white philanthropists whose agendas clashed with their own, African Americans often strived to translate their reform activities into a larger program of social action. In 1899, the distinguished Harvard University graduate W. E. B. Du Bois produced *The Philadelphia Negro,* a meticulously researched study of urban African American life. The project had been commissioned by the College Settlement Association, whose conservative wing was driven by the conviction that black people were somehow ridden with criminality and vice—an early version of the "culture of poverty" argument advanced in the 1960s to explain why economic misery persisted in much of the urban black community. But Du Bois consciously sought to set his findings within a historical and social context that acknowledged the importance of economic and political, not personal, solutions. Du Bois's sociological approach pioneered the use of scientific inquiry into the causes and effects of social problems.

The National Urban League—formed in 1910 as a merger of the

National League for the Protection of Colored Women, the Committee for Improving Industrial Conditions of Negroes in New York, and the National League on Urban Conditions Among Negroes—represented the application of professional social work to the kinds of social services that had long been practiced in the black community. It was founded by George Edmund Haynes, the first black graduate of the New York School of Philanthropy (later the Columbia University School of Social Work), and Ruth Standish Baldwin, a wealthy white reformer. The league offered counseling and other assistance to African Americans in housing, education, employment, health, recreation, and child care. It relied on scientific research techniques to document the exclusion of African Americans and press for greater opportunities.

The league also played an important role in the training and placement of black social workers. Formal social work education made its debut in 1903 with the University of Chicago's School of Civics and Philanthropy, later known as the School of Social Service Administration. In 1917 the National Conference of Charities and Corrections became the National Conference of Social Work. (In 1956 its name was changed to the National Conference on Social Welfare.) But because of racial segregation blacks were barred from social work education and training outside the north until the 1950s, and they were denied full participation in professional bodies.

Through the able leadership of Urban League personnel, historically black educational institutions stepped in to fill the void. Under Haynes's direction, Fisk University developed an undergraduate social service curriculum, including field placement with league affiliates. The Atlanta School of Social Work was founded in 1920 to provide instruction to black students, and it later affiliated with Atlanta University. By 1926, the Urban League itself employed one hundred fifty black social workers. Over the years, the league continued to preserve important ties to social work education; Whitney M. Young, Jr., for example, served as dean of the Atlanta University School of Social Work before becoming the league's executive director in 1961.

The devastating economic crisis generated by the Great Depression severely strained the capacity of private social service organizations to assist individuals in need. In an extension of the reform impulse of the Progressive period, the federal government under

President Franklin D. Roosevelt was forced to intervene with massive programs that placed social work firmly within the public domain. The Social Security Act of 1935 provided old age and survivors' insurance, unemployment insurance (known as entitlement benefits), and public assistance to the aged, the blind, and dependent children.

However, for African Americans the impact of government involvement was contradictory, since programs aimed at affected workers automatically excluded large numbers of black people. Nearly half of all African Americans worked in agricultural labor, casual labor, and domestic service, but these occupations were not counted as part of the covered workforce. The Urban League, the National Association for the Advancement of Colored People (NAACP), and others opposed the exclusion, arguing that it would single out black people as a stigmatized, dependent population, but their efforts were unsuccessful. They also openly criticized the unequal distribution of relief and segregated assistance programs.

The Civil Rights Movement of the 1960s, fueled by legal and social gains achieved by African Americans during the previous decade, attacked racism and discrimination on all fronts, and social work was no exception. Concentrated in segregated enclaves, crowded into dilapidated housing, and suffering from dramatically high rates of unemployment, black people in the inner cities had not reaped the benefits promised by the advent of civil rights. When Daniel Patrick Moynihan argued in 1965 that the black community was caught in a "tangle of pathology" resulting from "the deterioration of the Negro family," he was articulating a moralistic theme that had persisted in social welfare policy since at least the late nineteenth century. It was activist-oriented African Americans who led the challenge to such interpretations, defending the integrity of the black family and calling for a deeper understanding of the structural causes of poverty.

The antipoverty programs initiated under the Johnson administration's Great Society, while in part a response to Moynihan's analysis, also created new opportunities for contesting it. African American social workers condemned racism within the profession and demanded a greater commitment to issues of social justice. In 1967, because of opposition from the leadership of the National Association of Social Workers (NASW), a nondiscrimination amendment to the association's code of ethics was presented on the floor of the delegate assembly, where it passed. The following year, in San Francisco,

African Americans founded the National Association of Black Social Workers (NABSW). While some black individuals gained prominence within existing professional organizations—Whitney Young, Jr., for example, became president of the NASW in 1969—many African Americans turned to the NABSW as a vehicle for articulating the goals of effective, responsive service delivery in the black community and an end to racial exclusion and discrimination within the ranks of the profession.

Social work and social welfare programs, although widely believed to provide services on a nondiscriminatory basis, have always been influenced by larger historical trends and conditions. The historical exclusion of African Americans from social work schools and organizations virtually assured that concerned black people would continue to rely on their own methods for improving individual and community life. At the same time, the profession's dominant strategies and methodologies have reflected the racial, sexual, and class biases of the European American middle class, often to the detriment of those most commonly under the scrutiny of social workers.

An African American presence within the social work profession has helped to transform service delivery. Many black social workers have developed innovative models that acknowledge the importance of environmental factors—such as socioeconomic status and citizenship rights—in determining the well-being of African American people. By asserting positive recognition of extended family formations, they have been able to respond with new flexibility to individual and family concerns. And they have sought to extend these efforts throughout the profession, working to ensure that social work education and training incorporate information about the experiences of people of color. At the same time, many African Americans in social work have rejected the notion of adjustment to the status quo, calling for change in social institutions, laws, and customs that continue to keep African Americans from achieving their full potential.

In the 1990s, the assumptions that have guided social work theory and practice demand renewed attention. The problems facing the black community continued to reflect the racism that persists in employment, health care, education, and other areas. The unemployment rate among African Americans remains twice the national average; the AIDS crisis has reached disproportionately into the black community; and drug-addicted children are now entering an educational system whose capacities are severely constrained by diminishing resources. As in the past, however, the African American community has been left to tap its own potential in order to address these concerns. At the same time, mainstream social workers have adopted code words—diversity, multiculturalism, biculturalism—that obscure root causes and so fail to confront deep-seated racism, sexism, and class bias. Advocates of social work and social welfare can respond effectively to current problems by reclaiming a legacy of progressive social reform that acknowledges the need for structural, not personal, solutions.

Bibliography

Aptheker, Herbert, ed. (1971). *A Documentary History of the Negro People in the United States,* vol. 1. New York: Carol Publishing Group.

Axinn, June, and Herman Levin (1992). *Social Welfare: A History of the American Response to Need,* 3d ed. White Plains, NY: Longman.

Bell, Howard R. (1969). "National Negro Conventions of the Middle 1840s: Moral Suasion vs. Political Action," in August Meier and Elliott Rudwick, eds., *The Making of Black America: Essays in Negro Life and History,* vol. 1. New York: Atheneum.

Bennett, Lerone, Jr. (1988). *Before the Mayflower: A History of Black America,* 6th ed. Chicago: Johnson Publishing.

———. (1975). *The Shaping of Black America.* Chicago: Johnson Publishing.

Breul, Frank R., and Steven J. Diner, eds. (1980). *Compassion and Responsibility: Readings in the History of Social Welfare Policy in the United States.* Chicago: University of Chicago Press.

Clark, William E. (1923). "The Katy Ferguson Home," *Southern Workman* 52: 228–230.

Cromwell, Cheryl D. (1976). "Black Women as Pioneers in Social Welfare, 1880–1935," *Black Caucus Journal* 7(1): 7–12.

Franklin, John Hope, and Alfred A. Moss, Jr. (1988). *From Slavery to Freedom: A History of Negro Americans,* 6th ed. New York: McGraw-Hill.

Hornsby, Alton, Jr. (1977). *The Black Almanac: From Involuntary Servitude (1619–1860) to a Return to the Mainstream (1973–1976)?,* rev. ed. Woodbury, NY: Barron's Education Series.

Johnson, Audreye E. (1991). "The Sin of Omission: African American Women in Social Work," *Journal of Multicultural Social Work* 1(2): 7–15.

———. (1988). *The National Association of Black Social Workers, Inc: A History for the Future.* New York: National Association of Black Social Workers.

———. (1988). "Health Issues and African Americans: Surviving and Endangered," in John

S. McNeil and Stanley E. Weinstein, eds., *Innovations in Health Care Practice.* Silver Spring, MD: NASW Press.

———. (1977). "William Still—Black Social Workers: 1821–1902," *Black Caucus Journal* (Spring): 14–19.

Lewis, David Levering (1993). *W. E. B. Du Bois: Biography of a Race, 1868–1919.* New York: Henry Holt.

Lide, Pauline (1973). "The National Conference on Social Welfare and the Black Historical Perspective," *Social Service Review* 47:2 (June): 171–207.

Philpott, Thomas Lee (1991). *The Slum and the Ghetto: Immigrants, Blacks, and Reformers in Chicago, 1880–1930.* Belmont, CA: Wadsworth.

Still, William (1970). *The Underground Railroad,* orig. pub. 1872; reprint. Chicago: Johnson Publishing.

Weaver, Hilaryn N. (1992). "African-Americans and Social Work: An Overview of the Antebellum Through Progressive Eras," *Journal of Multicultural Social Work* 2(4): 91–102.

Williams, Leon F. (1983). "A Study of Discrimination in Social Work Education Programs," *Black Caucus* 14:1 (Spring): 9–13.

CHAPTER 10

Racially-Hostile Workplaces Under Workers' Compensation: When Race and Work Collide

Darryll M. H. Lewis

In 1995, white workers at an American company presented African American workers with a Ku Klux Klan Christmas card and hung a large, thick burlap rope in the shape of a noose and a black voodoo doll near a storeroom where African American employees frequented.[1] While these employees sought damages under Title VII,[2] if the African American employees had suffered a mental breakdown or some lesser form of neurosis or psychosis, workers' compensation law would have been invoked. Thus, this essay discusses claims under workers' compensation law available to employees who suffer physical or mental injuries as a result of workplace racism. Victims of workplace racism have a labyrinth of statutory remedies, including Title VII actions.[3] However, their options under workers' compensation laws are comparatively limited.[4] This is particularly true of conduct which would ordinarily give rise to a common law tort if the relevant conduct occurs away from the job.[5] Every state has a workers' compensation scheme that provides benefits for employees who are injured or disabled as a result of accidents that arise out of and in the course of the employment.[6] Notwithstanding the success of any Title VII claims,[7] if one is injured on the job as a result of racism, and if the injured employee can successfully establish the requisite elements for compensation under the respective state's workers' compensation scheme,[8] then, one may be entitled to compensation under workers' compensation law. Further, such injury does not guarantee that an employee has a recognizable cause of action outside of workers' compensation law.[9] Understanding the history of workers' compensation aids in comprehending its unique treatment of workplace injuries.

GENERAL HISTORY OF
WORKERS' COMPENSATION LAW

The genesis of the workers' compensation system is the industrial revolution. Industrialization dramatically increased workplace injuries. Lawsuits by employees seeking damages for injuries resulting from unsafe industrial sites predictably followed. In turn, employers delayed the conclusion (and ultimate compensation) of these suits by strategic but legal dilatory tactics. Thus, an employee may have sued successfully an employer, but only after a lengthy battle. The battle was neither pleasant nor easy. An injured worker faced legitimate common law employer defenses that implied that the employee was at fault or caused his or her own injuries. The common law denied damages to any employee who "assumed the risk," or "contributed" to the employee's plight. Nationwide, the legal system became a hindrance to productivity. Employees became the enemy of employers. This intolerance led legislatures to adopt workers' compensation systems, which required employers to compensate injured workers without delay. It established a statutory scheme that arbitrarily set the value of losses occurring on the job. In exchange for these plums, the legislatures abolished all employee common law cause of actions that arose out of and in the course of the employment, any reference to employee fault, and all employer common law defenses. In 1917, the United States Supreme Court upheld the constitutionality of such schemes.[10] In short, workers' compensation law became the exclusive[11] remedy for workplace injuries. Hence, the birth of our workers' compensation law system, but its apparent simplicity disguises its legalistic tentacles. The workers' compensation system was never designed to deal with nor is it efficiently capable of dealing with injuries resulting from workplace racism.

RACISM LEADING TO INJURY

There is no limit to the modern manifestations of workplace racism.[12] While some conduct may create a hostile work environment invoking the legal protections of Title VII, one does not necessarily require a hostile work environment to trigger the provisions of workers' compensation law.[13] A work environment is considered "hostile" under Title VII if an "objectively reasonable minority would find the environment hostile or abusive."[14] However, under workers' compensation law, a workplace injury or disability engages the legal applications. Varying results, discussed *infra,* derive thereafter.

OVERCOMING OR COMING WITHIN WORKERS' COMPENSATION LAW

Workers' compensation law may be either a burden or a benefit for one seeking recovery for psychological injuries due to workplace racism. The amount of recoveries for common-law torts is typically larger than judgments deriving from workers' compensation. Therefore, victims seek to sue their employers for common-law torts, such as intentional infliction of emotional distress. Often, workers' compensation will not permit such suits given the exclusive nature of the workers' compensation law. Even if one is successful eluding the exclusivity provision of the law, one may be unsuccessful fitting one's injury or the circumstances of one's injury into the requirements of compensability of workers' compensation law. The law is beneficial if the victim can overcome these obstacles.

EMOTIONAL DISTRESS UNDER WORKERS' COMPENSATION LAW

When racism leads to an injury on the job, the ideal claim is that the victim has suffered from the tort of intentional infliction of emotional distress. Typically, employers defend that the tort is barred by workers' compensation law.[15] Courts usually hold that the tort "sounds" in negligence and, in fact, dismiss the claim. Also, claimants fail because they are unable to establish that the employer "intentionally" committed the tort.[16] Courts have been unwilling to impute the intentional conduct of co-workers to their employers. They indicate that the doctrine of respondeat superior[17] is insufficient to establish the intent required to remove the tort from the grasp of workers' compensation law. Few claimants have been able to convince the courts that the racially-antagonist conduct is "outrageous," an indispensable element of the tort of intentional infliction of emotional distress.[18] They commonly state that:

> The liability clearly does not extend to mere insults, indignities, threats, annoyances, petty oppressions, or other trivialities. The rough edges of our society are still in need of a good deal of filing down, and in the meantime plaintiffs must necessarily be expected and required to be hardened to a certain amount of rough language, and to occasional acts that are definitely inconsiderate and unkind. There is no occasion for the law to intervene in every case where some one's feelings are hurt.[19]

When such claims are brought, employers move the court to grant a summary judgment.[20] If the motion is denied, the case is submitted to the jury to determine if the relevant conduct is outrageous. If this motion is granted, the jury is deprived of hearing the case.[21] Some courts have been willing to submit the claim to the jury.[22] The motion was denied in a case where a handicapped African American male dependent on insulin diabetes mellitus reported racial harassment at work, then placed in an unfair performance improvement plan and eventually discharged on the pretext that his performance was subpar.[23] Courts have also denied where a racial minority was subjected to:

> protracted harangues and verbal assaults from [his] supervising attorneys; was threatened, denied various perks, and privileges afforded to other persons with similar responsibilities; . . . was kept off of various distribution lists and organizational charts; was not afforded comparable secretarial or support staff services; did not receive comparable office or furniture; was not included in management functions, all on account of his race and national origin.[24]

In one case, an African American male restaurant worker expressed his dissatisfaction with the cook's soup. The employer responded that "all you niggers are alike. Plaintiff then walked into the kitchen, and [the defendant] followed him and called plaintiff a 'nigger.' Plaintiff told [the] defendant that he objected to the racial epithets and that he wanted to be treated 'like a human being,' to which [the defendant] replied, 'You're not a human being, you're a nigger.' "[25]

112

One court reasoned that racial comments "were not mere insults but rather an intentional pattern of harassment [where] the facts show[ed] that co-workers told racial jokes, one co-worker used the term 'dumb f*cking nigger' at least twice in plaintiff's presence, two racially-derogatory written items were placed at plaintiff's desk; [and] one derogatory cartoon was circulated among workers."[26]

Paradoxically, except for the Ninth Circuit Court of Appeals,[27] the federal courts of appeal have been more likely to grant the motion. Those courts often believe that conduct that may establish a racially-hostile work environment is not outrageous.[28] These courts have commonly quoted the following in refusing to submit the case to the jury:

> To present a successful claim for intentional infliction of emotional distress, "the conduct complained of must be of an extreme or outrageous type . . . so extreme in degree as to go beyond all possible bounds of decency and be regarded as atrocious and utterly intolerable in a civilized society" [citations omitted]. It is extremely rare to find conduct in the employment context that will rise to the level of outrageousness necessary to provide a basis for recovery.[29]

These courts balk at the claims of racial minorities who allege that their employers or co-workers have intentionally inflicted them to emotional distress. "[They allege] no more than racial discrimination, and courts do not consider such . . . allegations sufficiently outrageous to sustain a claim for intentional infliction of emotional distress."[30] "Moreover, the law intervenes only where the distress inflicted is so severe that no reasonable man could be expected to endure it."[31] Thus, the following allegations did not constitute intentional infliction of emotional distress where an African American female asserted that her white employer engaged in:

> suspending plaintiff for an offense for which white employees were not suspended, subjecting plaintiff to a physical altercation with a white female co-worker and disciplining only the plaintiff over the incident, sabotaging the plaintiff's work on a pay phone, refusing to treat plaintiff equally in disciplinary proceedings unless [the plaintiff] dismissed charges of racial discrimination pending before a local government agency, refusing to purge stale disciplinary actions from plaintiff's file, confining plaintiff to the supervision of the white woman who attacked her, thereby causing her to suffer a nervous breakdown on the job, intentionally

113

transporting plaintiff to the wrong hospital during her nervous breakdown in order to cause her further trauma, refusing plaintiff's request to transfer her to a different department, and constructively discharging her when she was physically and mentally unable to continue working under her tormentors.[32]

Similarly, the case was held that there was no intentional infliction of emotional distress where an African American male was "subjected to derogatory racial comments and jokes, . . . injured when he sat on a tungsten welding tip protruding vertically from his chair [when] the tip punctured his buttocks."[33] Nor was it considered sufficiently outrageous when a white co-employee threatened the African American with the "loss of her job, directed humiliating language, vicious verbal threats, and racial epithets at her, and called her 'nigger' when an argument arose concerning a parking space, [although the court described these acts as] extremely reprehensible."[34]

Understandably, a court does not consider these outlandish incidents as "outrageous." The courts that grant the defendants' motion to dismiss diminish the significance or impact of these despicable acts because they take place on the job. They proudly intimate that the statement of a prima facie Title VII case does not state a cause of action for the tort of outrage.[35] The absence of a reasonable black person standard is at the heart of these courts' failure to recognize the degree of pain inflicted upon minorities by workplace racists.[36] Vision would be restored to seemingly blind courts considering the tort of intentional infliction of emotion distress if the courts would emphasize, understand and appreciate that:

> [t]he omnipresence of race-based attitudes and experiences in the lives of black Americans causes even nonviolent events to be interpreted as degrading, threatening, and offensive [citations omitted]. Even an inadvertent racial slight unnoticed either by its white speaker or white bystanders will reverberate in the memory of its black victim. . . . [T]he factfinder must 'walk a mile in the victim's shoes' to understand those effects and how they should be remedied. In sum, the appropriate standard to be applied in [outrage] case[s] is that of a reasonable black person. . . . Because these racial beliefs and stereotypes pervade our society, employing a 'reasonable person' standard would permit discriminatory conduct and speech constructed on the foundation of these beliefs and stereotypes to stand unremedied.[37]

RACIAL INJURIES UNDER
WORKERS' COMPENSATION LAW

Given that common-law torts frequently are barred by workers' compensation law, the racial minority must seek compensation within the workers' compensation system. Under present law this route may be a difficult task.

Generally, an employee who seeks workers' compensation benefits for an injury resulting from workplace racism has four legal hurdles to overcome. First, an employee must be "injured." Second, a compensable injury must have happened "accidentally." In a lay sense, often workplace racism is an intentional act. In a law sense, conduct falling in this category may only be negligent. The distinction is critical since workers' compensation law seeks only to compensate "accidental" injuries. By definition, intentional acts are not accidental. This explains why plaintiffs typically allege *intentional* infliction of emotion distress. Traditionally, intentional acts have been excluded from coverage under workers' compensation law. Conversely, workers' compensation law has been the "exclusive" remedy for injuries resulting from negligent conduct. Nonetheless, such characterization of the injury-causing behavior or employment condition does not end the legal inquiry in workers' compensation law.

Third and fourth, the injury must "arise out of and be in the course of the employment." The phrase is usually conjoined and expressed in "one breath." However, it is clearly two distinct substantive standards. A compensable injury must "arise out of the employment."[38] Equally, the injury must have occurred during "the course of the employment."[39] The absence or failure of either prerequisite is fatal to a workers' compensation claim.

The interpretations of these requirements differ in each state. Therefore, this discussion is illustrative, rather than exhaustive of how workplace racism is treated under workers' compensation law. A Title VII hostile work environment certainly can be stressful to a reasonable minority. This stress can lead to psychic injuries requiring medical or psychiatric treatment or even disability. In workers' compensation parlance, these types of injuries are referred to as "mental-mental" injuries.[40] Mental-mental injuries are injuries to the psyche cause by non-physical employment stimulus (e.g., stress). The fact

115

that the stimulus is racially-motivated has not received any special consideration in workers' compensation courts. Instead, they are viewed simply as one form of an assortment of mental-mental injuries. The determination if such impairments is a recognizable "injury" is not uniform among the states. The ailment suffered must meet the statutory definition of an "injury."

WHAT IS AN "INJURY" UNDER WORKERS' COMPENSATION?

The most conservative view denies compensation to nonphysical injuries. In eight states,[41] for example, conditions that do not constitute "violence to the physical structure of the body" are not compensable "injuries." Thus, in those states, an emotional, mental, or psychological injury is not compensable under workers' compensation law. Accordingly, an African American male was unable to recover for his psychiatric injuries inflicted when white co-workers dressed in Ku Klux Klan attire causing him severe humiliation and embarrassment.[42] In addition, one state specifically has excluded any injuries resulting from racist-induced stimuli.[43] The most liberal position compensates these injuries so long as the claimant can establish their existence.[44] These states permit the claimant's own uncorroborated testimony to establish the existence of the injury. A hypersensitive racial minority who suffers psychological damage as a result of a mere racial insult, for example, being called a "boy," would simply have to establish that he was called "boy," which led directly to his mental incapacity.[45] Other states require that it is supported by independent psychiatric diagnosis. Between these two extremes, the definition of injury is integrally tied to how the disorder occurred.

Some states focus on the nature of the incident that induces the psychosis. These states inquire whether the incident was "unusual" or "extraordinary" in the context of the employee's normal work experiences.[46] A minority who is the victim of workplace racism must demonstrate that the racially-motivated incident or incidents are somehow an aberration to what is generally experienced in the job he or she works. Many courts have held that workplace racism is not uncommon. In such jurisdictions, the resulting injury may not be compensable. It fails to affirmatively answer the inquiry of whether or not the stressor is greater than the ordinary stress involved in the job?

There are some states that primarily concentrate on the reasonableness of the victim. These states postulate if a reasonable employee under similar circumstances would succumb to the precise stressor that caused the claimant's disorder.[47] In such states, a racial minority so victimized would have to establish that he or she is not eccentric, an eggshell, or thin-skulled.[48] Unlike cases under Title VII,[49] workers' compensation law has not differentiated between a reasonable employee and a reasonable minority employee. The fiction created by law assumes a colorless but reasonable employee. However, if the racial or ethnic culture of an employee is not factored, one can assume that the standard is biased. Hence, the benchmark of a "reasonable employee" is actually a "reasonable white employee."[50] The case law seems to reflect this slant. Courts err by failing to employ a reasonable black person standard to workers' compensation cases that purport to objectively measure the reactions of an African American claimant.

A few states compensate mental-mental injuries of eggshell workers.[51] This compensation would include hypersensitive racial minorities. These individuals would be considered unreasonable even by members of the same racial minority. However, in these states, courts have ruled that employers take employees as they find them.[52] They have held compensable a neurosis caused by an employment environment that exacerbates a preexisting condition.[53] A hypersensitive minority employee probably suffers from some sort of clinical paranoia, a preexisting mental condition, making him or her especially susceptible to further mental damage.

THE INJURY-BY-ACCIDENT REQUIREMENT

In all states, the injury must be "accidental." However, many states require that the incident that causes the injury be "untoward," "sudden," or "pinpointed." These requirements may pose a legal impediment for a racial minority who alleges that his or her psychic injury results from a racially-hostile work environment. In these states, stress that gradually leads to injury or disability is not a compensable injury since it is not "accidental."[54] The very nature of racially-hostile environment cases require that the incidents be repetitive,[55] which implies that the resulting stress is gradual. In states requiring unexpected or untoward events, a claim for injury or disability resulting from this environment may be defeated.[56] Conversely, some states compensate these gradually-developing disabilities. They analogize that stressful conditions, which gradually lead to mental injuries, are comparable to repetitive physical trauma (e.g., a typist who, over time, develops carpal tunnel syndrome) if it can be shown that the work environment substantially contributed to the victim's injury.[57]

DOES THE INJURY ARISE OUT OF THE EMPLOYMENT?

A racial minority who develops a psychic injury or disability due to a racially-hostile work environment must establish that the injury "arose out of the employment." Essentially, this means that the claimant's injury cannot result from risks or conditions common to those outside of the employment relationship. Thus, when a Mexican worker was physically assaulted by a white co-worker, it was argued that the resulting injury did not arise out of the employment.[58] The employer defended that racially-motivated attacks were a risk characteristic of everyday life. The Supreme Court of Illinois, in a split decision, ruled to the contrary:

> ... [A]ssaults by co-employees in the workplace that are motivated by general racial or ethnic prejudice are best treated as compensable "neutral" risks arising out of the employment. Prejudice of this sort does not usually result in physical attacks in the world at large: it would be incorrect to say that people run the everyday risk of assault on the street or in public places because of their Mexican heritage. However, when an assault by a co-employee rooted solely in ethnic prejudice occurs in the workplace, as here, it is presumably the result of an irrational human impulse toward violence which is as much a part of the victim's work environment as a defective tool would be. The victim may be unaware of the danger, but encounter it he must if the work to which he is assigned is to be completed. It is legitimately a hazard presented by the work. This is particularly true in our polyglot society in which employers are now required by Federal law to hire qualified minorities. . . . With more minori-

ties in the workplace, the potential for ethnic or racial friction is likely to increase. It would be anomalous for the law to address the problems of bigotry and lack of opportunity in society by requiring employers to hire qualified members of minority groups while not also requiring them to make the workplace as safe for minorities so hired as for other workers.[59]

Pennsylvania has carved out a third-party exception. It provides that:

> the term "injury arising in the course of his employment," as used in [the Pennsylvania Workers' Compensation Law], shall not include an injury caused by the act of a third person intended to injure the employee because of reasons personal to him, and not directed against him as an employee or because of his employment.[60]

Thus, when "racial epithets were used in [the plaintiff's] presence, an employee threatened to 'bury his hammer in [the plaintiff's] head' and that another employee told [the plaintiff] he would have him 'wiped out,' white workers deliberately discussed deer hunting and killing deer in [the plaintiff's] presence knowing of his aversion to the subject, . . . and that following such an episode, [the plaintiff] found a deer's head tied to the hood of his car," the court found that:

> [o]ppression or harassment because of a person's race is . . . [not employment related]. [The law] does not bar intentional infliction of emotional distress claims for racial harassment which fall within the ambit of the third-party exception.[61]

However, the third-party exception rule has also barred racial minorities' claims where the allegations fail to suggest that the racism was personal. In a case where several black claimants filed suit alleging intentional infliction of emotional distress as a result of the policies practiced by the employer, the court ruled that the claim was barred by the Pennsylvania Workers' Compensation Law:

> The basic motivation alleged [is] racial discrimination. The employee-Plaintiffs [fail] to establish personal animosity on the part of the third parties. The alleged "conspiracy" [is] to exclude blacks, as a class, from leadership or executive positions. The individual defendants are alleged to have promoted the policies, but nowhere are there any averments that they themselves [have] a personal animosity towards the particular employees. . . . The alleged discrimination is against black workers in general and the fact that there are five black employee-Plaintiffs named in

this suit confirms the notion that the third-parties' motivation was not personal.[62]

DOES THE INJURY OCCUR IN THE COURSE OF THE EMPLOYMENT?

To be in the "course of the employment," the worker must be tending to the employer's mission. Once an individual deviates from that task, he is considered outside the course of the employment. Engagement in personal matters, such as lunch or perhaps, horseplay, may take an employee out of the critical course. Thus, where a racial minority instigates or fuels racial controversy on the job, it is arguable that his or her activity is outside the course of the employment.[63]

CONCLUSION

Racial minorities who suffer injuries as a result of workplace racism certainly may file Title VII claims against their employers. However, in many cases, workers' compensation law deprives these same victims from seeking remedies for the tort of intentional infliction of emotional distress. Worse yet, a worker, injured as a result of workplace racism, may find that he or she cannot escape the exclusivity provisions of workers' compensation law. This same law may not provide any remedies. Workers' compensation law will compensate the victim for his or her medical expenses associated with the related injuries or disabilities. However, it denies compensation for economic loss or injuries to the psyche, reputation, integrity or raw outrage caused by workplace racism. The courts ought to employ a reasonable black person standard to assess reasonableness in potential outrage cases and where relevant in workers' compensation cases.

Notes

1. *Buchanan* v. *Sherill*, 51 F.3d 227 (U.S.C.A. Cir 10 1995). The case was dismissed because the plaintiff was unable to establish that racism was "sufficiently severe or pervasive."
2. The requirements for a prima facie case (the minimum pleadings that will survive dismissal) for a racially-hostile work environment is discussed *infra*, note 3.
3. A person who suffers racism on the job may be able to sue under several federal and state statutory laws. Under Title VII, 42 U.S.C. 2000-e, an employee who can demonstrate a "hostile work environment" may seek damages. In order to establish a hostile work environment, a plaintiff need not show injury *Merritor Savings Bank* v. *Vinson*, 477 U.S. 57, 91 L.Ed.2d 49, 106 S.Ct. 2399 (1986). Congress created the Equal Employment Opportunity Commission (EEOC) to conciliate such claims. Aggrieved workers must first file with the EEOC, which attempts to mediate the claims. Where the EEOC concurs that the employee has been improperly treated, it issues a Notice of the Right to Sue. In order to avoid dismissal, the plaintiff must adhere to several jurisdictional time periods (e.g., the suit must be filed within ninety [90] days of the issuance of the Notice of the Right to Sue). 42 U.S.C.A. Section 1981 provides for a cause of action against an employer whose intentional racial discrimination alters the terms or conditions of employment, hiring and promotion. 42 U.S.C.A. Section 1983 permits a similar cause of action when the employer is a government employer or an agent of a state that deprives employees of constitutional rights. 42 U.S.C.A. Section 1985 governs conspiracies by employers or co-workers to deprive individuals in a protected class of their civil rights. State laws generally permit parallel statutory actions against a discriminating employer. In addition, the conduct may be a ground for common law torts against the defendant-employer or defendant-co-worker. These torts may include assault, battery, and infliction of emotional distress. However, none of these options contemplate the interest that the government may have in prosecuting conduct, which constitutes a crime (e.g., hate crimes, criminal assaults, or violations of an individual's civil rights).
4. Unlike Title VII actions, under workers' compensation law 1) an employee must establish an injury or disability; 2) an employee may not sue an employer for injuries sustained as a result of common law torts; 3) the injury must be accidental; and 4) the injury must arise out of and in the course of the employment.
5. For example, a customer who slips and falls on a slick floor at the grocery may have a negligence claim against the store. However, for reasons explained *infra*, an employee who slips and falls on a slick floor at work cannot sue the employer for the common-law tort of negligence.
6. E.g., in Nebraska, these provisions are located at Nebraska Revised Statutes, Ch. 48–101 et seq. (1996).
7. E.g., a prima facie Title VII case must allege that 1) the plaintiff-victim-employee suffered intentional discrimination because of the plaintiff-victim-employee's membership in a protected class (e.g., racial category); 2) racial discrimination was pervasive and regular; 3) discrimination detrimentally affected plaintiff-victim-employee; 4) discrimination would have detrimentally affected a reasonable person of the same protected class in that position; and 5) existence of respondeat superior liability (i.e., the employer is responsible for its subordinate's inappropriate conduct) *West* v. *Philadelphia Electric Co.*, 45 F.3d 744 (U.S.C.A. Cir. 3 1995). A Title VII case is also stated when, based on the totality of the

circumstances, a plaintiff-victim-employee is able to establish a racially-hostile work environment by virtue of discriminatory ridicule, intimidation or insults *Merritor Savings Bank* v. *Vinson*, 477 U.S. 57, 91 L.Ed.2d 49, 106 S.Ct. 2399 (1986).

8. Generally, compensability under workers' compensation law requires 1) an injury; 2) by accident; 3) which arises out of the employment; and 4) which occurs during the course of the employment.

9. For example, one may suffer a mental breakdown due to workplace racism (perhaps compensable under workers' compensation law), however, unable to establish a hostile work environment sufficient to state or prove a prima facie Title VII case.

10. *New York Central R.R. Co.* v. *White*, 243 U.S. 188, 61 L.Ed. 667, 37 S.Ct. 247 (1917) (upholding the constitutionality of New York's workers' compensation scheme).

11. "Exclusivity" represents a legal term in workers' compensation law connoting that an employee is barred from suing his or her employer for injuries sustained on the job.

12. For example, racial joking, imitation of comedic black television characters *Love* v. *California*, 1996 U.S.App. LEXIS 8392 (U.S.C.A. Cir. 9 1996); verbal abuse "suck my d*ck, you black b*tch!" *EEOC* v. *Champion International Corp.*, 1995 U.S. Dist. LEXIS 11808 (U.S.D.C. N.D. Ill. W.D. 1995); racially-antagonistic displays (KKK signs, nooses) *Buchanan* v. *Sherrill*, 51 F.3d. 227 (1994).

13. An accidental injury triggers workers' compensation analysis; whereas, an injury is not required under Title VII analysis.

14. *Harris* v. *International Paper Co.*, 756 F.Supp. 1509 (U.S.D.C. D.Me 1991) (the court indicated that there are "two different perspectives on the question of unwelcomeness and pervasiveness: the perpetrator's perspective and the victim's perspective . . . necessitat[ing] a finding . . . from the standpoint of the employee. . . . The standard for assessing the unwelcomeness and pervasiveness of conduct and speech must be founded on a fair concern for the different social experiences of . . . white Americans and black Americans in the case of racial harassment. . . . Black Americans are regularly faced with negative racial attitudes, many unconsciously held and acted upon, which are the natural consequences of a society ingrained with cultural stereotypes and race-based beliefs and preferences. . . . As a result, instances of racial violence or threatened violence, which might appear to white observers as mere 'pranks' are, to black observers, evidence of threatening, pervasive attitudes closely associated with racial jokes, comments, or nonviolent conduct, which white observers are also more likely to dismiss as nonthreatening, and offensive. . . . [B]ecause Plaintiffs are black, the appropriate standard is that of a reasonable black person, as that can be best understood and given meaning by a white judge." Thus, when white co-workers posted a postcard of "Buckwheat" on Plaintiff's working machine, the testimony of the Plaintiff who viewed the gesture as a racial epithet was accepted by the court even though the Defendant did "not intend a racial slight." Accord, *Johnson* v. *Teamsters Local Union No. 559*, 1995 U.S.Dist. LEXIS 8181 (U.S.D.C. D.Mass 1995); *Lewis* v. *Gillette Co.*, 1993 U.S.Dist. LEXIS 10239 (1993).

15. In *Mass* v. *Martin Marietta Corp.*, 805 F.Supp. 1530 (D. Colo. 1992), where a black employee claimed racial mistreatment, the employer moved to dismiss the plaintiff's claim of intentional infliction of emotional distress on the ground that "the claim is preempted by the . . . Workers' Compensation Act."

16. In Pennsylvania, even intentional torts are barred by its workers' compensation law unless the claimant can establish that he or she is covered by an exception *Price* v. *Philadelphia Elec. Co.*, 790 F.Supp. 97 (E.D. Pa. 1992).

17. The common-law doctrine of respondeat superior holds that an employer is responsible for the negligent acts of its agents committed in the scope of the employment.

18. Many jurisdictions adopt the Second Restatement's version of the tort of intentional infliction of emotional distress. Section 46 of the Restatement 2d (1996) indicates that "[o]ne who by *extreme and outrageous conduct* intentionally or recklessly causes severe emotional distress to another is subject to liability for such emotional distress and if bodily harm results from it for such bodily harm" [emphasis supplied].

19. Section 46, Comment (d), Second Restatement of Torts (1965). Cited in *Howard* v. *National Cash Register Co.*, 388 F.Supp. 603 (S.D. Ohio 1975).

20. A summary judgment is a motion to the court that the case should be dismissed since, as a matter of law, the facts provide no basis on which the trier of fact could disagree as to the application of law.

21. The Restatement Second of Torts instructs that "[i]t is for the court to determine, in the first instance, whether the defendant's conduct may be regarded as so extreme and outrageous as to permit recovery, or whether it is necessarily so. Where reasonable [people] may differ, it is for the jury subject to the control of the court, to determine whether, in the particular case, the conduct has been sufficiently extreme and outrageous to result in liability."

22. In *Gomez* v. *Hug* 7 Kan. App.2d 603, 645 P.2d 916 (1982), where the Mexican plaintiff was subjected to a stream of vulgar comments, racial epithets, and threats of violence, the Kansas Court of Appeals offered the following rationale for its refusal to grant a summary judgment. "Certainly there is no occasion for the law to intervene in every case where someone's feelings are hurt. Certainly the rough edges of our society still need smoothing down and there must be freedom to blow off harmless steam. But this vituperation was well beyond the bounds of freedom to blow off steam. It is not a burden of American citizenship in the State of Kansas that such vitriolic bullying as was turned by [the defendant] against the [plaintiff], and its emotional and physical consequences, must be accepted without possibility of redress and accepted as often as it amuses the speaker to utter it. Kansas courts are not so impotent. *At the very least the victim of such an attack has the right to have his grievance heard by a jury of average members of the community to know whether they would exclaim "Outrageous!"* [emphasis supplied].

23. *Mass* v. *Martin Marietta Corp.*, 805 F.Supp. 1530 (U.S.D.C. D.Colo. 1992). (The court submitted the intentional infliction of emotional distress allegation to the jury.)

24. *Guzman* v. *El Paso Natural Gas Co.*, 756 F.Supp. 994 (W.D. Tex. 1990). (Mexican attorney brought suit for racial harassment and intentional infliction of emotional distress. The court ruled that the latter claim should be submitted to the jury.)

25. *Bailey* v. *Binyon*, 583 F.Supp. 923 (U.S.D.C. N.D. Ill. E.D. 1984). (Plaintiff brought Title VII and intentional infliction of emotional distress claims. The court concluded that the latter claim should be decided by a jury.)

26. *Mass* v. *Martin Marietta Corp.*, 805 F.Supp. 1530 (U.S.D.C. D.Colo. 1992).

27. In *Woods* v. *Graphic Communications*, 925 F.2d 1195 (U.S.C.A. Cir. 9 1991), a black worker requested that his union representative file a grievance against his white co-workers when they tolerated "racial jokes, cartoons, comments, and other forms of hostility directed at almost every conceivable racial and ethnic group, particularly Blacks. . . . He was subjected to several racial remarks and hostility, such as a karate chop and a racial joke by a [white co-worker], instructions by co-workers to wash his hands in a urinal, and the letters 'KKK' appeared on a

machine near his area. [The plaintiff] sought psychological counseling . . . and took several medical leaves." The union failed to file a grievance. In holding the union liable, the court ruled that the conduct was motivated by "discriminatory" and "evil" motives and that it was "outrageous and shocks the conscience of this society."

28. Despite the unacceptability of racial discrimination in a civilized society, [the court has] seen no indication that [it] would consider the conduct here 'outrageous' per se" *Martin* v. *Citibank*, 762 F.2d 212 (U.S.C.A. Cir. 2 1985). (A white employee refused to work under an African American supervisor and made the employment environment so unpleasant that the African American supervisor resigned and sued claiming intentional infliction of emotional distress.)

29. *Cox* v. *Keystone Carbon Co.*, 861 F.2d 390 (U.S.C.A. Cir. 3 1988). Interestingly, *Cox* did not involve a racial minority. The plaintiff was a corporate controller who was fired in order to deprive him of medical benefits. The plaintiff sought damages under the Employment Retirement Income Security Act (ERISA) as well as for intentional infliction of emotional distress. In denying the petition, the court cited the above language.

30. *Ramos* v. *Bell Atlantic Corp.*, 1996 U.S. Dist. LEXIS 18655 (U.S.D.C. E.D.Pa. 1996).

31. *Harriston* v. *Chicago Tribune Co.*, 992 F.2d 697 (U.S.C.A. Cir. 7 1993). (Black female plaintiff alleges that her employer intentionally subjected her to emotional distress by transferring her, giving her poor job evaluations and ultimately causing her resignation. The court granted the employer's motion for summary judgment.)

32. *Rollins* v. *McDonnell Douglas Corp.*, 907 F.Supp. 1514 (U.S.D.C. M.D.Fla. (1995).

33. *Bernhard* v. *Doskocil Companies, Inc.*, 861 F.Supp. 1006 (D.Kan. 1994).

34. *Vance* v. *Southern Bell Tel. & Tel. Co.*, 983 F.2d 1573 (U.S.C.A. Cir. 11 1993).

35. The tort of "outrage" is used interchangeably with the tort of intentional infliction of emotional distress.

36. See Note 14, *supra,* for explanation of the reasonable black person standard.

37. *Harris* v. *International Paper Co.*, 765 F.Supp. 1509 (U.S.D.C. D.Me. 1991). In essence, the author suggests the transplantation of the Title VII standard to cases involving the tort of intentional infliction of emotional distress and relevant workers' compensation cases.

38. An injury "arises out of the employment" if there is a sufficient connection between the injury and the employment. There are various tests utilized nationally to determine if an injury arises out of the employment. The "positional-risk" test is employed by most jurisdictions: did the employment require the victim to be at the place and at the time the injury occurred? A. Larson, *The Law of Workers' Compensation*, Section 6.

39. In general, at the time of the injury, the employee must be engaged in his employer's business rather than activities personal to the worker. *Ibid.*

40. There are three types of "mental-mental" injuries: 1) mental disorders induced by emotional stimulus (e.g., a black man suffering psychological injury resulting from being called a racial epithet); 2) mental disorders induced by sudden emotional stimulus (e.g., suffering a nervous breakdown by virtue of witnessing the murder of a colleague); and 3) mental disorders induced by nonsudden emotional stimulus (e.g., psychosis brought on by repetitive, persistent, and enduring racially-hostile environment) Zupanec, D., "Mental Disorders As Compensable Under Workmens' Compensation Acts," 97 A.L.R. 3d 161.

41. Alabama, Texas, Georgia, Kansas, Minnesota, Nebraska, Ohio, and Louisiana

require "injury to the physical structure of the body" or "violence to the physical structure of the body."

42. *Marshall* v. *Ormet Corp.*, 1991 Ohio App. LEXIS 4338 (C.A. Ohio, A.D. 1991).

43. ". . . [A] disease that manifests itself in the fear of or dislike for an individual because of the individual's race, color, religion, sex, national origin, age, or handicap is not an injury by accident arising out of the employment" Fla. Stat. Ann. Section 440.02(1). In *Colorcraft Corp. and Fuqua Industries* v. *Jandrucko*, 576 So.2d 1320 (C.A. Fla. Dist. 1 1991), *Tomlinson* v. *Jandrucko*, 983 F.2d 236 (U.S.C.A. Cir. 11 1992) (affirmed), the claimant successfully argued that she developed a disabling phobia of black men when she was assaulted by a black man in the company parking lot. The quoted statute is a legislative response to that determination, disallowing such future claims. Whether this provision would bar claims by a victim of workplace racism who suffers a mental disability, particularly since such injuries do not derive from "fear of or dislike for an individual because of [another's] race" is questionable.

44. Michigan and Hawaii are representative of this position. Although many states recognize the compensability of mental-mental injuries. These states stand apart because they permit the claimant's subjective testimony to establish the causative nexus between the injury and the employment *Deizel* v. *DIFCO Laboratories, Inc.*, 403 Mich. 1, 268 N.W.2d 1 (1978); *Ratliff* v. *General Motors Corp.*, 339 N.W.2d 196 (Mich.App. 1983); *Royal National Insurance Co.* v. *Labor and Industrial Relations*, 487 P.2d 278 (Haw. 1971).

45. Judge Gene Carter expressed concern over the appropriate standard to employ when dealing with racial minorities possessing thin skin. ". . . [E]mployers cannot be expected to respond to the concerns of hypersensitive employees, some objective standard of unwelcomeness and pervasiveness must be applied" *Harris* v. *International Paper Co.*, 765 F.Supp. 1509 (U.S.D.C. D.Me. 1991).

46. For example, the Supreme Court of Wisconsin has held that "in cases of nontraumatically caused mental injuries, . . . out of the ordinary work stresses must be shown in order for the claimant to recover" *Swiss Colony, Inc.* v. *Department of Industry, Labor & Human Relations*, 72 Wis.2d 46, 240 N.W.2d 128 (1976). (Claimant was exposed to a humiliating, overbearing, negative, brusque, and belittling supervisor, which led to the claimant's mental incapacity. The court held the disability was not compensable.)

47. In *Darnes* v. *Industrial Commission of Arizona*, the Arizona Supreme Court intimated that "[t]here simply must be a hypothetical 'reasonable person' working alongside claimant by whom we can judge the stressfulness of work-related events and the reasonableness of the employee's reaction thereto, so as to assure the work-related nature of the injury as compared to non-work related stress" 156 Ariz. 179, 750 P.2d 1382 (Ariz.App. 1988).

48. "Instead, as expressed by the Wyoming Supreme Court, [the court] need only decide whether . . . disciplinary procedures and worker harassment suffered by claimant as a result of [working conditions are] the same as would be suffered by any other worker in a similar job under [similar] circumstances," *Graves* v. *Utah Power & Light Company*, 713 P.2d 187 (Wyo. 1986).

49. See Note 14, *supra*.

50. In *Harris* v. *International Paper Co.*, Judge Carter indicates that since "racial beliefs and stereotypes pervade our society, employing a 'reasonable person' standard [rather than a reasonable black person standard] would permit discriminatory

conduct and speech constructed on the foundation of these beliefs and stereotypes to stand unremedied" 765 F.Supp. 1509 (U.S.D.C. D.Me. 1991).

51. An "eggshell" person is an individual who is especially sensitive to normal influences.

52. Our [Workers' Compensation] Act . . . is not merely objective covering the average person; it is also subjective and protects even the eggshell. With adequate safeguards to shield the employer, even those predisposed to mental injury should be able to recover for ordinary work-related stress to which others would not succumb. We conclude that ordinary work-related stress and strain could be compensable if it were shown by clear and convincing evidence that the trauma generated by the employment predominated in producing injury. And less showing, however, would be insufficient to adequately protect the employer" *Townsend* v. *Maine Bureau of Public Safety*, 404 A.2d 1014 (Me. 1979).

53. In *Albertson's Inc.* v. *Workers' Compensation Appeals Board*, 131 Cal.App.3d 317, 182 Cal.Rptr. 309 (1982), the Supreme Court of California was faced with an employee who was diagnosed as possessing a "mild obsessive-compulsive personality." The employee subjectively believed that she was subjected to intentional harassment. She developed a mental disability. In holding that the disability was compensable, the court said "job harassment may be thought of as a species of potentially stressful circumstances, like a repetitive job, or an abundance of deadlines. The amount of stress exerted by such circumstances varies from individual to individual; what is stressful to one is not to another. . . . To one experiencing it, such an injury is as real and disabling as a physical injury [citations omitted]. . . . Because industry takes the employee as it finds him, . . . [t]he proper focus of the inquiry, then, is not on how much stress *should be* felt by an employee in his work environment, based on a 'normal' reaction to it, but how much stress *is* felt by an individual worker reacting uniquely to work environment" [emphasis original].

54. Thus, in *Yates* v. *Life Insurance Company of Georgia*, the Supreme Court of South Carolina explained that "the word 'accident' as used in workers' compensation, means an unlooked for and untoward event that the person who suffered the injury did not expect, design, or intentionally cause. . . . Assuming that a mental disorder is compensable if it is caused by an unexpected, injury-causing event, a mental disorder is not compensable as an 'injury by accident' if it either results from exposure to normal working conditions or is brought about by the gradual build up of emotional stress over time" 353 S.E.2d 297 (S.C.App. 1987).

55. A prima facie Title VII case mandates that racist activity be regular and pervasive implying that they exist over a period of time.

56. The Supreme Court of Illinois held that a black employee was not entitled to compensation for injuries due to racial epithets and abuse by his supervisor. "While mental stimulus, such as fright, shock or excessive unexpected anxiety resulting in injury might justify a compensation award, . . . we do not permit recovery for every nontraumatic psychic injury from which an employee suffers merely because the employee can identify some stressful work-related episode which contributes in part to the employee's depression or anxiety. . . . Compensation for nontraumatic psychic injury cannot be dependent solely upon the peculiar vicissitudes of the individual employee as he relates to his general work environment. . . . The episode which allegedly precipitated the disability involved an argument between a supervisor and an employee over working conditions, something not uncommon in the normal workplace environment" *General Motors Parts Division* v. *Industrial Commission*, 168 Ill.App.3d 678, 119 Ill.Dec. 401 (1988).

57. The New Jersey Supreme Court explained that "[t]he employee's subjective reaction is not to be disregarded but it cannot be the sole ingredient of the formula for compensability. There must be objective evidence which, when viewed realistically, carries petitioner's burden of proof to demonstrate that the alleged work exposure was to a material degree a contributing factor" *Williams* v. *Western Electric Company*, 178 N.J.Super. 571, 429 A.2d 1063 (1981).

58. *Rodriguez* v. *The Industrial Commission*, 95 Ill.2d 166. 447 N.E.2d 186, 68 Ill.Dec. 928 (1983). (A white co-worker struck the Mexican claimant over the head with a two-by-four. The co-worker had no provocation for the assault; his only motive was prejudice against the claimant because he was Mexican.)

59. *Rodriguez* v. *The Industrial Commission*, 95 Ill.2d 166, 447 N.E.2d 186, 68 Ill.Dec. 928 (1983). The dissent contended that racially-motivated assaults were common to society at large as "there are thousands who are capable of disproving this 'verity' by a display of their scars and bruises."

60. 77 Pa.Stat.Ann. Section 411(1) (1996).

61. *Price* v. *Philadelphia Elec. Co.*, 790 F.Supp. 97 (E.D. Pa. 1992).

62. *Hicks* v. *Arthur*, 843 F.Supp. 949 (E.D. Pa. 1994).

63. Thus, where an African-American worker called his co-worker a "white hillbilly motherf*cker who runs the KKK" and, in response, the white co-worker burns a cross of wire, one might conclude that the employees' activities are outside the course of the employment. Facts taken from *Newton* v. *Air Force,* 85 F.3d 595 (U.S.C.A. Cir. D.C. 1996).

••••••••••••••••••
CHAPTER 11

Social Issues of Children in Poverty

Alva Barnett

Poverty in the United States has overwhelming effects on black life, especially children and families. Two of the primary reasons that poverty has such a pervasive impact on black life in America are: 1) the consistent inequities in economic, educational, and health areas regardless of the strength of the economy; 2) some of the historical views and opinions, stereotypes and rationale, and ignorance about blacks in America have not been sufficiently modified in practice so that structural as well as cultural pluralism could abound for all peoples. An explanation of some of these areas mentioned, how they affect blacks, impact growth, and social functioning is very crucial. The fact that there will be a call to interact and unite is expected along multidimensions: not to isolate, individuate, and separate. An understanding of some of these factors will hopefully encourage a forward and upward movement.

Here in the United States of America, in the 1990s, global diversity, economic redistribution, population shifts, lack of jobs or adequate wages, lack of educational opportunities and adequate incomes, and governmental and middle-class consumer indebtedness are realities that suggest poverty is steadily on the rise. One example is that 77.5 percent of all blacks who are poor live in a central city, while there is a more even distribution of poor whites living in and outside a central city, 49.7 percent and 50.3 percent, respectively (Bennett 1991). Another example is the income inequality seen in 1982, the first time in twenty-five years, when the poorest families (twenty-six million or 40 percent) were living on less money than the richest of families (3.25 million or 5 percent); the latter receiving the largest share of the national income (*Dollars and Sense* 1988).

Simultaneously, there has been a resurgence of the stereotypical views and ideology of the black family and community in relationship to increased poverty and a declining sense of personal economic strength. These views include the culture of poverty as discussed by Oscar Lewis and Herbert Gans who have dealt with adaptation to circumstances, more acquiescence with a discouraging generational pattern and an apathetic mood (Rainwater 1970). Only 21.1 percent of the U.S. population are black Americans (Bennett 1991). However, more recently, Kilborn (1992) described some one hundred and fifty million people, about 60 percent of the population, who are identified as middle class yet hurting economically. They tend to suffer in silence, which suggests a mood of alienation and apathy, and a sense of hopelessness. King (1967) aptly discusses alienation as one of the dangerous evils in the world today, in part, he states:

> . . . All of the forces of good in the world are founded in interconnectedness and unity—of man and man, man and woman, man and nature, man and God. Growth requires connection and trust. Alienation is a form of living death. It is the acid of despair that dissolves society. (1967: 44)

More insidious is the second view, which focuses on the breakdown of the black family, lifestyle, behaviors, and attitudes that negatively affect well-being and is often related to value changes. In connection with this view, the poor are easier to blame for their circumstances as opposed to looking squarely at the practices and failures of the nation's economy and the identified leaders (Ryan 1968; Gorman 1991; Wright-Edelman 1992).

These current views have a tendency to de-emphasize the socio-structural changes that have a direct effect on the peoples of this nation, while fueling the fires of overt racism. King states: "Racism and its perennial ally, economic exploitation, provides [sic] the key to understanding most of the international complications of this generation" (1967: 173).

Something that transcends intercoastal waterways and the international interactions is the mythological dogma that has been refuted of the notions of superiority and inferiority between racial groups, and even economically different groups called classism (King 1958). The use of these man-made categorizations has resulted in attitude and behavior that leads to practices of discrimination and injustice; these practices make difficult the permeability of many opportunities for labor force, income involvement, and equity; family health and well-being; and education and training.

Race, discrimination, and injustice are salient factors in the maintenance and increase of inequities particularly between black and white America. Frederick Douglass reflected this concern over a century ago: "Where justice is denied, where poverty is enforced, where ignorance prevails, and where one class is made to feel that society is organized in a conspiracy to oppress, rob, and degrade them, neither persons nor property will be safe" (Raspberry 1993: 16). According to Jacobs (1991), the process for there to be equal income levels for white and black American families will take about 169 years, given the speed and the direction the rate of change is taking place.

Further considerations of the issue of poverty, the selected factors that do contribute to the poverty-rate of Black Americans, and the changing composition of the population will be made in this essay. However, an understanding must be established that the United States is not a poor country that cannot take care of its people. Poverty, while deeply embedded into our capitalistic society, can be eliminated. There are more millionaires in the United States than at any other time in its history (United Way of America 1989); there is also an alarming and growing number of people who have a high level of technical and social skills. But there is also isolation for people with fewer family and community ties, who do not participate in the economic market (i.e., homeless), and many are hopeless with a sense of economic distress. Along with the basic needs for food, clothing, and shelter, there are many needs and concerns of those who have gained materially more than emotionally, spiritually, or culturally; a balance is needed on all sides.

Other evidence that this country is able to take care of its economically poor can be seen with our growth since World War II. The United States is the biggest exporting nation and it has a partnership within the world trade arena (Hearst 1993). More specifically, Fosler (1989) indicates that more than 40 percent of the world gross product was produced in the United States, even though that figure has declined somewhat and that there have been increases in foreign investments into this country.

Thirty years ago, Bagdikian (1963) spoke about the invisible, poor Americans in every region and city; they were described as being hidden by the new looks of the metropolis, generally unseen in the core of cities in the midst of their comfortable townspeople. During this period, the national average gross national product kept people thinking that the country with the highest standard of living in the world had eliminated poverty. While this fact may have been true for 80 percent of the population, the change to mechanization of operations has put many farmers off their land, family loyalty is being tested and shaken, and the unskilled jobs with good pay are going by the wayside—urban misery yet unknown. Both social and economic upheaval occurs and continues at a rapid rate of change.

In 1991, the United States was identified as the richest country among the developed countries, even though 24.2 percent of the population was poor or near poor. The top three countries under the United States showed 21 percent of their populations were poor or near poor. These countries were Israel, United Kingdom, and Australia. The United States had the smallest middle class of the ten countries listed (*Dollars and Sense* 1991).

The population patterns of world urbanization is growing and changing. For example, in 1950 the largest urban population was in New York-New Jersey with 12.3 percent, followed by London. In 1984, Mexico City was first at 18.1 percent, while New York-New Jersey was fourth at 15.3 percent. By 2000, Mexico City is projected as number one at 26.3 percent and New York-New Jersey number six at 15.5 percent.

On the heels of this urbanization is the steady growth of the immigrant population. The majority of the 4,822,000 babies projected to be born in the United States by 2030 will be born to people of color. The proportion of births to Hispanic and Asian women is expected to grow steadily due to young immigrants who are starting their families in the United States. More than 27 percent will be Hispanic babies, 8 percent Asian babies, while black births are expected to remain steady at 17 percent. During this time period, the proportion of non-Hispanic white births will shrink 47 percent (U.S. Bureau of the Census 1996). Increased attention to urban centers is occurring, while the poverty is worsening in smaller cities and rural areas. As we look at the southern region, there are more poor whites than poor blacks, however, poverty falls much more heavily upon the black population. For example, in the Inland South in 1993, the poverty rate of 45.1 percent was far beyond the national poverty rate of 33.1 percent for blacks (see figure 2.1) (Current Population Survey 1997). More recent

Figure 2.1

Poverty Rates by Race—Atlantic South, Inland South, and the United States

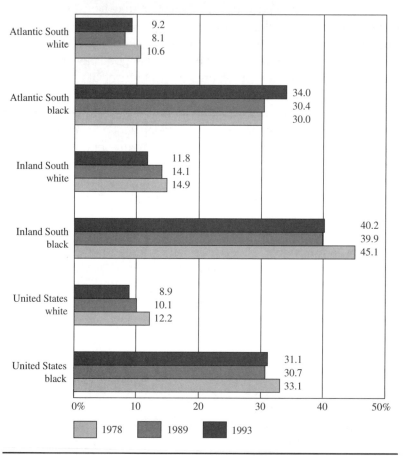

Source: U.S. Bureau of the Census (1979, 1990, 1994). *Current Population Survey.* Washington, DC: U.S. Department of Commerce.

statistics indicate that among seventeen developed countries, in the midst of broader affluence, America has the highest rate of child poverty. The childhood poverty rate of our children (21 percent) are reliable predictors of infant mortality, poor health, school dropout, and death by violence. As this level of poverty remains among our children, there are estimates that our nation loses $33 billion to $177 billion in the employment and worker productivity of the future. One of the contributing factors for this rate of childhood poverty is the lack of regular enforcement efforts by the state for child support. In 1995, 54 percent of the cases in this state system had court orders for child support; collection was 18.3 percent of those cases (Sconyers et al. 1997).

The fastest growing segment of the poor are women and children. The rates of child poverty in the midst of broader affluence is alarming. One in five children is poor, representing 14.4 million U.S. children (Children's Defense Fund 1991). One-third of poor children are black; in fact, the poverty rate for black children has been over 40 percent since 1982.

In 1989, female-headed households with no spouse represented 46.5 percent of black families; this was not statistically different when the figure was 49.4 percent ten years earlier. The rate of poverty for this type of family has been consistently higher than that for other black family types. In 1988, there were 5.2 million black children living with one parent, which was up from 950,000 in 1980. For the white population, children in this type of living situation were 9.9 million up from 1.7 million and for Hispanics it was 2.0 million up from 895,000. Over 90 percent of black and hispanic children in one-parent living situations live with their mother; for the white American population it is 85 percent. A characteristic of this situation is that for black children, 54 percent in one-parent situations are living with a never married parent, while 50 percent of white children in single parent dwelling are with a divorced parent (U.S. Bureau of the Census 1989).

An economic characteristic of these one-parent households is the median income for black female-headed households with no spouse, which is $9,710, but for whites it is $17,020 (see figure 2.2) (U.S. Bureau of the Census 1988). Also, women with no spouse in the household have a lower median family income than either the married couple households or households with men and no spouse present.

In 1995, 31 percent of the total population were identified as children through the age of twenty-one years. Even though there are approximately twenty-seven million more children twenty-one years old and younger than in 1950, this age group is declining relative to other age groups in the population. For example, by year 2000, this group is expected to remain at 31.5 percent from the 31.6 percent in

Figure 2.2

Related Children under Eighteen Years of Age Living in Families Below 100 Percent of the Poverty Level—1995

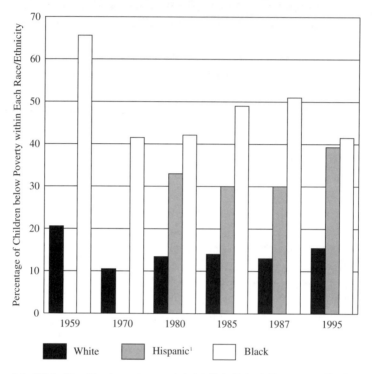

White   Hispanic[1]   Black

1. For 1980, the data on Hispanic percentages was also included in the black and white percentages. Therefore, the overall percentages for this year are not accurate in terms of exclusivity.

Note: Data is not available on ethnicity prior to 1979.

Source: U.S. Bureau of the Census (1989, 1996). *Current Population Survey.* Washington, DC: U.S. Department of Commerce.

1995. Over 55 percent of the population in 1995 are adults ages 22–64 years (Health Resources and Services Administration 1996). Due to the dramatic rise of the incidence of children living in poverty between the early 1970s on into the 1980s, the number of young families living below the federal poverty guidelines has increased more than 40 percent since 1980 (*The Ford Foundation Letter* 1987). In 1995, fourteen million related children younger than eighteen years of age lived in families with income below $15,569, which represents the federal poverty level for a family of four. Between 1980 and 1995, the children living in poverty increased by about 2.9 million. However, those who were sixty-five years old or older living in poverty decreased by nearly six hundred thousand (Health Resources and Services Administration 1997). Since 1978, the steady climb of the number of poor people has risen from twenty-five million to forty million. This increase includes the working poor who represent 10.1 percent of Americans.

The growing number of people in poverty is considered more than twice the official levels. Included in this group are people who live in squalid and overcrowded conditions, which contribute to major health problems like tuberculosis; malnutrition due to diets and nutritional intake levels, many of which barely keep children and families alive; chronic stress, which puts them at greater risk of social maladjustment; inadequate job training and placement; and educational failure. The poverty line has not reflected the depth of the problem nor the issues addressed (*The New Federalist* 1995). Another relevant description of its impact was stated by Bagdikian: "Poverty is like cancer: left to itself, it will only get worse" (1963: 38). The population is older as indicated by the average life expectancy from thirty-five years in 1956 to sixty-eight years in 1976 and seventy-six years of age in 1991. During the Post World War II era, between 1946 and 1964, some seventy million baby boomers were born. They now represent 33 percent of the U.S. population and by year 2005, they will be in the majority at ages between fifty and seventy-four years. By 2010, the over sixty-five population group will more than double. This now middle aged "Boomer" group is receiving a great deal of attention and resources are being developed. This group has been described as living well and generally not incapacitated (Janes 1997; Stark 1996). A recent survey indicated that individuals born between this period, 1946 and 1964, are among the top one percent of the wealthiest Americans (Nest Egg Series 1993). The population group of people of color is younger than the average U.S. population and is growing at a faster rate. The growth rate is significantly increasing due to the steady flow of immigrants into the United States. Blacks continue to be the largest people-of-color population group.

There exists a distinct correlation between poverty and academic achievement. Also, the level of educational attainment is associated with the type of entry-level jobs and the amount of salary. There is a continuing educational gap between white and black Americans; the ability of a child to maintain an expected grade level has been found to be affected by long-term poverty, which tends to be more characteristic of blacks (United Way of America 1989; Baskerville 1991). There is a significant gap between the average monthly income and educational attainment; regardless of educational level, black people's income is lower than it is for white people. For example, in 1987 the average monthly income for blacks with a master's degree earned $2,180 and the white counterpart was $2,830; whites with a bachelor's degree earned $2,160; blacks with a high school diploma earned on average per month $880, while whites with no high school diploma were earning $800 (U.S. Bureau of the Census 1990).

Between 1976 and 1986, black males enrollment fell by thirty-four thousand, which represented the largest decline in college participation of any group; however, the high school completion rate increased from 68 percent in 1976 to 76 percent in 1986. In the next few years there will probably be a steady decline of overall college enrollment because older students will no longer offset the younger student enrollment decline (United Way of America 1989). Dropping out of high school is linked largely with Hispanics between the ages of sixteen to twenty-four years old. In 1995, young people between the ages of sixteen and twenty-four years old who had not completed high school represented 3.9 million students—12 percent of the young adult population. The high school drop out rate for Hispanics was one-third of this population or 30 percent; and for blacks the rate was 12.1 percent (see figure 2.3) (Health Resources and Services Administration 1997).

By the year 2000, the labor force will consist of 26 percent nonwhite groups. Blacks will account for 12 percent of the total labor force. In the 1990s, 57 percent of new workers will be racial minorities; Hispanics will have the fastest growth in labor force participation representing 10 percent of the entire labor force (United Way of America 1989). For younger children, 64 percent of black children attended public nursery school compared to 30 percent of white children in 1985; during the same period, about 64 percent of black kindergarten students attended all day, which was twice the proportion of whites (U.S. Bureau of the Census 1988). Two of the contributing factors related to the black participation rates in nursery school

Figure 2.3

School Dropout Rates for Young People (Ages Sixteen to Twenty-Four) by Race/Ethnicity—1975 to 1995

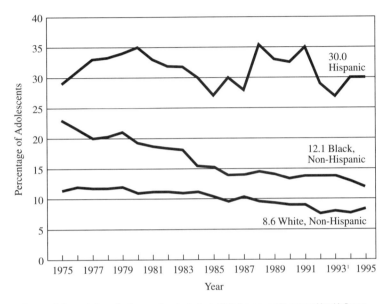

1. Because of changes in data collection procedures beginning in 1992, data may not be comparable with figures for earlier years.

Note: Status rates measure the proportion of the population who have not completed high school and are not enrolled at one point in time, regardless of when they dropped out.

Source: U.S. Department of Education (1996). *Digest of Education Statistics.* Washington, DC: National Center for Education Statistics.

and kindergarten are: 1) there is a larger proportion of the black population under eighteen years of age; in 1990, this proportion was 33.1 percent, and for whites, 24.9 percent. The median age for the black population was 27.9 years for this same period and for whites, 33.7 years; 2) there are a large number of black women working outside of the home and black females tend to work longer hours with longer job tenure as compared to white women (U.S. Bureau of the Census 1988; Bennett 1991). Also the fertility rate for younger black women is higher than that of their white counterpart, and both black and white women with infants are more likely to be in the labor force.

Defining the problem of poverty is a major determinant on what strategies to develop that are likely to be most appropriate, effective, and efficient. Starling (1993) has looked at the defined "poverty" in the following ways: 1) poverty seen as a lack of money—a guaranteed income is likely to contribute to a greater sense of well-being within and among people; 2) poverty is defined in terms of unemployment, a lack of jobs—provide incentives and encouragement to businesses, the private sector into the inner cities, and the job corps to make available jobs for all who are able to work; 3) poverty is a lack of basic necessities and opportunities such as food, clothing, shelter, and comprehensive health care—the solution is to develop and implement programs to provide needed services; and 4) poverty is a breakdown of what many call family values, while other areas are Biblical, the sacred testament of faith and commitment or humanism, which focuses more on the view of self, the secular emphasis. This focus looks more at individual behaviors, attitudes, understanding why we do what we do, and self-acceptance.

This country is going to depend on its children to be policy makers, bankers, business executives, social services and health care providers, and marriage partners and parents a few years from now. Black Americans' choices, actions, attitudes, commitments, and the risks taken today all represent role modeling and courageous examples to the children who must understand the complexities of the problems, tackle them, and generate and make use of the resulting opportunities. Furthermore, the focus is to continue with 1) fortitude and not complacency or apathy; 2) education and training targeting excellence, not immediacy; 3) family, community, and self awareness, not isolation. Life "ain't no crystal stair," but with constant vigilance and struggle or agitation, we continue forward in spite of difficulties and adversities, now more than any other time in historical legacy. We must resist despair.

What happens to black Americans, the largest racial group in this country and growing slowly, is significant in its ability to fully participate locally, nationally, and internationally. This group of the population has its largest proportion under age eighteen years and a smaller proportion aged sixty five years and older. The dangers of continued poverty has taken its toll; in addition to the young dying or becoming disabled from various health and environmental ailments, the life span, though lengthened over the decades, is comparably less than that of whites. A man living in Bangladesh has been said to have a better chance of reaching the age of sixty-five than a man in Harlem (Gorman 1991).

For centuries, black Americans have survived hard work, severely cruel behavior from others, unavailable and inadequate foods and shelter, high rates of poverty, lack of accessible health care, and inequitable opportunities in employment and education. Yet, there has been progress with many advances through the years. These areas are not insurmountable, but the focus should be more towards community building, self-help, neighborhood organizing, and other preventable strategies, self awareness, and development representing an historical legacy that has helped to keep us grounded and focused—such as getting an education and knowledge building of a broader diversity of cultures; getting involved in policy and political activities; and becoming familiar with structural interventions that are likely to assist in the maintenance of the disparity (e.g., medical tests and trials, legal rulings, and population studies). Black Americans are not destined to poverty nor a life of despair and hopelessness.

The primary recommendation for the handling of poverty is to analyze it as a process. This process involves:

1. understanding what poverty is from various perspectives. What is the context that poverty is viewed and addressed, which is interactional in nature?

2. identifying and isolating factors that influence the presence of poverty. Understanding how each factor and component of the factor can be dealt with to eradicate its strength can impact the prevalence of poverty, relational components, and relevant factors within the environment that are operating. This knowledge represents an assessment of the relational components that are operating.

3. the diagnosis tends to give more meaning to the obstacles and strengths, representing an assessment of the relational components and relevant factors. The concern becomes how do you provide an objective analysis without major negative biases and labeling. Understanding the whole, qualitatively and quantitatively is crucial.

4. the treatment plan and its timeliness refers to the appropriate and potentially effective intervention strategies that are alternatives. The fluidity of patterns, perceptions and relations of personal and interpersonal interactions are important to know and recognize as one maintains

consistency of intervention. The emphasis is on the whole, both qualitatively and quantitatively.

5.   regarding prescriptions, once you know the story and the validity of it through meanings, perceptions, beliefs and attitudes the tendency toward accuracy is greater. By staying on the scene, consistent observation as environmental or personal stresses may occur, changes in the prescribed intervention will also change as needed.

6.   a valid prognosis is more likely as one recognizes and acknowledges that change is heard but there is no more inertia. When satisfying gains are made prognosis is good, hope abounds.

7.   the re-evaluation process with great expectations and acceptance of self and others creates an atmosphere of motivation and cooperation. This process tends to lead to voluntary termination due to effective intervention and treatment. It is important to remember that the meaning of great differs one from another.

As King recognized many years ago, as recently quoted by Bonner: "It is not what they call me that matters, it is What I answer to" (1992: 18).

By 2010, eighty percent of the global population will live in poorer nations. This country may well be a leader in helping to create positive effective change in employment, job readiness and most important respectful, humane treatment of humanity.

Bibliography

Alter, Jonathan et al. (1988). "Why We Can't Wait Any Longer" in *Newsweek* (March 7): 42–43.

Bagdikian, Ben H. (1963). "The Invisible Americans," *The Saturday Evening Post* (December 21–28): 28–38.

Baskerville, Dawn (1991). *Blank Enterprise* (March): 37.

Bennett, Claudette E. (1991). "The Black Population in the United States: March 1990 and 1989. *Current Population Reports*, series P-20. no. 448.

Bonner, Dale (1992). "Conquering the Enemy Within," *Upscale* (January): 18.

Bruce, Reginald (1997). "Managing Change in the Coming Millenium," *1997 National Meeting of the American Red Cross*, invited address. Louisville, KY.

Burtless, Gary (1987). "Inequality in America: Where Do We Stand?" *The Brookings Review* (Summer): 9–16.

Chicago Tribune (1993). "Toward a Richer North America." (February 7): D–2.

Children's Defense Fund (1991). "Leave No Children Behind."

Creigs, Beverly and Howard Stanback (1986). "The Black Underclass: Theory and Reality," *The Black Scholar* (September/October): 24–32.

Current Population Survey (1997). "The State of the South 1996." Chapel Hill, NC: MDC.

Dollars and Sense (1991). "Poverty Champ." (October): 7.

——. (1988). "The Economy in Numbers: Crossing the Line on Equality." (December): 56.

Ford Foundation Letter, The (1987). "Children in Poverty." (June): 6, 8.

Fosler, R. Scott (1989). "Demographics of the 90s: The Issues and Implications for Public Policy," *Vital Speeches of the Day* 55 (July 1): 572–576.

Gans, Herbert J. (1992). "Fighting the Biases Embedded in Social Concepts of the Poor," *The Chronicle of Higher Education* (January 8): 56A.

Gitterman, Alex (1987). "Public Health Social Work in Maternal and Child Health," in St. Denis, ed., *Proceedings: Implementing A Forward Plan-A Public Health Social Work Challenge*. Pittsburgh, PA: University of Pittsburgh School of Public Health. (April): 3–4.

Gorman, Christine (1991). "Why Do Blacks Die Young?" *Time* (September 16): 50–52.

Health Resources and Services Administration (1997). "Child Health USA '96–'97," Department of Health and Human Services. Washington, DC: U.S. Government Printing Office.

——. (1996). "Child Health USA '95," Maternal and Child Health Bureau. Washington, DC: U.S. Government Printing Office.

Hearst, Randolph (1993). "U.S. Prosperity and Global Trade." *San Francisco Examiner* (February 7): IIA.

"Households, Families, Marital Status and Living Arrangements" (1998). Washington, DC: U.S. Government Printing Office, p. 20, no. 433.

Jacobs, John (1991). "Children's Needs Neglected," *The Omaha Star* (August 15): 7.

Kilborn, Peter T. (1992). "The Middle Class Feels Betrayed, But Not Enough to Rebel," *New York Times* (January 12): D–1.

King, Martin L. (1967). *Where Do We Go From Here: Chaos or Community?* New York: Harper & Row.

——. (1958). *Stride Toward Freedom: The Montgomery Story.* New York: Harper and Brothers.

Janes, Daryl (1997). "Graeber Simmons and Cowan Targets Aging Baby Boomers," *Austin Business Journal* (October 10): 31, 35.

Kleiman, Carol (1991). "Demographics Lead Push for Diversity," *Chicago Tribune* (September 15): G–1.

Levy, Frank (1987). "The Middle Class: Is It Really Vanishing?" *The Brookings Review* (Summer): 17–21.

Liederman, David (1997). "Welfare Reform: Target Poverty, Not Families," *Children's Voice*. Washington, DC: Child Welfare League of America.

Macpherson, David and James B. Stewart (1991). "The Effects of Extended Families and Marital Status on Housing Consumption by Black Female Headed Households," *The Review of Black Political Economy* 19: 3–4 (Winter-Spring): 65–81.

"Marital Status and Living Arrangements" (1988). Washington, DC: U.S. Government Printing Office, p. 20. no. 433.

Mullaney, Timothy J. (1992). "Middle Class Should Stop Whining," *The Wichita Eagle* (June 21): 17A.

Nest Egg Series (1993). "Survey of the Savings and Spending Attitudes and Behaviors of Affluent Baby Boomers," Equitable Life Insurance Society.

New Federalist, The (1995). "Target: America's 40 Million Poor," (June): 9–12.

New York Times. (1993). "Attitude Adjustment: Presidents Money and the National Mood," (January 31): 3E.

Omaha World Herald (1991). "Politicians Debate Economic Dip," (September 29): 23A.

Page, Clarence (1993). "Coming Soon: The New Underclass," *Chicago Tribune* (October 31): D–3.

Pulsuk, March and Phyllis Pilisuk, eds. (1973). *How the White Poor Live*. New Jersey: Transaction Books.

Raspberry, William (1993). "What Would Frederick Douglas Say Of Today?" *Omaha World Herald* (February 19): 16.

Rainwater, Lee (1970). *Behind Ghetto Walls*. New York: Aldine Publishing.

Ryan, William. *Blaming the Victim*.

Sconyers, Nancy et al. (1997). "Ready or Not Here It Comes," *Child Welfare* (Winter): 8–9, 21.

Stark, Judy (1996). "Fulfilling the Wishes of Empty Nesters," *San Jose Mercury News* (August): G–1.

Starling, Grover (1993). *Managing the Public Sector*. Belmont, CA: Wadsworth.

Steele, Shelby (1992). "The Dividing of America," *Destiny Magazine* (August/September): 26–29.

Thomas, Evan (1986). "Growing Pains at 40," *Time* 127(20) (May 19): 22–41.

U.S. Bureau of the Census (1996). *Current Population Survey*. Washington, DC: U.S. Department of Commerce.

———. (1990). "Black Americans." Washington, DC: U.S. Department of Commerce.

———. (1988). *Current Population Survey*. Washington, DC: U.S. Department of Commerce.

U.S. Department of Education (1988). "Trends in the Well Being of American Youth." Washington, DC: U.S. Government Printing Office.

United Way of America (1989). "What Lies Ahead: Countdown to the 21st Century." Alexandria, VA: United Way Strategic Institute.

Wright-Edelman, Marian (1992). "Poverty, Values and Leadership," *The Omaha Star* (July 23): 6.

CHAPTER 12

The Team Approach to Black Liberation

Jerome H. Schiele

Despite the progress made by some African Americans over the last two decades, African Americans collectively still lack considerable control over their lives and destiny. The doctrine and practice of white supremacy, which provide whites, especially white men, with inordinate control over American political, economic, and educational institutions, continue to be major impediments to the collective advancement of and greater power for African Americans (Akbar 1991; Welsing 1991; Wilson 1990; Baldwin 1985). Not only do African Americans collectively wield little power in predominately white institutions, they exert little political and financial control over predominately black institutions, with the possible exception of the black church. In addition, conspicuously lacking in the African American community are organizations—business, educational, political, and so on—that affirm an Africancentric world view, which affirms philosophical assumptions endemic to the culture and necessary for the liberation, survival, and prosperity of African Americans. Whether referred to as liberation or advancement of the race, most African Americans would probably agree that their status here in the United States should be significantly improved.

Although most African Americans might agree with the latter statement, considerable disagreement exists over the means through which African Americans can best attain liberation and/or advancement. Indeed, the means advocated by African American leaders often correspond with the goals they seek for African Americans. What has developed from this debate over means and goals is a historical split of the African American leadership into primarily two camps: inside advocates and outside advocates. Inside advocates, generally known as integrationists, civil rights leaders, or cross racial coalition builders, maintain that the best chance for advancing African Americans is through political advocacy within the American system. They attempt to exert pressure on the government and existing white institutions to integrate and to provide equal treatment for African Americans in all areas of life. Although inside advocates may acknowledge racism, they generally believe that efforts toward separation and the establishment of black controlled institutions hinder the progress of African Americans by furthering racial divisions. Furthermore, inside advocates believe that, because African Americans have made significant contributions to this country and have internalized its values and principles just as much as whites, America "owes" African Americans equal treatment and equal opportunities for upward mobility.

Outside advocates, generally known as black nationalists, racial separatists, or self-help traditionalists, view efforts toward assimilation and social justice within the American system as futile. Their efforts are usually targeted more at building and supporting organizations that are exclusively controlled by African Americans. These persons, unlike the inside advocates, usually have little or no faith in white America changing. They believe that white Americans are inherently insincere and/or deceptive and that white Americans desire to continue the exploitation of African Americans because they benefit politically, economically, and psychologically from the oppression of African Americans. Moreover, many in this camp believe in the power and necessity of self-help, that self-help serves to enhance the confidence, pride, and the political/economic status of a people.

An unfortunate consequence of this rift is that the activities of inside and outside advocates are often presented as mutually exclusive, uncomplimentary methods of social change. That is, outside advocates view working within the system to affect change as compromising the political and economic interests of African Americans, and attempting to establish some separate "black nation" or black controlled organizations is viewed as impractical and divisive among many inside advocates. Furthermore, negative images of both camps abound: outside advocates often view inside advocates as "sellouts" and inside advocates frequently view outside advocates as "radicals." A tragic corollary of not viewing these different methods as complimentary is that the efforts of African Americans toward liberation and advancement remain fragmented and absent of coordination.

This article provides a conceptual framework to illuminate a more coordinated strategy African Americans can use to bring about liberation and advancement: the team approach. It examines the importance and necessity of the team approach, identifies offensive and defensive functions of the team, and discusses some offensive and defensive roles African Americans should assume on the team. This article builds on and expands Akbar's (1992) call for the practice of a team approach for black redemption.

DEFINITION AND NECESSITY OF A TEAM

A team is a group of people working in coordination in a contest or some competition. We generally think of teams in the athletic sense, but the team approach is frequently used in other segments of society, especially in business and politics. Teams are needed when there is an opposing force or forces that vie for some mutually desired object or goal. The major themes in team work are identification of the desired object or goal, the identification of other teams or groups of people that want the same goal and/or that desire to prevent the opposition from attaining its goal (i.e., the competitor), and the need to strategize and coordinate activities.

In the United States, the team approach is especially needed for historically oppressed groups of which African Americans are a part. This fact is primarily because of the insincere and hypocritical character of the United States government and those who hold political and economic power, who most often are white and male. But more fundamentally than that is the world view that pervades the United States. This world view, known by some as the Eurocentric world view (Schiele 1994; Baldwin and Hopkins 1990; Asante 1990; Baldwin 1985; Akbar 1984; Richards 1979; Dixon 1976; Carruthers 1972), is based on the geohistorical and sociophilosophical origins of Europe. This world view is said to be inherently oppressive in its cosmological and axiological character, because it emphasizes values such as domination and control over nature and other people, excessive competition, exclusion, materialism, and insular individualism (Schiele 1994; Kambon 1992; Baldwin and Hopkins 1990; Meyers 1988; Akbar 1984). In essence, this world view is said to be inconsistent with val-

146

ues that promote equality and the inherent worth of all people (Schiele 1994). It has created political and economic institutions that do not give all people equal access to material resources (1994), nor has it created socioeducational institutions that affirm the experiences and contributions of groups of color, especially people of African descent (Asante 1991).

With this in mind, the United States, as a political and social entity, can be viewed as antiblack. This fact is not only because of the domination and control aspects of the Eurocentric world view, but also because of its inherent value of black or African inferiority (Baldwin 1985). Black inferiority, therefore, is seen as a normative phenomenon within the Eurocentric world view (Baldwin 1985; Kambon 1992), and it is this value that provides the political and economic justification to exploit and oppress black people in this country and throughout the world. Furthermore, if internalized by blacks, this value becomes an insidious tool used to keep in check the African American's level of confidence and motivation to do for self. It also impedes the development of self-love and a collective consciousness that are needed for any ethnic group to achieve liberation and advancement.

Because they live in a sociophilosophical and political/economic context that underscores competition and inequality and that defames their worth and cultural reality, the team approach becomes necessary for African Americans. This approach is not only needed for liberation and advancement but also survival. Its primary thrust should be to protect African Americans from the antilife forces that threaten African Americans as a biological and cultural entity. Furthermore, in order for the team approach to be successful, it must include both offensive and defensive dimensions.

FUNCTION AND ROLES OF THE OFFENSE

The primary function of any offensive dimensions of a team is to score. It moves the ball by making progressive or sweeping steps toward the ultimate goal—a touchdown in football terms, which is liberation and advancement in political/economic terms. Its function is not reactive but rather proactive. The offense is the initiator of activities, and, as the initiator, it seeks to build autonomous organizations and institutions that ensure the perpetuation of the group. The offense, therefore, comprises the efforts of outside advocates.

If one considers economic development and independence to be a major goal of the American survival game, and if one would peruse the data on economic development in the black community, it would appear that the African American community generally lacks a strong offensive force in this area. Data indicating that African Americans represent roughly a third of those below the poverty line (U.S. Bureau of the Census 1991) demonstrates that in many major cities over 70 percent of the businesses in African American communities are controlled by non-African Americans (Kunjufu 1991), and showing that blacks rely more on public sector employment than do whites (Landry 1987) demonstrates that African Americans have not been proactive enough to do for self economically. Besides the dearth of economic institutions and businesses, African Americans lack philosophical and political control of the schools in which their children and future professionals are socialized and trained. Thus, the African American community is in dire need of dedicated African Americans who will take the responsibility of initiating self-help activities in a proactive and offensive way to help the African American community put some points on the score board.

Although there are many ways to do this, at least three roles are important to fully cultivate a viable offensive team: knowledge producer, oratorical persuader, and community engineer. These roles must not be seen as mutually exclusive but rather interchangeable. However, one of the problems that has plagued the liberation and advancement efforts of African Americans is lack of support for and reinforcement of the notion that human talents vary considerably among people; not everybody is cut out for the same thing, and very few people can do many things very well. To this end, African Americans must be honest with other African Americans who believe they have a talent in one area but in actuality do not. This misbelief only leads to misdirected energy that ultimately brings about an unproductive team.

Another consideration is that the greater the number of African Americans on the offense—indeed on the entire team—the greater the ability to develop specific talents and skills. Too often in organizations that seek to liberate and advance African Americans a few people take on the responsibilities of the entire organization. African Americans must understand that in order for liberation and advancement to become a reality, more people have to be motivated and dedicated enough to work, to execute their specific tasks and talents. Indeed, work is the behavioral manifestation of the psychological dimensions of motivation and dedication. Thus, all of the roles are important, but their significance is only enhanced when team members coordinate their talents and skills and become steadfastly motivated and dedicated to work.

The Knowledge Producer (Offense)

The knowledge producer serves as a foundation for the offense and the defense. For the offense, however, the major role of the knowledge producer is to generate ideas and values that serve as the infrastructure for the construction of a community, a nation, a society. Ideas and values are important because they are used to develop societal roles, norms, mores, institutions, and customs, which are the basic building blocks of a social system (Longres 1990). Without these building blocks, the ability of African Americans to develop a social system of integrity is limited. Moreover, the ideas and values that lay the foundation for the social system of African Americans must be Africancentric. They must reflect traditional African philosophical assumptions that project a more holistic, spiritual, and affective mode of understanding phenomena (see Schiele 1994; Meyers 1988; Akbar 1984; Zahan 1979; Mbiti 1970). These ideas and values must be shaped by the cultural experiences of both traditional Africa and historic African America. As Nobles (1974) reminds us, African Americans are of African root and American fruit. African Americans are of African root in that the core or foundation of their cultural reality is African. However, the nurturing and free expression of that reality has been adversely affected by the American practice of cultural oppression and white supremacy that has produced peculiar fruit (i.e., people), both black and white. Thus, knowledge generated to liberate and advance African Americans must take into account the relics of traditional Africa as well as the deleterious effects of almost four hundred years of cultural oppression and human degradation here in the United States.

The knowledge producer generates ideas and values, consistent with an Africancentered world view, that serve to support the material creations and manifestations of the "community engineer," which is discussed later. She is a researcher, not only in the quantitative sense, but also in the sense that she is intensely inquisitive about exploring new ideas or reshaping old ones. Moreover, the knowledge producer must have excellent command of written and verbal communication. She must be especially skilled at writing and have an intense desire to write. Knowledge producers should come from all backgrounds; they should be interested and trained in social science, physical science, medical science, law, business, social work, the arts, entertainment, and so on. Whatever their field of interest, the hallmark of the knowledge producer is scholarship. They are the ones who define and illuminate social, physical, cultural, and spiritual reality. It is especially important that knowledge producers be ideologically and philosophically correct (i.e., Africancentered), for if they are not, they will formulate a knowledge base that merely mirrors the political agenda and philosophical traditions of others who seek to oppress and exploit African Americans.

The Oratorical Persuader

The oratorical persuader is that person on the offense who is the team's inspirational force. He is the orator through which the message of hope, faith, and confidence is promulgated. In other words, he is the messenger, the griot who orally communicates the needs, desire, and agenda of the group. This person must be talented and skilled in the art and science of rhetorical and mind persuasion. He must be able to read an audience and clearly articulate ideas and the emotional and psychological needs of the people.

For African Americans, the appeal to psychological needs is important. Almost four hundred years of oppression has had devastating effects on the collective psyche of African Americans (see Welsing 1991; Akbar 1984; Muhammad 1965). Notwithstanding the adverse political and economic oppression, cultural oppression has been African Americans' worst enemy. Cultural oppression, which for African Americans has been the imposition and universalization of European American cultural reality, has left African Americans ignorant of the greatness of their people and has caused many African Americans to degrade themselves, especially relative to European Americans. This has caused many African Americans to believe that the white or Eurocentric world view is the exclusive view of reality. To this extent, a considerable number of African Americans, especially the professional class, suffer from what Kambon (1992) calls psychological/cultural misorientation. This misorientation occurs when African Americans accept the definitions of reality avouched by European Americans without any regard for or consideration of an Africancentered view of reality (1992). Hence, the person is conceptually and philosophically incarcerated and functions within an alien definitional system that does not affirm her or his African personhood (1992).

The oratorical persuader must be able to successfully address psychological/cultural misorientation in African Americans. This should be a primary goal of her oratorical persuasion. In other words, her goal should be 1) to persuade the audience that there is psychological/cultural misorientation and that it is a primary obstacle to African Americans' liberation and advancement; 2) to help the audience defeat psychological/cultural misorientation so that they can recapture and affirm their Africancentered view of reality; and 3) to inspire the audience towards action aimed at community building and maintenance based on Africancentric principles and philosophical assumptions.

To coordinate their activities, the knowledge producer and the oratorical persuader must be in frequent contact with one another. Indeed, the message that is written and published by the producer should be consistent with that which is verbally disseminated by the persuader. And, of course, sometimes the oratorical persuader and the knowledge producer can be one in the same. Dr. Martin King, Jr. is an example of someone who was skilled in both rhetorical persuasion and written communication. However, people like Dr. King are rare and usually people are more skilled in one over the other. The point is that specialization should be the hallmark of the team, allowing some room, however, for skill flexibility and interchangability.

Both the oratorical persuader and knowledge producer function to generate, validate, and disseminate knowledge. Knowledge, however, has to be anchored in action for it to have any material relevance, especially for an historically oppressed group seeking liberation and advancement. The materialization of knowledge leads us to the next role of community engineer.

The Community Engineer

The community engineer is the component of the offense that puts what the oratorical persuader and knowledge producer have said and written into action. This is not to imply that the roles of the knowledge producer and oratorical persuader are not action oriented. All behavior is action. Action for the community engineer, however, is direct behavior that leads to the establishment and continuation of organizations and institutions, that is, things that can be seen and felt. The community engineer is the builder of schools and businesses; he or she is the electrician, plumber, building contractor, teacher, pilot, lawyer, social worker, dentist, world processor, farmer—anybody who has a skill, whatever it may be.

There are two categories of community engineers: 1) those who actually create businesses and schools, and 2) those who are employed in these businesses and schools, who actually execute professional roles and responsibilities that sustain the business or school. This bifurcation raises important questions about African Americans' application of capitalism as the mode through which goods and services are produced and disseminated. If the Africancentered world view serves as the philosophical model of the team—especially its focus on collectivity and spirituality—to what extent can capitalism conform to Afrocentric tenets and values? Can there be such a thing as Afrocentric capitalism? Does disparity in income automatically lead to the exploitation of those ho have less? and, as Karenga (1993) notes, can there be the practice of cooperative economics? I support the practice of cooperative economics (Ujamma), which emphasizes the need for African Americans to draw on a communal, economic strategy that underscores and establishes "1) social ownership; 2) strong family and group ties; 3) consumer unions; 4) economic planning; 5) socialized medicine; 6) cooperative organization of black professionals for social service; 7) the elimination of private profit; 8) a black controlled educational system; and 9) the essentiality of collective self-reliance" (1993: 381).

I believe that although there might be some income disparity,

African Americans should attempt to distribute goods, services, and power evenly. However, management and decision making are skills, and, therefore, one could argue that some people are better skilled or talented to be in positions of power than are others. If this is true, then can there be "compassionate power wielders" who are not concerned with ego inflation and exploitation but rather collective preservation? In other words, does power automatically corrupt all people, regardless of race/ethnicity and culture? If the Africancentered world view serves as the framework for the liberation and advancement of African Americans, then every effort must be taken to prevent the emergence and destroy the existence of rugged individualism, inordinate greed, and conspicuous consumption. Williams' (1987) master plan and his discussion of African democracy, Karenga's (1993) kawaida theory, and Schiele's (1990) theory of Afrocentric organizational structure should be examined for ways to implement a truly Africancentered world view in politics, economics, and the everyday world of work.

Whatever economic and political theory the team decides to employ, community engineers are the backbone to any substantive effort towards black liberation and advancement. Their establishment and operation of businesses and schools will give a material sense of autonomy that for too long has been scant in the African American community. Moreover, as African Americans establish more businesses and independent schools, the ability of those on the defense to be effective in their political advocacy of African American concerns becomes greater. In other words, there is no political freedom in America without first having economic freedom. Thus, the offense, especially via the community engineer, serves to ensure economic autonomy, while the defense, which is examined in more detail below, seeks to advance and protect the group politically.

FUNCTION AND ROLES OF THE DEFENSE

Whereas the offense functions to build and establish businesses and schools for cultural affirmation and self-sufficiency, the defense functions to neutralize and intercept political forces aimed at preventing the self-help and self-sufficiency activities of the offense. The defense is the watch dog; it constantly monitors the activities of those who seek to obviate the rise of African Americans and who seek to continue their exploitation and oppression. Thus, the defense is more reactionary than proactionary, albeit it should be proactionary too. The point is that whereas the offense should function regardless of opposition—in that all people/groups should want to perpetuate their culture through self-help and self-affirming institutions—the defense functions primarily to mediate or eliminate the effects of opposition on the group's ability to survive, advance, and prosper. Those who function more defensively can be generally referred to as inside advocates.

In a society like the United States where racism becomes a major oppositional force to people of color, the defensive component of black liberation fights to protect the African American community from racist attempts at controlling and manipulating the lives of African Americans. In this regard, African Americans who function more defensively are more likely to interact and to be employed in predominately white organizations and institutions than are African Americans who function more offensively. Although the effects of racism imbue all American organizations and institutions, most of the decisions made in the United States that affect the masses of citizens are made by white people, especially white men, in predominately white organizations, both public and private. This implies that those who work on the defense must be especially skilled at communicating and interacting with white people, knowledgeable of all of the communicative and cultural nuances that characterized European American culture. This does not imply that these persons should internalize European American culture—especially those features that jeopardize the survival of African Americans—rather it means that the person must be well adapted to European American culture.

In order to have a successful team, African Americans must remain mindful that Eurocentric cultural adaptation is not the same as Eurocentric cultural adoption (i.e., cultural internalization). Although adaptation can place one at risk of adoption, adoption is not a necessary outcome of adaptation. African Americans on the defense— but also on the offense—must maintain a sense of biculturalism: the ability to adapt and function successfully under conditions of Eurocentric cultural oppression while simultaneously maintaining the remnants of traditional West African culture and philosophical assumptions. Of course, as the offensive dimension of the team develops more fully, cultural oppression will be less of a factor in the lives of African Americans. However, it is the defense that keeps cultural oppression in check. To maintain this stance, there are at least three roles that can and should be assumed by those who function more defensively. They are the knowledge producer, the spook, and the political thorn.

The Knowledge Producer (Defense)

As the reader can discern, knowledge production is an important activity from my perspective. Just as it is important to produce and disseminate knowledge on the offense, it also is important to produce and disseminate knowledge on the defense. Unlike the knowledge producer on the offense, the knowledge producer on the defense functions to produce knowledge that primarily describes and demonstrates the injustices levied against African Americans by America's racial oppression and discrimination. In other words, this knowledge producer functions not to build a foundation for community development—as does the offensive knowledge producer—rather she functions to identify and explain the various manifestations of racial oppression to justify the need to end such oppression. The defensive knowledge producer, therefore, conducts statistical analyses that demonstrate racial oppression, analyzes policies and other mandates that reinforce racial oppression, and/or produces position papers, newsletters, and so on that illuminate racist attitudes and practices and that call for their immediate end. The defensive knowledge producer's efforts aim at reminding and convincing American citizens that racism is still alive and that governmental and private programs are needed to atone for historic and contemporary injustices against African Americans.

That knowledge producers who are more defensive locate themselves in predominately white organizations/businesses is an important fact. Although the location of an African American knowledge producer in predominately white organizations may restrict the strength of his discussion of and advocacy against racism, there are advantages. First, information that is critical for building intellectual arguments against racism, that otherwise would not be present in predominately black organizations, is frequently disseminated in predominately white organizations. This information could take the form of statistical analyses of employment practices or more clandestine data such as efforts aimed at spying on and undermining certain black organizations. Predominately white organizations tend to have more of this information because 1) many of these organizations function—whether officially or unofficially—to exploit and disunite African Americans, and 2) these organizations are prominent in producing, disseminating, and validating most of the knowledge generated in the United States. Second, personal conversations and experiences with white colleagues can be important sources of information. For the African American knowledge producer in predominately white organizations this means that his personal contact gives him or her a window through which to discern the attitudes and to predict the future behavior of white people, especially as it concerns activities that place black people in political, economic, and biological jeopardy. In short, because of his physical intimacy with white people, the defense knowledge producer can access data that the offense knowledge producer can not.

Knowledge producers of both the offense and defense establish think tanks that are financially independent of the white power structure is also essential. African American knowledge producers must remember that a group's level of financial independence is directly related to its level of ideological and intellectual independence. African Americans should not continue to rely solely on white-controlled foundations to fund their research, because although some foundations will allow open dialogue on race and cultural issues, most function unofficially to maintain European American cultural and political dominance. In addition, many of these foundations implicitly restrict definitions of "open" and "critical" dialogue. It is imperative, therefore, that a working relationship be developed and maintained between African American entrepreneurs and African American knowledge producers so that the African American community can develop foundations that fund the kind of research and scholarship that speak specifically to the liberation and advancement of African Americans.

Nonetheless, it is important for the knowledge producer who functions defensively to maintain intimate contact with organizations and foundations controlled by European Americans. This intimate physical contact and its implications for black liberation is underscored more in the next role of the spook.

The Spook

Greenlee's (1993) *The Spook Who Sat By the Door* provides an excellent fictional example of how African Americans can use their intimate contact in white organizations to gain strategic information that can be used to bring about black liberation and advancement. The book primarily centers on one character, Freeman, who becomes one of the first African American Central Intelligence Agency (CIA) agents. Although he appears to others to be quite loyal to the agency and gung ho in the execution of his assigned duties, Freeman is really spying on the spies. He uses the information and knowledge gained from his affiliation with the C.I.A. to establish and launch a counter black resistance movement in Chicago that militarily confronts the police and other law enforcement officials, who have brutalized and unfairly treated the black community. Because of top secret information Freeman received while an intelligence agent, Freeman's militia was well organized, well equipped, and well prepared, and launched a formidable fight against the white-controlled police department and national guard.

African Americans can learn considerably from this fictional novel. If African Americans are to have a successful and viable defense, they must have people to serve as spooks or informants who provide needed information for the team's progression and who serve to undermine, sabotage, and expose organizations that aim to manipulate and destroy African Americans. This person, who works clandestinely, must be a member or have intimate access to all kinds of organizations, including, but not limited to, educational, legal, health, military, intelligence, and business organizations, and must have the uncanny ability to deceive coworkers and supervisors, just as Freeman did in *The Spook.* They must be exceptionally skilled in their area of expertise and be able to maintain unquestionable allegiance to the mission of black liberation.

The role of the spook is probably the most important and historically underutilized role in the African American community. African Americans must keep in mind that in spite of the official documents and political propaganda that profess equality for all people in the United States, the advancement and liberation of black people is in conflict with the unofficial agenda of white hegemony and supremacy. The United States politicizes race: it distributes power,

157

resources, and legitimation based on one's skin hue. Thus, as long as European Americans benefit collectively and individually from the oppression of African Americans, the political interest of European Americans will remain oppositional to the political interest of African Americans.

Political elections across this country demonstrate this point when there are white and black candidates vying for the same elected position. In most of these elections, whites overwhelming cast their votes for the white candidate and blacks overwhelmingly cast theirs for the black candidate. This is especially true when the black candidate advocates vociferously for the poor and the oppressed, of whom are disproportionately black (U.S. Bureau of the Census 1991). In addition, symbolic codes are now used regnantly by politicians to sway the white vote by instilling fear and hostility. Although these codes superficially appear race neutral, they carry racist connotations. Some of these codes are affirmative action, urban crime/violence, youth violence, welfare cheats/frauds, and drug addicts (McConahay and Hough 1976), all of which are thought to be associated primarily or exclusively with African Americans.

Throughout the history of the United States, governmental and private officials have often spied on and infiltrated black organizations that have been seen as threats to white hegemony. Indeed, many of these spies were (are) influential persons in these organizations. For example, it has been reported that Joel Spingarn, who was one of the founders and executive directors of the National Association for the Advancement of Colored People (NAACP) for many years, gave the FBI information on NAACP activities and operations (see Martin 1993). The apartment plan of the Chicago Black Panthers party headquarters, which was drawn up by a black spy who infiltrated the Panthers, was given to the Chicago police department and was a major weapon used to assassinate Black Panther leader Fred Hampton. In addition, the FBI under J. Edgar Hoover's orders, forged Malcolm X's signature to several inflammatory letters that were mailed to Elijah Muhammad to exploit and exacerbate the unfavorable relationship between the two men after Malcolm was suspended from the Nation of Islam (see Evanzz 1992; Carson 1991).

For African Americans to be continually spied on but yet not employ intelligence methods to undermine and spy on organizations that seek their destruction is imprudent. Moreover, for African Americans to believe that their civil rights are intact and that America offers equal opportunities politically and economically for all is also foolish and politically immature. In order to promote the political interest and survival of African Americans, it is important that the role of spook, spy, informant, be fully developed and applied by African Americans.

The Political Thorn

The political thorn is the defense's counterpart to the offense's oratorical persuader. Like the oratorical persuader, the political thorn should be skilled and trained in oral communication and rhetorical persuasion. Unlike the oratorical persuader, the political thorn functions to agitate the system of racism and to advocate the interest of African Americans in whatever work or professional setting. Therefore, there are two roles of the political thorn: agitator and advocate. In her role as agitator, this person functions to upset the free flowing pursuit of racist stereotypes and practices that cast African Americans as impotent, unintelligent, and immoral. The political thorn does this by publicly exposing and calling out racist practices in hiring, promotion, and other areas of business and education. She leads protests and rallies the community to fight against racist practices in government, the private sector, or in the broader community. In other words, the political thorn is African Americans' bullhorn, the perpetual thorn in the side or buttocks of those who wittingly or unwittingly seek to continue racist practices and discrimination.

The political thorn is more proactive in her role of advocate than in her role of agitator. The critical difference is that whereas agitation functions to neutralize or diffuse hostile gestures toward African Americans, advocacy functions to prevent those gestures from occurring in the first place. Politicians, other governmental officials, and private administrators are probably the best examples of political advocates. Their role is or should be proactive in protecting the rights and interest of their constituency by establishing and passing legislation and/or developing organizational policies that seek to advance values of equality and justice for all. For those who advocate on behalf of African Americans, their advocacy should focus primarily on the protection of the rights of African Americans as citizens and human beings, the establishment of policies that redistribute wealth and resources to African Americans—who have the highest percentage of people under the official poverty level than any other group (U.S. Bureau of the Census 1991)—and the support of policies that target greater and more influential employment opportunities for African Americans.

The African American advocate who becomes a politician must not lose sight of her or his commitment to the African American community first, even if the district he represents has a white majority. Moreover, if the offense develops the kind of business and economic strength needed to enhance a people's political status, then the ability of the advocate to argue a more convincing case on behalf of African Americans to the broader population is enhanced. African Americans must understand that political advocacy and economic empowerment go hand in hand. The economic force provided by the offense will give the advocates and the entire African American community the leverage needed to fight in a hostile and competitive sociopolitical milieu.

Although the sub roles of advocate and agitator were presented separately, they are really two transparent and interactive sides of the same coin. They are symbionic and represent the core behavioral thrust of the role of political thorn. Albeit oratorical skills are important in this role, so too are skills in persuading non-African American audiences to support the upliftment of the African American community. This persuasion must be couched in moral terms to appeal to the moral desires—no matter how repressed—of those who benefit from the oppression of African Americans. Farrakhan's (1993) *A Torchlight for America* is an excellent example of one who uses the call for moral consciousness to not only redeem African Americans but to also demonstrate to non-African Americans the interconnectedness of the destinies of Americans of diverse racial and ethnic backgrounds. However, African Americans must understand that any moral appeal without economic leverage lacks strength in persuading and forcing others to act morally towards them. Thus, in order for the political thorn to be effective, she or he must never reject the importance of the offense and group self-determination in making his or her work easier.

CONCLUSION

The team approach to black liberation is necessary for African Americans to uplift and advance themselves as a truly self-determined people. This article has presented some beginning ideas as to how this team could function and the roles it might possess. Considerable work, however, is still needed to more fully develop the team approach.

Two areas needing further attention are the phenomenon of the Uncle Tom and the role of fair-minded and sincere European Americans. Uncle Toms, who are African Americans that demonstrate the most extreme form of cultural/psychological misorientation and black self-hatred, pose a major danger to the collective progress of African Americans. Because of his addiction to materialism and recognition from the white power structure, the Uncle Tom is an easy prey for cooptation by antiblack elements and, thus, is used to undermine efforts aimed at black self-determination. Further work on the team approach should be dedicated to 1) better identity of the Uncle Tom by clearly delineating psychological and behavioral characteristics associated with this person, and 2) identify strategies to expose the Uncle Tom and to neutralize her efforts of sabotage.

The team approach also must consider the role of fair-minded and sincere European Americans who have overcome the psychological effects of racial oppression (i.e., feelings of superiority) or who have learned how to confront and successfully cope with those effects. Just as the tom is used to sabotage and undermine black liberation efforts, sincere European Americans can be used on the defense to undermine and sabotage efforts to continue white supremacy and racial oppression. Their physical appearance gives them easy entry into and movement in organizations that seek to maintain white supremacy and racial oppression. As we consider the role of European Americans, however, we must remember that because of the pervasiveness of racism and its corollary of affording European Americans comfort and privilege, European Americans who are sincere and fair-minded towards African Americans are deviants from the European American norm and should be considered in rebellion (Akbar 1992). Thus, sincere and fair-minded European Americans are hated by most other European Americans, especially if they demonstrate their sincerity and support for African Americans publicly and uncondi-tionally.

If these two areas are fully explored, along with the other ideas of this article, then African Americans have a better chance at liberation and advancement. At this point in time, the team approach offers the best strategy to improve the condition of African Americans, at least until another sociopolitical and cultural reality emerges. Although many African Americans appear to have no faith in the redemption of the African American community, we must remember that the dark-est part of the night is just before dawn. The team approach offers a viable method to usher in the dawn of a new reality, one that will af-ford African Americans greater self-determination and power to con-trol their destiny and to ensure their survival as a people.

Bibliography

Akbar, N. (1992). *Redemption of the Black Mind.* Speech presented at the April United African Movement's weekly lecture series, Brooklyn, NY.

———. (1991). *Visions for Black Men.* Nashville, TN: Winston-Derek.

———. (1984). "Africentric Social Sciences for Human Liberation," *Journal of Black Studies* 14(4): 395–414.

Asante, M. K. (1991). "The Afrocentric Idea in Education," *Journal of Negro Education* 60(2): 170–180.

———. (1990). *Kemet, Afrocentricity, and Knowledge.* Trenton, NJ: African World Press.

Baldwin, J. (1985). "Psychological Aspects of European Cosmology in American Society," *The Western Journal of Black Studies* 9(4): 216–223.

Baldwin, J., and R. Hopkins (1990). "African-American and European-American Cultural Differences as Assessed by the Worldviews Paradigm: An Empirical Analysis," *The Western Journal of Black Studies* 14(1): 38–52.

Carruthers, J. H. (1972). *Science and Oppression.* Chicago: The Center for Inner City Stud-ies.

Carson, C. (1991). *Malcolm X: The FBI File.* New York: Carroll & Graf.

Dixon, V. (1976). "World Views and Research Methodology," in L. King, V. Dixon, and W. Nobles (eds.), *African Philosophy: Assumptions and Paradigms for Research on Black Persons.* Los Angeles, CA: Fanon Center Publications.

Evanzz, K. (1992). *The Judas Factor: The Plot to Kill Malcolm.* New York: Thunder's Mouth Press.

Farrakhan, L. (1993). *A Torchlight for America.* Chicago: Nation of Islam.

Greenlee, S. (1993). *The Spook Who Sat by the Door,* revised ed. Laurelton, NY: D & J Books.

Kambon, K. (aka Joe Baldwin, 1992). *The African Personality in America: An Africancentered Framework.* Tallahassee, FL: Nubian Nation Publication.

Karenga, M. (1993). *Introduction to Black Studies,* 2d ed. Los Angeles, CA: The University of Sankore Press.

Kunjufu, J. (1991). *Black Economics.* Chicago: African American Images.

Landry, B. (1987). *The New Black Middle Class.* Berkeley: University of California Press.

Longres, J. F. (1990). *Human Behavior in the Social Environment.* Itasca, IL: F. E. Peacock.

Martin, T. (1993). *The Jewish Onslaught: Despatches from the Wellesley Battlefront.* Dover, MA: The Majority Press.

Mbiti, J. (1970). *African Religions and Philosophy.* Garden City, NY: Anchor Books.

McConahay, J. B., and J. Hough (1976). "Symbolic Racism," *Journal of Social Issues* 32 (Spring): 23–45.

Meyers, L. J. (1988). *An Afrocentric World View: Introduction to an Optimal Psychology.* Dubuque, IA: Kendall-Hunt.

Muhammad, E. (1965). *Message to the Black Man.* Chicago: Nation of Islam.

Nobles, W. W. (1974). "African Root and American Fruit: The Black Family," *The Journal of Social and Behavioral Sciences* 20: 66–77.

Richards, D. M. (1979). "The Ideology of European Dominance," *The Western Journal of Black Studies* 3(4): 244–250.

Schiele, J. H. (1994). "Afrocentricity as an Alternative World View for Equality," *Journal of Progressive Human Services* 5(1): 5–25.

———. (1990). "Organizational Theory from an Afrocentric Perspective," *Journal of Black Studies* 21(2): 145–161.

U.S. Bureau of the Census (1991). *Money Income of Households, Families, and Persons in the United States: 1990.* Washington, DC: U.S. Government Printing Office.

Welsing, F. C. (1991). *The Isis Papers: The Keys to the Colors.* Chicago: Third World Press.

Williams, C. (1987). *The Destruction of Black Civilization: Great Issues of a Race from 4500 B.C. to 2000 A.D.,* revised ed. Chicago: Third World Press.

Wilson, A. N. (1990). *Black-on-Black Violence: The Psychodynamics of Black Self-annihilation in Service of White Domination.* New York: Afrikan World Inforsystems.

Zahan, D. (1979). *The Religion, Spirituality, and Thought of Traditional Africa.* Chicago: University of Chicago Press.

PART III

The African Diasporic Experience Through Autobiography and Black Studies Narratives

CHAPTER 13

An African-Centered Analysis of W. E. B. Du Bois's *Darkwater: Voices from Within the Veil* by Utilizing Molefi Kete Asante's Proposed Africalogical Framework

Ahati N. N. Toure

THE CONTEXT

The publication of W. E. B. Du Bois's *Darkwater: Voices From Within the Veil* (1969) occurred at a time of great moment in the lives of U.S. Africans and in the world. For one, there was the shattering trauma of the first European World War, which shook to the very foundations the faith of those whose hope lay in the impregnable fortress of European civilization. For U.S. Africans, it was a time in which they found themselves increasingly under duress in the suffocatingly ubiquitous atmosphere of white supremacy, the victims of unbridled violence, lawlessness, and unremitting oppression. The masses of Africans in the northern cities flocked to the Hon. Marcus Mosiah Garvey's brand of Pan-Africanism, and to his inspiring and rival program for national resurrection. And, for a decade, Du Bois himself had emerged from the relatively sedate halls of academia to immerse himself in the thick of political battle and propaganda, most notably, as the eloquent and passionate editor of the National Association for the Advancement of Colored People's *The Crisis*. Du Bois, "artist and black Christian, radical democrat and cultural pluralist,"[1] was hailed in the United States—despite Garvey's following of six million Africans[2]—as the leading spokesman for U.S. Africans at the time of *Darkwater*'s publication. With a circulation of one hundred thousand in 1919, Du Bois, through *The Crisis*, was capturing the attention of "something like 250,000 people [who] read him each month."[3]

167

Du Bois had also become the chief propagandist and organizer of a Pan-Africanist movement, the first conference of which was held in 1900. The second—following nearly twenty years later, one year before *Darkwater* was published—was held in Paris in 1919, and out of it emerged a proposal to provide international supervision to the former German colonies in Africa, with a view to their eventual independence contingent upon African "readiness" for self-governance.[4] "This [proposal of Du Bois's] received worldwide publicity in the months preceding the book's appearance."[5]

Du Bois conceived of *Darkwater*, in large part, as a polemic against the white supremacist anxiety over the imagined rising tide of color threatening to engulf the European world.[6] Hence, its title, *Darkwater: Voices From Within the Veil*, underscores it as a refutation of this European dread; the book presented the explication by Du Bois (who spoke for the U.S. African element of that rising tide) of the voices and viewpoint of those humans amassed behind the veil, beyond which Europeans were abysmally ignorant. The veil represented the superficial knowledge Europeans possessed of Africans, distorted as it was by irrational caste prejudice. It was a barrier to human understanding, the color line beyond which the humanity of the dark tide could not be contemplated or comprehended by the "civilized" European mind. *Darkwater*, like *The Souls of Black Folk*, represented Du Bois's priesthood function and mission, his mediation with the European Americana world of the concerns, feelings, aspirations, even humanity of African Americans, made invisible and inaccessible by a veritable iron curtain of color caste.

The caliber of thought, moreover, against which Du Bois battled in *Darkwater*—articulated in books like Madison Grant's *The Passing of the Great Race or the Racial Basis of European History* (1916) or Lothrop Stoddard's *The Rising Tide of Color Against White World Supremacy* (1921)—held to a deep-seated hostility towards and suspicion of democracy and egalitarianism. As Aptheker put it, Grant's book "was a classical affirmation of extreme right-wing thinking and served, indeed, as one of Hitler's inspirations."[7] Filled with assertions of Anglo-Saxon superiority, anti-African and anti-Jewish sentiments, and male gender supremacy, Grant's work argued for the sterilization of "unfit" humans—including, of course, U.S. Africans—and the elimination of "defective" infants.[8] Stoddard, likewise, in his book, voiced the classic, maniacal, paranoiac, and psychotic European American terror of people of color, with the obligatory warning that the insidious machinations of bolshevism were behind a plot to undo the purity of the white race.[9]

Such works merely expressed ideas of accepted currency in the south, and indeed, throughout the whole of the United States, as was evidenced by the widespread brutalization of African people during this period. Rabid European American mobs, amid general governmental indifference, ruthlessly slaughtered several hundreds of Africans in twenty-seven incidents or racial violence in both the north and south during what later became known as the Red Summer of 1919.[10] Lynching had reached an all-time high between 1914 and 1918 such that "approximately every fourth day somewhere in the United States a Black man, woman, or child was tortured, hanged, or burned by a mob—and accounts of every one of these reached the desk and seared the brain of the editor of *The Crisis*."[11]

Darkwater, like *The Souls of Black Folk,* represents a collection of essays—ten in all—some of which appeared in the *Atlantic*, the *Independent, The Crisis*, and the *Journal of Race Development*.[12] These essays, interspersed with poems and short stories, address the general question of European American caste (race) prejudice and the European American oppression of U.S. Africans, its injustice and irrationality—and, indeed, immorality—as well as the rapacity of European civilization and its failure to live up to the ideals it purports to uphold.

THE AFRICALOGICAL FRAMEWORK FOR AFROCENTRIC ANALYSIS

The analytical framework for determining whether Du Bois's work can be considered Afrocentric, or manifests "the groundedness of observation and behavior in one's own [African] historical experiences,"[13] will draw upon Molefi Kete Asante's formulation in his working paper *Afrocentricity and Human Knowledge: An Introduction to Africalogy*, which seeks to provide a methodology for the Afrocentric analysis of any phenomenon of human inquiry. According to Asante, any Afrocentric analysis must consider four principal issues: 1) cosmological, under which are subsumed concepts of racial forma-

169

tion, culture, gender and class; 2) epistemological, under which are subsumed language, myth, and dance-music-art; 3) axiological, under which come the conceptions of the good and right conduct; and 4) the aesthetic, under which are seven aspects: polyrhythm, polycentrism, dimensional, repetition, curvilinear, epic memory, and wholism.[14]

Further, the discipline of Africalogy divides inquiry into six general fields of knowledge: social, historical, cultural, political, economic, and psychological. All have three paradigmatic approaches to research: functional, categorical and etymological.[15] "The functional paradigm represents needs, policy, and action. In the categorical paradigm are issues of schemes, gender, class, themes and files. The etymological paradigm deals with language, particularly in terms of word and concept origin.[16]

Asante's scheme further permits knowledge areas to be divided into the categories of the cultural/aesthetic, dealing generally with the arts and the humanities,[17] and social/behavioral, which refers "to the area of knowledge that deals with human behavior in relationship to other humans, living or dead, relationship to the cosmos, and relationship to self."[18]

Based on this schema, Du Bois's work can be said to be, in the main, a social treatise in the social/behavioral field (although it has elements of the cultural/aesthetic), for it assumes the problem of the color line to be a domestic social problem between two groups of people presumed to be culturally linked and of the same society in unequal relationship to one another. Although a social treatise, Darkwater also treats of political, cultural, economic, psychological, and historical aspects of the problem of African integration into European American society, and the resistance to that integration consequent of European caste prejudice and oppression. This problem of the color line, or the problem of caste status within European society, also assumes an international dimension in Du Bois's thought. Further, Darkwater falls under the functional paradigm as outlined by Asante, for its principal aim is to achieve a policy objective in European American society and global European culture: the integration or acceptance of Africans as equal, as "raceless" partners, as, at the very least, "colored" or "ethnic" Europeans; it seeks the abolition of invidious proscriptions of color distinction and oppression, the extirpation of caste.

Also, according to Asante's schema, *Darkwater* treats principally of cosmological issues, including the concepts of race formation, culture, gender, and class; axiological questions of the good and right conduct; and epistemological questions, dealing primarily with the issue of the myth of democracy and justice in European culture.

Finally, *Darkwater* is a Eurocentric work, for Du Bois does not proceed from the epistemic stance of African-centeredness, but from one of Europe-centeredness in which the African is seen as "living on someone else's terms."[19] As Asante argues, "We are either existing on our own terms or the terms of others."[20] Clearly, in this work Africans are seen as existing only in relationship to the European world.

CHAPTER SUMMARIES

Du Bois's "Credo" at the beginning of the work establishes the ideological framework for his intellectual and literary assault. He espouses the oneness of God and the brotherhood of all peoples on the earth. "I believe that all men, black and brown and white, are brothers—differing in no essential particular, and alike in soul and the possibility of infinite development."[21] He further affirms his faith in "the Negro Race," in the beauty of its genius (which is vague), "the sweetness of its soul, and its strength in meekness [which suggests an untoward and unpalatable docility in the face of oppression] which shall yet inherit this turbulent earth."[22] While affirming his faith in race, lineage, and self, Du Bois also declares his faith in work, in the Devil and his angels, who afflict the lives of U.S. Africans, in pacifism, in democracy, in the training of children, and in patience.[23]

Du Bois begins his argument in his first chapter, "The Shadow of Years," with an autobiographical essay, the purpose of which is, apparently, to set forth his credentials to the European public. Through this brief autobiographical account he establishes several significant points:

1. He is not hostile to Europeans qua Europeans, having grown up among them and, hence, having been socially intimate with them.
2. He is personally familiar with the sting of caste (color) prejudice.

171

3. He is equipped by the finest preparation in European education, both at Harvard University and the University of Berlin, to treat on any subject with authority and erudition.
4. He did live, study, teach, and work in the south, making him quite familiar with the conditions there (and perhaps, as well, making him an authentic Negro).[24]
5. His work as an activist-scholar makes him eminently qualified to discuss the problem of European caste (race) prejudice and the U.S. African with unquestioned authority.

In this regard, Du Bois recounts his family history with the rather curious observation that he is the product of both African and European ancestry, noting, with apparent relish, that "having finally gotten myself born, with a flood of Negro blood, a strain of French, a bit of Dutch, but, thank God! no Anglo-Saxon, I came to the days of my childhood."[25] One ponders the significance of this revelation with the speculation that it may serve—in his mind at least—to establish the authenticity of his humanity, of his biological connectedness to the Europeans to whom he was representing himself as the advocate for those voiceless Africans incarcerated behind the veil. Du Bois seems, in so establishing his identity, to be astride two worlds, to claim by virtue of his heredity and his white New England background to be as much a part of the European world from which he is debarred as of the "Negro" one to which he is ineluctably shunted by virtue of the color line.[26]

As a growing youth Du Bois lived intimately with Europeans, "cordially despised the poor Irish and the South Germans, who slaved in the mills,"[27] and generally saw himself as equal to all those in the community of which he was a part. But while Du Bois appears to attempt to mask through his lofty prose the psychological impact of untoward caste (color) distinction as it impinged upon his developing psyche, without a doubt his awareness of the meaning his white peers attached to his being chromatically different was a searing experience. While undaunted, he was, nonetheless, reactive. *"If they beat me at anything, I was grimly prepared to make them sweat for it!"* [emphasis mine].[28] Increasingly, as the young Du Bois matured, his skin color grew into an insuperable social barrier, and his response was to affect an outward air of superiority and indifference. But, inwardly, there were occasional tears. And, he admits: "I flamed! I lifted my chin and strode off to the mountains, where I viewed the world at my feet and strained my eyes across the shadows of the hills."[29] Du Bois keenly felt the offense of the color line and of the caste status; yet, during these days he, nevertheless, describes himself as "happy."[30]

From the quiet, white New England world of his youth, Du Bois journeys to Fisk University (Harvard University, for the moment, a dream deferred) in Tennessee and to that exotic and foreign "land of slaves," for his first, sustained encounter with and sojourn among his own kind.[31] Du Bois himself recalls the south appeared to him "a far land" where he would be "among strangers who were regarded (and in truth were) 'mine own people.'" Fisk University, in Du Bois's periodization of his life, represented the beginning of "The Age of Miracles," ending with his Ph.D. at Harvard University and his doctoral studies in Germany at the University of Berlin. It was followed by "The Days of Disillusionment," which involved his tenure at Wilberforce University; "The Discipline of Work and Play" saw his marriage and his sociological work on the "Philadelphia Negro" and at Atlanta University for thirteen years; and finally, "The Second Miracle Age" witnessed his political activism, commencing with his work in the Niagara Movement and, closely following, in the NAACP.

In his second chapter, "The Souls of White Folk," Du Bois endeavors to explicate the American racial situation for his European readers and to peer into, dissect, and present to them their own souls as a dispassionate observer, from a stance of scientific objectivity, "[h]igh in the tower, where I sit above the loud complaining of human seas."[32] Interestingly, as in the first chapter, Du Bois asserts his competence to comment upon the European psyche because of his identity with Europeans. "Of them I am singularly clairvoyant," he writes. "I see in and through them. I view them from unusual points of vantage. Not as a foreigner do I come, for I am native, not foreign, bone of their thought and flesh of their language"[33] [emphasis mine]. Thus, while he is, on one hand, a removed observer high in a tower, he is also an intimate by blood, by education, and by experience. And what he sees in the American European psyche is the ugliness of race (caste) prejudice, a nineteenth- and twentieth-century phenomenon he argues would have been considered curious, if not ludicrous, in the medieval European world. Further, in advancing this argument, Du Bois uses the European "we." And thus, while claiming detachment and objectivity, he simultaneously asserts his identity with the history and culture of the people whose ugliness he decries.

Caste (race) prejudice and the notion of white supremacy are absurdities, Du Bois argues, and faith in their validity and moral rightness leads to violent, brutal, and inhuman acts against others so deprecated. As well, it leads to ethnocentrism, to the European monopolization of history, and to its distortion, to the warped notion that history is the singular chronicle of the greatness of those people deemed to be white.[34] And in the progression from comic absurdity to tragic seriousness, this psychosis engenders a culture of virulent madness and fury, and a people possessed of an "ungovernable lust of blood; mad with murder, destroying, killing, and cursing." It leads to the withering of justice and the pollution of civilization, to "orgy, cruelty, barbarism, and murder done to men and women of Negro descent."[35]

Du Bois further indicts European American society, with its pretensions to egalitarianism, as hypocritical, charging its recent war to preserve democracy in the world, and its protest of human rights violations abroad, were glaringly contradicted by its treatment of Africans within its own borders. Du Bois, now, becomes the "we" of the darker peoples, victims of the white man's grand delusion of inherent and inimitable superiority. The Christian religion, as well, fails the test under European practice. The engine of European rapacity is economic, he asserts, and this rapacity leads to war, to conquest, to imperialism, and to the subjugation of African peoples; because of this foundation the flowering of Europe subsists. He states: "[W]e darker men said: This is not Europe gone mad; this is not aberration nor insanity; this *is* Europe; this seeming Terrible is the real soul of white culture—back of all culture—stripped and visible today"[36] [emphasis his].

That conclusion notwithstanding, Du Bois (incredibly) asserts that European culture is superior to anything that arose from Africa or Asia, not because Europeans are inherently superior to Africans or Asians, but because they have built upon the great accomplishments of Africa and Asia.[37] Europe for Du Bois—despite its inherent violence and barbarity against African peoples—represents the historic pinnacle of all human civilizations, the apex of all human development. There is not, for him, the remotest contemplation of an independent and exalted African existence that is uniquely Afrocentric. And yet, he is unequivocal in his charge that the notion of color (caste) superiority fueled the European colonization of Africa, and that its imperial exploitation was the chief cause of the European world war, that the war represented, at bottom, a scrambling of European nations for colonial possessions to secure economic advantage and nationalistic prestige.[38]

In his third chapter, "The Hands of Ethiopia," Du Bois pursues this theme in greater detail as he contemplates the rich and glorious African past: the genius of its civilizations, its technological innovation, and its highly developed agriculture and trade at a time when Europe was but a wilderness.[39] But Africa, the fount of human world history, is now the victim of unspeakable European aggression. There are four hundred years of "that trade in human beings which first and last robbed black Africa of a hundred million human beings,"[40] distorting and crippling social, economic, and governmental life and cultural development. "Today, instead of removing laborers from Africa to distant slavery, industry built on new slavery approaches Africa to deprive the natives of their land, to force them to toil, and to reap all profit for the white world."[41]

By its continued imperialism, Du Bois warns, Europe faces the threat of war against it by the world's exploited masses that could portend its destruction; Europe's criminal exploits cannot go long unchallenged. As a pacifist and a democrat, therefore, Du Bois calls for continental African self-determination. In particular, he advocates that Africans of the former German colonies, with the immediate addition of Belgian and Portuguese possessions, be permitted to form a new African state[42]—with room for discussing the voluntary surrender of other European holdings. But Du Bois's proposal (incredibly) envisages "international" (i.e., European) tutelage and guardianship with either eventual incorporation into the politicoeconomic structure of the metropolitan powers, or bona fide independence once the "natives" are deemed "capable" (by the European tutors) of self-rule. Du Bois is, thus, a committed Europeanist (and, one must admit, imperialist)—albeit a liberal one—and his is "an Africa for Africans guided by *organized* [that is to say, European] *civilization*"[43] [emphasis mine].

Hence, the insoluble contradiction in Du Bois's epistemic posture both as an intellectual and as a "Negro": while Europe is rapacious and brutal, it is also civilized and deserving of deference. While its exploitation of Africa is both criminal and unrelieved, it can, apparently, be trusted to steward Africa's humane and independent development. Moreover, states Du Bois, "no one would expect this state to be independent and self-governing from the start."[44]

Two cardinal principles must, in addition, be acknowledged. First, the proposed experiment must accept the solidarity of international labor across racial lines, and a recognition that "no industrial democracy can be built on industrial despotism."[45] Second, Du Bois insists, it does not suggest, in contradistinction to Garvey's proposal, the "vast transplantation" of twenty-seven million Africans of the Western world. These "Western" Africans, however, could easily furnish "from time to time technical experts, leaders of thought, and missionaries of culture for their backward brethren in the new Africa"[46] [emphasis mine].

Returning to domestic issues, that peculiar alchemy of industrial capitalism, labor and caste (race) prejudice are the subjects of Du Bois's focus in his fourth chapter, "Of Work and Wealth." The city of East St. Louis sets the stage for the interaction between three groups—industrial capitalists, European organized labor, and African workers—symbolized as the powerful man from the north, the unwise man from the east, and the black man from the south. East St. Louis, that squalid industrial city to which the working poor are confined, that "feverish Pittsburg in the Mississippi Valley—a great, ruthless, terrible thing!" with its "crude, cold and ever hateful aspect,"[47] serves to generate the glittering wealth of the industrial capitalist class. "In fact, East St. Louis is a paradise for high and frequent dividends and the piling up of wealth to be spent in St. Louis and Chicago and New York and when the world is sane again [speaking of the European world war] across the seas."[48]

Proceeding in the chapter in parabolic fashion, Du Bois highlights the contradictions inherent in the three-way relationship between the groups and decries the outbreak of racial violence against U.S. African workers and their labor. European organized labor, however, blinded by race (caste) prejudice, is effectively manipulated by the industrial capitalist elite such that it is unable to recognize its interest in a joint struggle with U.S. African workers to extract equitable wages and other concessions from their common enemy. Consequently, "unwise" and exploited organized labor, like industrial capitalism, becomes an agent of oppression and violence against African people. European organized labor's struggle for justice, writes Du

Bois, degenerated "suddenly from a fight for wage and protection against industrial oppression [and] East St. Louis became the center of the oldest and nastiest form of human oppression—race hatred."[49]

Despite Du Bois's formulation, he, nonetheless, makes a general appeal to European organized labor, to industrial capitalism and to European American society, arguing U.S. African labor is essential to the development of American society, and its exclusion is irrational and economically unsound. "The vision of industrial democracy has come to the giants who lead American industry and finance. But it can never be realized unless the laborers are here to do the work. . . . American Negroes stand today as the greatest strategic group in the world. Their services are indispensable."[50]

The central problem for Du Bois is that racism (or caste) is but a chimera that cloaks the true nature of oppression in the world. In his internationalist socialist vision, Du Bois asserts that there are no races as such; instead, fundamentally, there are economic groupings or classes in varying relation to each other and to the means of production. They are "the imperial commercial group of master capitalists, international and predominantly white; the national middle classes of the several nations, with strong blood bonds, common languages, and common history; the international laboring class of all colors; the backward, oppressed groups of nature-folk, predominantly yellow, brown and black."[51]

The great question of justice in the world, then, centers around the equitable distribution of wealth to all the peoples of these groups. And because Du Bois's paramount goal is inclusion, the extirpation of caste, he is forced to cling tenaciously to the belief that European progress (understood in his mind as "human progress") is predicated upon U.S. African inclusion, which necessarily follows the abandonment of race (caste) prejudice. "All humanity must share in the future industrial democracy of the world. For this it must be trained in intelligence and appreciation of the good and the beautiful."[52] Hence, while Du Bois in the beginning of the chapter purports not to trust Europeans,[53] he, nonetheless, fervently hopes in them for the world's salvation as well as that of African people in the United States.

Du Bois's fifth chapter, "The Servant in the House," continues the discussion of labor with an indictment against African menial servitude in the United States, its demeaning social significance, and the attendant caste presumptions of European American employers. Re-

177

counting his personal experience as a bus boy at a Minnesota hotel during his Fisk years, Du Bois argues that such servitude is consistent with European American supremacist notions that relegate U.S. Africans to the caste status of menials perpetually in European American employ. It presents, for him, a continuation of the legacy that spawned American enslavement: the assumption that Africans possess no humanity and were, in fact, born to serve superior racial masters. "Negroes are servants; servants are Negroes,"[54] Du Bois objects. "Menial servitude is an anachronism—the refuse of mediaeval barbarism."[55] Furthermore, many forms of menial labor, including domestic labor, are not deemed serious enough either to warrant the attention or protection of organized labor, Du Bois notes, leaving such workers (mostly women) to the despotism of the employers in whose homes they work. In Du Bois's view, menial service—and domestic service in particular—should be eliminated.

Moving from the issues of labor and socioeconomics, in chapter six, "Of the Ruling of Men," Du Bois explores the concept and the practice of democracy in European history and culture and the impact of the distorting factors of racism (caste prejudice and oppression), class, and the oligarchic tyranny of industrial capitalism in its historical and ideological unfolding. If Afrocentricity is, in fact, placing Africa at the center of the human experience and of issues in human inquiry, this chapter represents the centering of Europe, with Africans mendicants pleading at the gates (through the supplicant voice of Du Bois) for entry. "Infinite is human nature," he states. "We make it finite by choking back the mass of men, by attempting to speak for others, to interpret and act for them, and we end up acting for ourselves and using the world as our private property."[56] And thus, states Du Bois, the experience of Europe, despite its shimmering ideals, has been the privileging of an elite to the benefits of democracy and to the exclusion of others deemed unfit to participate in self-governance—women, Africans, and the poor. While democracy "is a method of realizing the broadest measure of justice to all human beings,"[57] the "world" has generally chosen another course. "Democracy alone is the method of showing the whole experience of the [human] race for the benefit of the future and if democracy tries to exclude women or Negroes or the poor or any class because of characteristics which do not interfere with intelligence, then that democracy cripples itself and belies its name."[58]

Interestingly, Du Bois employs the European "we" in this chapter, arguing against European caste prejudice and toward European liberality. Democracy in the United States and elsewhere has failed because "*we* have attempted to enthrone any chance majority and make it rule by divine right. *We* have kicked and cursed minorities as upstarts and usurpers when *their* sole offense lay not in having ideas or hair like *ours*. . . . Surely, too, the remedy for absolutism lies in calling *these* same minorities to council" [emphasis mine].[59]

Hence, for Du Bois, democracy is the extirpation of all privilege, of all exclusivity within domestic and international European culture. It is radical and universal inclusion; it is global and domestic egalitarianism; it is humanism unbounded, justice on a grand, world scale. This is the Du Boisian vision, punctuated with the ever indefatigable plea (faith?) that however "desperate the temptation, no modern nation can shut the gates of opportunity in the face of its women, its peasants, its laborers, or its socially damned."[60] His is a socialist democratic vision: "The Will to Brotherhood of all Colors, Races, and Creeds; the Wanting of Wants of All. Perhaps the finest contribution of current Socialism to the world is neither its light or its dogma, but the idea back of its one mighty word—Comrade!"[61]

Expanding his egalitarian vision to encompass the matter of gender, Du Bois in chapter seven, "The Damnation of Women," attacks sexism (also a form of caste) and the male dominance and tutelage of women:

> All womanhood is hampered today because the world on which it is emerging is a world that tries to worship both virgins and mothers and in the end despises motherhood and despoils virgins. The future woman must have a life work and economic independence. She must have the right of motherhood at her own discretion. The present mincing horror at free womanhood must pass if we are ever to be rid of the bestiality of free manhood; not by guarding the weak in weakness do we gain strength, but by making weakness free and strong.[62]

In addition, Du Bois calls for respect and offers praise for the African woman, who, for him, symbolize motherhood—indeed, the motherhood of humankind. With this idea, Du Bois looks to African culture and history for values and exemplars—from antiquity to contemporary continental figures and U.S. African heroines like Tubman, Truth, and Wheatley. Despite the reverence for the African woman as mother in African culture, "this mother idea" explains why "the west-ward slave trade and American slavery struck like doom. . . . The crushing weight of slavery fell on the black woman. Under it there was no legal marriage, no legal family, no legal control over chil-dren."[63] Enslaver domination represented the most degrading viola-tion of African womanhood, of the sanctity of women so repugnant that Du Bois is moved to declare: "I shall forgive the white South much in its final judgment day . . . but one thing I shall never forgive, neither in this world nor in the world to come: its wanton and con-tinued and persistent insulting of black womanhood which it sought and seeks to prostitute to its lust."[64]

African women, further, are the strength of the African people in the United States. Their courage, personal freedom, strength of char-acter, and leadership provide exemplars for the race, and are a source of its vitality and progress. "As I look about me today in this veiled world of mine, despite the noisier and more spectacular advance of my brothers, I instinctively feel and know that it is the five million women of my race who really count."[65]

Despite the triumph of African women, however, the U.S. African community is faced with the disruption of the family due to economic constraints that tend to pull apart husband and wife, and sociocul-tural mores that tend to designate the woman's role as homemaker and the husband's as income earner. Nonetheless, this view of gen-der roles within the family is ill-adapted to economic realities. "The Negroes are put in a peculiarly difficult position, because the wage of the male breadwinner is below the standard, while the openings for colored women in certain lines of domestic work and some indus-tries, are many."[66] Consequently, husband and wife find themselves living in different geographical areas to secure work. Whatever the solution to this dilemma: "we cannot abolish the new economic free-dom of women. We cannot imprison women again in a house or re-quire them on pain of death to be nurses and housekeepers," Du Bois maintains. "The uplift of women is, next to the color line and the peace movement, our greatest modern cause."[67]

Furthermore, Du Bois comments—albeit with some degree of am-biguity—on the issue of the beauty of African women. There inheres in the racist presumption that African women are not beautiful both an advantage and a disadvantage, he argues. The disadvantage, of course, lies in the perverse insistence that beauty is European, but that insistence simultaneously freed African women from the patron-izing and suffocating constraints of the "cult of the lady," permitting them to exercise—as whole and authentic persons—freedom of will, of individual character and intelligence, so that, as Du Bois writes, we have "a vast group of women of Negro blood who for strength of character, cleanness of soul, and unselfish devotion of purpose, is today easily the peer of any group of women in the civilized world. And more than that, in the great rank and file of our five million women we have the up-working of new revolutionary ideals, which must in time have vast influence on the thought and action of this land."[68]

Du Bois's tribute to African women is poignant:

> No other women on earth could have emerged from the hell of force and temptation which once engulfed and still surrounds black women in America with half the modesty and womanliness that they retain. I have always felt like bowing myself before them in all abasement, searching to bring some tribute to these long-suffering victims, these burdened sisters of mine, whom the world, the wise, white world, loves to affront and ridicule and wantonly to insult. . . . [N]one have I known more sweetly feminine, more unswervingly loyal, more desperately earnest, and more instinctively pure in body and in soul than the daughters of my black mothers.[69]

In his eighth chapter, "The Immortal Child," Du Bois, again, mar-shals his arguments against the cruelty of European caste (race) prej-udice and the irreparable harm it causes its victims. Using the life of Coleridge-Taylor, the great African English musical prodigy, Du Bois illustrates how his music, his human creativity and genius, would have been cruelly crushed—with an immeasurable loss to European culture—were it not for the tenuous thread of chance, and had the ugly specter of racism (caste) triumphed to impose its unreasoned tyranny upon his life. So unremitting is that tyranny that U.S. African parents question the wisdom of giving birth to children, a sentiment against which Du Bois argues, stating in "the treatment of the child the world foreshadows its own future and faith. All words and all thinking leads to the child—to that vast immortality and wide sweep of infinite possibility which the child represents."[70] And, consistent with that truth, Du Bois urges that Africans bear children as a sacred duty in the struggle against European caste prejudice and oppression "to accomplish the immortality of black blood, in order that the day may come in this dark world when poverty shall be abolished, privilege be based on individual desert, and the color of a man's skin be no bar to the outlook of his soul."[71] The sacred duty of African parents, moreover, requires not simply the begetting of children, but their training and nurturing towards authentic adulthood.

Du Bois's discourse on the child provides him with a forum for discussing the purpose of education, which is not merely to preserve conformity with the status quo, but to achieve cultural and human advancement. Accordingly, "the object of education is manhood and womanhood, clear reason, individual talent and genius and the spirit of service and sacrifice, and not simply a frantic effort to avoid change in present institutions."[72] Its goal is to instill in the hearts of men and women the ideals of fairness, justice, and equality. The very access to education, moreover, must be just. It must not simply be the privilege of the wealthy, but the opportunity of the talented, regardless, as well, of color (caste). Indeed, the immortal child, for Du Bois, is "that child of all races and all colors. All children are the children of all and not of individuals and families and races. The whole generation must be trained and guided and out of it as out of a huge reservoir must be lifted all genius, talent and intelligence to serve all the world."[73]

From this, Du Bois explores the psychological impact of caste upon its victims in chapter ten, "Of Beauty and Death," the vexation and agony of being African in European, racist America. "Imagine spending your life looking for insults or for hiding places from them— shrinking (instinctively and despite desperate bolsterings of courage) from blows that are not always but ever; not each day, but each week, each month, each year."[74] For Du Bois, beauty is the beauty of nature and of God's creation, while death is the life an African must constantly endure in the maddening world of hatred, oppression, unrelieved insults, lynchings, and mob violence.

But part of Du Bois's anger, which seems to smack of elitist contempt, is directed towards his fellow Africans, who are suspended somewhat helplessly in the world between beauty and death:

> Pessimism is cowardice. The man who cannot frankly acknowledge the "Jim-Crow" car as a fact and yet live and hope is simply afraid either of himself or of the world. There is not in the world a more disgraceful denial of human brotherhood than the "Jim-Crow" car of the southern United States; but, too, just as true, there is nothing more beautiful in the

universe than the sunset and moonlight on Montego Bay in far Jamaica. And both things are true and both belong to this world and neither can be denied.[75]

In one aspect of Du Bois's conception of beauty one sees Du Bois's Eurocentrism. Beauty, for him, is also sitting among Europeans in conversation, in normal human exchange in Paris of 1919, without the haunting presence of caste prejudice. "It was simple human decency and I had to be thankful for it because I am an American Negro, and white America, with saving exceptions, is cruel to everything that has black blood," he recalls. *Fellow blacks, we must join the democracy of Europe*" [emphasis mine].[76] And similarly, France is called "the worthiest nation of the world."[77]

The death of the veil, or the curse of caste status, distorts life for the African in the United States, scarifies it with hatreds, misunderstandings, violence, and grief. "It drops as drops the night on Southern seas—vast, sudden, unanswering. There is Hate behind it, and Cruelty and Tears. . . . Listen, O Isles, to these voices form within the Veil, for they portray the most human hurt of the Twentieth Cycle of that poor Jesus who was called the Christ!"[78]

Despite Du Bois's apparent optimism, the physical death is what finally serves as the consummation of beauty for the African, for in physical death inheres an imperturbable peace, an escape from the living death of a tortured life.

The tenth and final chapter of his work is a short story "The Comet," a fanciful tale of the end of the world in New York City, in which a comet's tail sweeps poisonous gas into the earth's atmosphere, killing all except an African man, who works as a messenger at a Manhattan bank, and a young, wealthy, and "beautiful" European woman. Du Bois presents a disturbing image. Although one understands its message, which is reiterated endlessly and in variation throughout the book—the essential racelessness of humanity—it is no less regrettable. This Du Boisian preoccupation with European women is evident in some of the literary vignettes interspersed throughout the work; the notion of the union of the African man and the European woman appears to be the quintessential representation of the Du Boisian goal of race reconciliation, or caste abolition, within European society. This young, rich, and "beautiful" European woman, at first repulsed by this African man because of caste prejudice, must consent to the inexorability of the world as it is, viewing him and herself, as a consequence, with a heart transformed. The European woman begins to see the African not as a mere beast, but as a companion with whom she could live and be united and whom she could love, purged of notions of color caste or class.

> She was no mere woman. She was neither high nor low, white nor black, rich nor poor. She was primal woman, mighty mother of all men to come and Bride of Life. She looked upon the man beside her and forgot all else but his manhood, his strong, vigorous manhood—his sorrow and sacrifice. She saw him glorified. He was no longer a thing apart, a creature below, a strange outcast of another clime and blood, but her Brother Humanity incarnate, Son of God and great All-Father of the race to be.[79]

There is something irrepressible about Du Bois' regard for European women. In them, it seems, lies his hope for caste abolition—were it not for the corrupting influence of European men. Within the European woman Du Bois finds exquisite tenderness, sensitivity, and delicate beauty both of form and of soul. For example, the European woman in "The Princess of the Hither Isles" (a short fictional vignette) takes pity on the suffering and degraded African masses cruelly mocked by her insufferable male companion, the King of Yonder Kingdom. Du Bois's first words are: "Her soul was beautiful, wherefore she kept it veiled in light-laced humility and fear, out of which peered anxiously and anon the white and blue and pale-gold of her face—beautiful as day break or as the laughing of a child."[80]

Similarly, there is the little, European girl in "Jesus in Texas," a short story in which Du Bois remarks on the religious hypocrisy of Europeans, who reject Jesus of Nazareth—whom they meet in darkness—only after they discover in the light that he is a "mulatto." This female child, to the contrary, clings to the "nigger Jesus" without the revulsion of the adults of her caste. In the same story, a poor white woman who feeds and confides in the "mulatto" Christ is scandalized to discover she has been socializing with a "nigger." Du Bois, again, writes of her: "[s]he was a little woman, and once had been pretty."[81] (No similar descriptions of African women are found in Darkwater.) This European woman is later moved with the vision of a lynched Christ to abandon her racist convictions.

In Du Bois's summing up of the aspirations of the voices within the veil, one can see not an African man and an African woman

184

brought together in a world cleansed and righteous, but the vision of an African man and a European woman, brought together under an extreme and unlikely circumstance, forced to replenish the earth with a "mulatto" humanity that would make the caste distinctions between African and European irrevocably ambiguous. Perhaps, in Du Bois's vision of race reconciliation (or caste abolition) lies the notion of race suicide, of the mixing of African and European to create one great "colored" race. Perhaps, as well, for Du Bois, the white woman represents the purity and hope of European civilization, and the white man its degradation and corruption.

There is, however, a twist to the story. The young European woman is reunited with her father and her wealthy young lover (again the specter of the racist and corrupting influence of European males), and the African man, subsequently, with his African wife. Upon the arrival of the woman's father and her young lover, the African devolves from a man, a human, into—in the reascendant white perception—a "nigger," while the European woman becomes, by virtue of her color, a superior being. The world returns, unhappily, to what it was, as the veil, the reinstallation of caste, once again, descends with a chilling finality.

ANALYSIS AND CONCLUSION

Du Bois's *Darkwater,* to reiterate, can be identified according to Asante's schema as a social/functional work within the social/behavioral field of knowledge and treating specifically of cosmological, axiological, and epistemological issues relating to global and domestic European culture and the resistance of Europeans to African inclusion. It is, thus, a Eurocentric work. Specifically:

1. Cosmologically, Du Bois sees race formation as ambiguous because of the pejorative and hegemonic nature of caste (racial) distinctions and their lack of scientific specificity. For him, the notion of race is a means by which to establish ideological and structural relations of power based on a caste system. In addition, Du Bois identifies himself as belonging genetically, at least in part, to the European group. Class distinctions based on economic relations seem

much more compelling for him, and these distinctions approximate, as well, ideological caste (racial) hierarchization on a global scale. At all points, Du Bois thinks and argues within the assumptions of European culture. On the question of gender he is progressive and nonsexist.

2. Axiologically, the good and right conduct are premised on egalitarianism or democracy across racial lines and on all levels of European culture and society. The goal is the extirpation of caste (racial) distinctions, or "racelessness," in the European hegemonic conception of human groupings, as well as the elimination of discriminatory class distinctions. Du Bois's values are both democratic and socialistic.

3. Epistemologically, Du Bois's egalitarian views on race and African acceptance within European society (or the abolition of caste) are tied to his conception of the myth of democracy as the central feature of European civilization. Democracy, for Du Bois, embodies Europe's highest ideal and, perhaps, one of its greatest intellectual and practical achievements. This myth of democracy fuels his vision of the possibility of African inclusion. While cognizant of European rapaciousness, Du Bois is confronted with the confounding myth of democracy that leaves him unable, intellectually, to resolve the dialectical conflict that exists between European ideals and practice. And because the myth of democracy is so compelling for him, Du Bois is unable to determine whether the hope of African inclusion as equal, "raceless" partners in European society is a chimera or a real possibility. His is, in some ways, a desperate faith.

Unquestionably, then, *Darkwater* is centered in the European experience, and this is Du Bois's epistemological stance. Du Bois seeks acceptance for himself and his fellow Africans of the west as Europeans in culture and in the abandonment of the significance of caste (color distinction) that separates African from European in the European social order. One sees, for example, that in his discussion of the

Continent and its people, Du Bois's identification with both is, indeed, rather tenuous. Continental Africans are viewed as "backward brethren" in need of leadership in thought and culture from the European world. In contrast to Garvey's historical and cultural identification with Africa and Africans, Du Bois asserts the maximum involvement of U.S. Africans with the Continent and its peoples would be to supply technical experts and cultural leadership "from time to time." Even his call for continental African independence, which requires European supervision, Du Bois makes as a pacifist and a democrat—political positions that have meaning only with respect to European ideological movements—and not as a Pan-African nationalist. Simultaneously, his identification with Europeans is much more culturally and epistemologically complete; he is "bone of their thought and flesh of their language." In addition, Du Bois boasts an ancestry that includes "a strain of French" and "a bit of Dutch" for good measure to add to his "flood of Negro blood." In contrast, the people of whom his ancestry is predominant, for whom he has elected to speak, he described as "strangers."

In *Darkwater*, Du Bois is, in fact, a European in everything other than in skin color and in the European American caste hierarchy, against which *Darkwater* is addressed. For him Europe embodies the highest level of civilized human development. From Du Bois one gets the feeling that African culture is a dead culture, a relic from the past, which contributions to the world are historical but not living and, therefore, devoid of contemporary relevance except insofar as this "particularistic past" can demonstrate the validity of African humanity to Europeans and serve as a refutation of the necessity of the caste system. Even in Du Bois's notions of particularism can one see the valorization of European modalities as central and as universalistic.

Further, for Du Bois the principal political issues of the age are: 1) the resolution of the color line (which, again, refers to the problem of African inclusion in European society, or the abolition of caste); 2) the success of the peace movement (which concentrates on intra-European world peace and peace between European nations and other nations); and 3) the women's movement (which concern is obviously larger than the plight of "western" African women). Hence, in Du Bois's list of priorities, the liberation of Africa that more closely ap-

proximates Garvey's level of faith in Africans and in their human pos-
sibilities, the unity of African peoples worldwide, and the independent
progress of the U.S. African people toward self-determination and
collective struggle are not his paramount objectives. To the contrary,
Du Bois operates thoroughly within the context of the European
world.

While Du Bois in "The Damnation of Women" expresses his great
love and affirmation of African womanhood, the piece seems more a
panegyric to the memory of his mother, whom he dearly loved, than
to the total aspect of African womanhood. Du Bois's emphasis is on
African motherhood, and for this he harks back to African motifs and
cultural values. But the notion of African woman as companion, as
beautiful, as beloved to the African man seems incompletely expressed in the chapter. This notion is in rather striking contrast to loving, sensitive, and somewhat romantic portrayals of European
women that appear within the text.

In fact, there is a general feeling of distance from African people
in the book. One senses that Du Bois is much more concerned with
establishing his identity with Europeans than with Africans. This
view is certainly a direct implication of his struggle to abolish his
caste status within European society. But it may also be a consequence, perhaps, of his mediation role with Europeans on behalf of
Africans. Despite Garvey's mass following, Du Bois, like Washington
before him, was proclaimed by Europeans to speak for the African
masses. The nature of the designation of his spokesmanship constitutes a very material consideration in contemplating Du Bois's por-
trayal or distortion of the African voice. The spokesperson is obliged
to the authorizing agent, and one senses in Du Bois that this feeling
of obligation is primarily to Europeans. And, thus, there is an element of inauthenticity (bordering on fraudulence) in Du Bois's representation to Europeans of the African voice. There is a sense in
which one feels that Du Bois, in *Darkwater: Voices From Within the
Veil*, is articulating to Europeans what the African voice should be
saying as opposed to what it actually was saying to Europeans and
to the world.

Notes

1. Manning Marable, *W. E. B. Du Bois: Black Radical Democrat* (Boston, MA: Twayne Publishers 1986), p. 91.
2. Maulana Karenga, *Introduction to Black Studies* (Los Angeles: Kawaida Publications 1984), p. 118.
3. Herbert Aptheker, *Introduction.* In W. E. B. Du Bois, *Darkwater: Voices from Within the Veil* (Millwood, NY: Kraus Thomson Organization Limited 1973), p. 5.
4. W. E. B. Du Bois, *The World and Africa* (New York: International Publishers 1965), pp. 11–12.
5. Aptheker, *Introduction,* p. 5.
6. Ibid.
7. Ibid., p. 6.
8. Ibid.
9. Ibid.
10. Karenga, *Introduction,* p. 109.
11. Aptheker, *Introduction,* pp. 7–8.
12. Ibid., p. 11.
13. Molefi Kete Asante, *Afrocentricity and Human Knowledge: An Introduction to Africalogy* (Working Paper 1989), p. 13.
14. Ibid., pp. 8–13.
15. Ibid., p. 14.
16. Ibid., p. 14.
17. Ibid., p. 23.
18. Ibid., p. 25.
19. Ibid., p. 9.
20. Ibid.
21. Du Bois, *Darkwater*, p. 3.
22. Ibid.
23. Ibid., p. 4.
24. See David Levering Lewis, *W. E. B. Du Bois: Biography of a Race* (New York: Henry Holt 1993), p. 73. Lewis notes that Du Bois claimed to have solidified his "racial" identity during his years at Fisk University, although his sense of identification with the African group appears somewhat "porous" and "labile," never wholly solid. Indeed, "Willie's ambivalence [about his own identity as belonging to the U.S. African group] endowed him with a resilient superiority complex, and that complex convinced Willie himself, as well as many others, that his lifelong espousal of the 'Dark World' was an *optional commitment* based above all upon principles and reason *rather than a dazzling advocacy he was born into*" [emphasis mine].
25. Du Bois, *Darkwater*, p. 9.
26. See Lewis, *Du Bois,* pp. 72, 148. Du Bois was enthralled with the discovery that his paternal heritage boasted French aristocratic ancestry from the Caribbean. In importance his strain of French far outweighed his flood of African blood. Further, notes Lewis: "This subtext of proud hybridization is so prevalent in Du Bois's sense of himself that the failure to notice it in the literature about him is as remarkable as the complex itself."
27. Du Bois, *Darkwater*, p. 10.
28. Ibid., p. 11.
29. Ibid., p. 12.

30. Ibid., p. 9. See also Lewis, *Du Bois*, p. 28. He calls *Darkwater* "the most passionate but least candid of his autobiographical writings."
31. See Lewis, *Du Bois*, p. 56. Du Bois "always minimized the role that Great Barrington's African-American community had played in his growing up." Nonetheless, he agrees that Du Bois's "knowledge of the larger world of black people—especially of southern black people—was as indirect and negligible as he said it was."
32. Du Bois, *Darkwater*, p. 29.
33. Ibid.
34. Ibid., p. 31.
35. Ibid., p. 33.
36. Ibid., p. 39.
37. Ibid., p. 40.
38. Ibid., p. 49.
39. Ibid., p. 56.
40. Ibid., p. 57.
41. Ibid., p. 58.
42. Ibid., p. 66.
43. Ibid., p. 68.
44. Ibid.
45. Ibid. p. 70.
46. Ibid.
47. Ibid., p. 84.
48. Ibid., p. 85.
49. Ibid., p. 94.
50. Ibid., pp. 96–97.
51. Ibid., p. 98.
52. Ibid., p. 103.
53. Ibid., p. 82.
54. Ibid., p. 115.
55. Ibid., p. 116.
56. Ibid., p. 140.
57. Ibid., p. 142.
58. Ibid., p. 144.
59. Ibid., p. 152.
60. Ibid., p. 154.
61. Ibid., p. 159.
62. Ibid., pp. 164–165.
63. Ibid., pp. 168–169.
64. Ibid., p. 172.
65. Ibid., p. 179.
66. Ibid., p. 180.
67. Ibid., p. 191.
68. Ibid., p. 185.
69. Ibid., p. 186.
70. Ibid., p. 202.
71. Ibid., p. 203.
72. Ibid., p. 206.
73. Ibid., p. 213.
74. Ibid., p. 223.

75. Ibid., p. 230.
76. Ibid., p. 241.
77. Ibid.
78. Ibid., p. 246.
79. Ibid., p. 269.
80. Ibid., p. 75.
81. Ibid., p. 131.

CHAPTER 14

The Paradox of Separate and Unequal: African Studies and Afro-American Studies

Guy Martin and Carlene Young

The relationship between Africa and the West is complex, ambiguous, and unequal. From the fifteenth to the nineteenth centuries, the Atlantic slave trade constituted the essence of this relationship. For some four hundred years, European nations conquered and divided the whole of the African continent among themselves. The dark cloud of colonialism descended over Africans, whose land, labor, and economic wealth were methodically and thoroughly exploited and stripped by European colonial powers. It was left to European missionaries, educators, and enlightened administrators to win the hearts and minds of the African people. This so-called civilizing mission, which was seen as an essential aspect of the "white man's burden," implied that the indigenous Africans' mores, cultures, and values were considered inherently inferior and backward, and that consequently these people had to be "uplifted" to a more advanced state of civilization, based on the European culture that the missionaries perceived to be ideal. In support of this blatantly Eurocentric attitude and policy, the colonial administration called upon anthropologists whose major function was to provide the colonial administration with the socio-ethnographic data necessary to better subdue and control the indigenous people. Thus, in Africa as in other parts of the colonial empire, anthropologists were the founders of the new discipline that became known as "African Studies" and the forerunners of the new breed of area specialists referred to as "Africanists." Some of the major contradictions inherent in the colonial situation began to be exposed, toward the end of the colonial era, by certain scholars using the method of sociological analysis.[1] At about the same time, African studies began to emerge progressively from the anthropological and ethnographic ghetto in which colonialism had confined them. Thus, specialists on Africa began to appear in disciplines such as sociology, philosophy, religion, geography, linguistics, the arts, history, economics, and political science.

The advent of independence in Africa in the early 1960s gave fresh impetus to African studies. Until then, the field had been largely dominated by European—mostly British and French—scholars who were still very much tainted with the biases and prejudices inherent in the colonial mentality. A new breed of Africanists, much more open-minded, enlightened, and sympathetic to the aspirations and concerns of the African nationalists, began to appear on the scene: the American scholars in the United States and the African scholars in Africa.

AFRICAN STUDIES IN THE NEO-COLONIAL ERA AND PREEMINENCE OF THE UNITED STATES

While legally and politically independent, African states continued to be victims, though of a more indirect and subtle form of domination by political, economic, social, cultural, military, or technical means. In this neo-colonial situation, minor political and administrative powers were entrusted to the indigenous African elites, while major political and economic power remained firmly fixed within the hands of the former colonial powers. In this context, however, European supremacy was declining while the United States's power was steadily rising throughout the world. This was due to the fact that the United States progressively gained control over what are considered to be the crucial elements of power in the modern age, namely, economic and financial resources, science and technology, and communication systems. Thus, inevitably, the United States began to show a growing interest in the non-Western parts of the world, particularly in Africa, which possessed tremendous mineral wealth and offered vast and expanding economic opportunities in terms of markets and investments. It is worth noting here that the birth of African studies in the

United States—the African Studies Association (ASA) was created in 1957—was coincidental with the advent of the neo-colonial era during which United States imperialism progressively superseded European imperialism in the political, economic, and technological control of most of the African continent.

It might be useful, at this juncture, to specify the purpose and function of African studies in this neo-colonial context. Just as in the old colonial days, the "Africa specialists" were assigned the task of gathering, analyzing, and evaluating a vast amount of data on the sociological, cultural, political, and economic aspects of the newly-independent African states to be passed on to Western decision makers for their use in organizing and readjusting their continuing control over these states. By the sheer variety and amount of financial, human, and institutional resources mobilized for that purpose, the United States was definitely leading the growth and development of the discipline named African Studies in the world. Through Title VI of the National Defense and Education Act (NDEA) of 1958, the United States federal government induced the creation of a significant number of African Studies centers linked to universities throughout the country. The federal government was also instrumental in the creation of the African Studies Association (ASA), which was set up on March 22, 1957, in New York City by a relatively small group of American social scientists involved in the study of African affairs.

Progressively, a whole complex of public, private, and semiprivate institutions became increasingly involved in the organization, financing, and utilization of African studies centers in the United States. Most prominent among these were the Department of State, the Agency for International Development (AID), the Central Intelligence Agency (CIA), and the Ford and Rockefeller Foundations, which, together, constitute what one study has appropriately termed "the extended family."[2] Together, these institutions provide the bulk of the funding for foreign area studies. It is this money, doled out in the form of grants, contracts, salaries, and fellowships, which has shaped and influenced the direction of most studies undertaken about Africa in the United States. As most U.S. scholars involved in research on Africa became increasingly dependent on these institutions for financial support, and as they came to play a growing role as official or unofficial advisers on African affairs to various government agencies, it became obvious that a major contradiction was developing between academic neutrality and political involvement and constraints. This dilemma has been well captured by the African Research Group, authors of the earlier-mentioned study: "Nurtured by foundation and government grants, they (American social scientists) operate under the cover of a false neutrality of academic scholarship, which permits them to camouflage their ideological biases and the strategic-policy implications of their work."[3] Indeed, as one of these social scientists, René Lemarchand, readily admits: ". . . there is no doubt that the increase in government-sponsored research directly infringes on the autonomy and the professional integrity of researchers."[4]

In fact, African studies have continuously and persistently been permeated by a dominant theory—or ideology—which is generally referred to as the "developmentalist paradigm." This "ideology of development," as some authors call it, appears as nothing more than an updated version of the colonial "civilizing mission." It is based on a conception of unilinear evolution according to which all societies—following the example of Western societies—must necessarily follow the same historical evolution, which will take them from "savagery" to "civilization." Thus, the industrialized societies appear as the quintessential models which must absolutely be emulated by other, non-industrialized societies if they wish one day to taste the coveted fruits of economic growth and development, and technological and scientific progress.[5] Most of the research on Africa during the past twenty years has been inspired, in one way or another, by this blatantly Eurocentric paradigm and has resulted in countless studies on various aspects of economic "development," political "modernization" and social and cultural "change" in Africa.

PURPOSE AND FUNCTION OF AFRICAN STUDIES
AND THE SEARCH FOR ALTERNATIVES

This carefully built ideological and institutional edifice was shattered to the point of near-collapse when in 1969, at the Montreal meeting of the ASA, a group of concerned African and Afro-American scholars questioned the whole concept and function of African Studies. This revolutionary group justifiably saw the existing institutional framework as one designed to perpetuate the multidimensional exploitation of African and Afro-American peoples. Beyond the purely legal claim of a more equal representation of blacks in the decision-making apparatus of the ASA was the more profound questioning of the whole concept, purpose, and function of African Studies in general.[6] What was the essence of these claims?

What responsible African and Afro-American scholars were, and are now, basically concerned with is the improvement of the socio-economic condition of the majority of black people through the elimination of all forms of exploitation and the control of political, social, and economic institutions and processes likely to effect such changes. In short, they aim at the progressive recovery of political and economic power in order to achieve revolutionary changes in their respective societies. Consequently, police-relevant research in Africa (and in the United States) must be geared toward that aim. Basically, such research should give African and Afro-American decision makers the relevant information—and thus the means—necessary for them to transform radically both their internal societies and their relations with Western powers to the benefit of their countries and peoples. This implies, *inter alia,* the adoption of an entirely new research perspective and approach on the part of the Africa experts. The Africanist must become extremely attentive to the expression of the demands, priorities, and the needs of ordinary African people. His task would then be that of a mediator, namely, to faithfully translate what Jean Copans has appropriately called "the truth of the masses"[7] into information and data of direct policy-relevance to the African decision makers.

At the institutional level, groups of concerned Africanists have set up specific organizations more attuned to the interests, priorities, and needs of their respective communities and peoples. Among these are the African Heritage Studies Association (AHSA) and the Association of Concerned African Scholars (ACAS) in the United States, and the African Political Science Association (APSA) in Africa.

At the individual level, the Africanist must thoroughly reevaluate, question, and redefine his subjective role and objective function both in the society being studied and in the society of origin to bring these in tune with the new priorities outlined above.[8] In short, a new breed of "African scholars" must come into being. As Mazi Ojiaku has aptly remarked, ". . . to be an African scholar, one need not be an African. One must, however . . . be able to describe and analyze the system of thought and way of life of the people and culture one is studying from the African angle."[9]

Finally, it seems both necessary and urgent to free Africanist research from the outdated, inappropriate, and culturally-biased conceptual and methodological frameworks in which it still largely operates and which result in an inaccurate and Eurocentric image of contemporary African society. Consequently, a priority task of this reoriented research should be to develop new and original concepts and theoretical frameworks firmly grounded in African history, society, culture, and values and perfectly adapted to the objectives sought. The social and political thought of such brilliant and original African thinkers and activists as Amilcar Cabral, Frantz Fanon, Kwame Nkrumah, and Julius Nyerere could serve as a basis for the elaboration of these new concepts and theories. In this formidable task, it is hoped that all Africanists of good will, from whatever discipline, nationality, and cultural background, will contribute in an objective and constructive spirit. This, in our opinion, is the direction in which African Studies in the 1980s should be oriented if it is to make a significant and meaningful contribution to the progress of African and Afro-American peoples.

TRANSITION AND CHANGE IN THE
UNITED STATES' SPHERE OF INFLUENCE

The gestation and birth of African and Afro-American Studies in the United States are as diametrically opposed as the experiences that shaped the colonizers and descendants of enslaved Africans. African Studies efforts were designed to provide knowledge to assist colonial interests, but Black Studies was the direct result of a liberation struggle by persons of African ancestry.

An investigation of African and Afro-American/Black Studies is instructive and perhaps even prophetic insofar as it represents a microcosmic view of the dialectics of power and the never ending struggle of the colonizer and the colonized. The very nature of the introduction of these two disciplines into academia provides insight into the character of the society which produced them.

African Studies, in its initial conceptualization and subsequent

197

implementation, had a key role to play in the overall strategy of sub-jugation. The historical precedent for institutions of higher learning to take an active leadership role in the achievement of goals consonant with "Manifest Destiny" expectations of Euro-Americans is long-standing and fully documented in the literature.

In the specific instance of African Studies in the United States there was the expressed intent to develop experts and advisors for American businesses and the U.S. Department of State who under-stood the fast breaking developments on the African continent. There was a concerted move by the State Department, key foundations, and strategically placed academicians to establish formal structures capa-ble of acquiring sufficient knowledge to develop programs that would keep Africa within the framework of the Western world. These devel-opments were taking place during the early 1950s when the African continent was moving to break the chains of colonialism.

AFRICAN STUDIES IN HISTORICALLY BLACK COLLEGES

Several of the historically black colleges offered a form of African Studies that pre-dated the concerted efforts of the U.S. government to ensure the development of establishment-oriented experts and advi-sors on African affairs. The efforts of Afro-American scholars at these institutions were distinctively at variance, both in terms of objectives and content, with the subsequent African studies programs that were encouraged by the U.S. government.

In the late 1930s and early 1940s, the political thought of Kwame Nkrumah was shaped at Lincoln University (Pa.), where he studied the ideas of Marcus Garvey. Garvey felt that a free and independent Africa was the only salvation for the Negro, and that a Pan-Africanist philosophy was essential to the success of African people. By 1950, Lincoln University had instituted an African Studies program that was expressly directed to the study and understanding of Africa.

By the second World War, Fisk University had begun an African Studies program under the direction of Lorenzo Turner, whose pri-mary interest was cultural contributions to the New World and the study of African survivals. The publication of his classic work in the field of linguistics, *Africanism in the Gullah Dialect,*[10] was the culmination of outstanding scholarship. African Studies at Fisk University ended when Turner left to accept a position at Roosevelt University in 1946.

Although Howard University had no organized program in African Studies until 1953, there was a heavy concentration on the subject, as reflected particularly in the scholarship of William Leo Hansberry, Rayford W. Logan, and Mark Hanna Watkins.[11] A former student of Hansberry who became the first African governor general of Nigeria, Nnamdi Azikiwe, named the new school of African Studies at a Nigerian university, Nsukka, in his honor.[12]

The involvement of the United States in the Korean War during the early 1950s, the onset of the Cold War, and the contest for control of the resources and loyalties of the Third World were the backdrop for the exigency of the State Department-sponsored African Studies in this country. The first ten years were dominated by American political scientists studying political mobilization and political socialization in specific African nations. The focus has since shifted to southern Africa.

BLACK STUDIES IN AMERICAN UNIVERSITIES

The blatant racial inequalities that existed in the U.S. were exposed to the world following the second World War. The civil rights struggles of American blacks in the 1950s and 1960s were made known to the world community through television, and the assassination of such black leaders as Malcolm X and Martin Luther King, Jr., stirred hearts and minds around the globe.

This was the setting in which the student rebellions and black consciousness movement gave birth to Black Studies programs in the 1960s. There is no doubt that another factor was the identification of U.S. black students and intellectuals with African liberation struggles and the demise of colonialism on the African continent. There was a general perception that the survival of peoples of African ancestry was essential to all discussion and the fundamental basis for broadbased development of a nascent but potent global perspective. African languages, history, religions, and culture experienced a resurgence in interest and assumed their proper place in the Pan-African curricula of Afro-American/Black Studies programs as they struggled for acceptance in the universities and colleges. Community activists and students stormed the citadels of education and demanded entry. Exclusion, distortion, and specialized interests that benefited from Afro-American subordination were challenged and subsequently determined to be unacceptable.

The birth of Afro-American/Black Studies as a discipline was reminiscent of the tortured beginnings of the black community itself as it attempted to make a claim for the citizenship that the Thirteenth and Fourteenth Amendments promised but had not delivered. The struggle for Black Studies programs has been an arduous one fraught with many battles, small but sometimes significant successes, and the knowledge that although the struggle is relentless there are no acceptable alternatives. Universities and colleges were reluctant to accept those students who were interested in Black Studies, and most often defined them as deviants and outsiders in the natural order of superiority and ability. Despite the fact that the Ford Foundation gave a one-time-only, one-year allocation to fifteen institutions for Afro-American Studies in 1969, there was no move by the community of established scholars to embrace this fledgling discipline.

It is commonly known that there were a general body of knowledge, outstanding scholarship, and resource materials available long before the civil rights movement and rebellions in American cities brought Black Studies programs to institutions of higher learning. Despite that reality, the demands of Afro-Americans for an accurate and complete recounting of their history, contributions, experience, culture, and continuing role in the development of American society were met with incredulity, resistance, and resentment on the part of the university community.

POWER AND POWERLESSNESS

Analysis of the dissimilarity in the inception and implementation of African Studies and Afro-American/Black Studies may be approached from an understanding of power and powerlessness. Power has been defined as the ability to determine the behavior of others in accord with one's own wishes, regardless of the others' wishes. Power may also be distinguished by the type of influence brought to bear upon subordinated individuals or groups. This may involve the exercise of force such as assaults and confinement, domination through commands, requests, and so forth, which make explicit the behavior wanted, utilizing symbols, and propaganda. Implicit in the concept of power is the fact of uneven and unequal reciprocity. In other words, the action on one side of the interaction equation is effective and decisive to a degree greater than that found on the other side. This inequality is inherent in relationships characterized by oppression.

Black Studies, as it personified the oppressed, offered a "solution" in the words of Paulo Freire, "not to integrate them into the structure of oppression, but to transform that structure so that they can become beings for themselves."[13] Indeed, Freire informs us that "the interests of the oppressors lie in changing the consciousness of the oppressed, not the situation which oppresses them; for the more the oppressed can be led to adapt to the situation, the more easily they can be dominated."[14] This perspective allows for a better understanding of the historic role and function of African Studies. However, this posture now can best be described as anachronous.

It is no longer possible for people of good will to discharge themselves of any responsibility for world conditions by disclaiming individual involvement in the subjugation and exploitation of Third World peoples. The people themselves no longer are in a mood to accept such terms for mere survival. They know how they have been victimized. A common theme which has demonstrated the universality of relief-seeking is the cry for "liberation." This plaint is voiced by citizens and scholars from Latin America, Asia, Africa, the Caribbean, and the United States.

The nature of the relationship between Third World nations and the super powers has entered a unique phase. No longer can the technological giants be assured that their agendas will be met without challenge, disruption, or even rejection. Third World nations are reassessing their roles. Heretofore, they were forced to give even when giving was not in their best interest. Their leverage is grounded in the wealth of natural mineral resources which are essential for the continued productivity of the industry of the developed nations. The inherent nature of power is its inevitable instability—because it is not authorized it belongs only to those who can take and hold it. This truism is well known to those who have exercised power on a global basis. It is increasingly known to those who seek to control their own destiny.

The potential that lies in strong productive Afro-American/Black Studies programs, and the new breed of "African scholars" is formidable. Afro-Americans constitute one of the largest constituencies of persons of African ancestry outside the Continent, have some of the highest levels of education and training, generate one of the largest gross national products among Western nations, and have the latent potential of nationhood. These factors, allied with the land base, natural resources, and progressive leadership in Africa could change the posture of each individual African regardless of his current residence. At the same time, they could irrevocably change the substance and character of interaction between Western powers and all peoples of color. One may be assured that the vantage ground which these circumstances offer has not gone unnoticed by the dominant powers, who have no intention of relinquishing that position. This is the promise and the challenge of the present.

Notes

1. Most prominent among these were: Georges Balandier, "La situation coloniale: Approche theorique," *Cahiers internationaux de sociologic* XI (1951); and Michel Leiris, "L'ethnographe devant le colonialisme," *Les temps modernes* 58 (August 1959).
2. Africa Research Group, *African Studies in America: The Extended Family* (Cambridge, MA, 1970). This group has compiled a most revealing dossier on the overt and covert activities of these institutions in the field of African studies.
3. Ibid., p. 1.
4. Rene Lemarchand. "Le pianiste et le chef d'orchestre: l'africanisme et le pouvoir aux Etats-Unis," *Politique Africaine* 12 (December 1983): 68 (G. Martin's translation from French).
5. On this point, see: Guy Martin, "Theories, Ideologies and Strategies of Development in Africa," *Africa Development* VIII (April 1983): 36–45; Alf Schwarz, "La sociologie en Afrique ou les veritables enjeux du paradigme du developpement international," in Alf Schwarz, ed., *Les Faux Prophetes de l'Afrique ou l'Afr(eu)canisme* (Quebec: Presses de l'universite Laval 1980), pp. 89–160.
6. A useful historical survey of the evolution of African studies in the United States is provided by Immanuel Wallerstein, "The Evolving Role of the Africa Scholar in African Studies," *Canadian Journal of African Studies* 17:1 (1983): 9–16.
7. Jean Copans, "D'un africanisme a l'autre," in Schwarz, *Les Faux Prophets,* pp. 53–68; Jean Copans, "les Afriques des africanistes," *Le monde diplomatique* (April 1982): 2; and Wallerstein, "The Evolving Role of the Africa Scholar."
8. Ibid.

9. Mazi O. Ojiaku "Traditional African Social Thought and Western Scholarship," *Presence Africaine* 90 (1974): 209–210.
10. Lorenzo D. Turner, *Africanisms in the Gullah Dialect* (Chicago: University of Chicago 1973; orig. pub. Arno Press 1949).
11. Personal interview by Carlene Young with St. Clair Drake, who was a key participant in these developments, April 1984.
12. Robert G. Weisbord, *Ebony Kinship: Africa, Africans, and the Afro-American* (Westport, CT: Greenwood Press 1973), p. 184.
13. Paulo Freire, *Pedagogy of the Oppressed* (New York: Seabury Press 1970), pp. 60–61.
14. Albert Memmi, *The Colonizer and the Colonized* (Boston, MA: Beacon Press 1967), p. 114.

• • • • • • • • • • • • • • • • • •
CHAPTER 15

Segregation and Scholarship: The American Council of Learned Societies' Committee on Negro Studies, 1941–1950

Robert L. Harris, Jr.

The American Council of Learned Societies' (ACLS) designation of its Committee on Negro Studies in 1941 held out the prospect of anchoring both the black scholar and the study of Afro-American life and culture in American scholarship. Although black scholars had pioneered the scientific examination of the Afro-American past, they encountered numerous restrictions in their work, especially in the south. They were generally denied access to libraries and the meetings of professional and scholarly organizations (Winston 1971: 702). E. Horace Fitchett, for example, was barred from the Charleston Library Society in 1936 while researching materials for his dissertation "The Free Negro in Charleston, South Carolina." He was able to read in a special room at the Charleston Free Library, but he had to enter and exit from the rear of the building. A black janitor took his requests for books and brought them to him. At the College of Charleston Library, he was permitted use of its facilities only after regular hours, when the white students had left for the night (Fitchett 1950: 14–18).

W. E. B. Du Bois resigned from the American Association of University Professors (AAUP) in 1945 to protest meetings held in places that excluded its black members. The AAUP had met six years earlier in a New Orleans hotel that refused to serve black people. The crowning insult for Du Bois came when the Washington, D.C., AAUP affiliate held a dinner in a segregated hotel. To avoid embarrassment, the

AAUP Chapter decided not to invite its black members (Aptheker 1978: 32). These incidents made it difficult for black scholars to function within the broader academic arena and thereby confined the study of Afro-American life and culture to a remote corner of American scholarship.

The ACLS's Committee on Negro Studies was established as a counterweight to the Carnegie Corporation study of the Negro in America, directed by the Swedish political economist Gunnar Myrdal. The Carnegie Corporation invited Myrdal in 1937 to conduct a comprehensive investigation of black people in this country. This project was the brainchild of Newton D. Baker, former Cleveland mayor (1912–1916) and secretary of war under President Woodrow Wilson. His administrative experience gave him special insight into the problems resulting from the mushrooming black population in the nation's northern cities. He was particularly distressed by the race riots that shook the country after World War I. The Carnegie Corporation, of which Baker became a board member in 1931, had granted $2.5 million to black institutions, primarily in the south, from its inception in 1911 to 1937. Baker believed that accurate information was necessary for decision on allocating funds, especially for programs affecting the growing black urban population (Myrdal 1944: xlviii; Garraty 1974: 50–51).

As Myrdal's project was getting under way in 1939, Waldo G. Leland, ACLS secretary, suggested that Melville J. Herskovits, Anthropology professor at Northwestern University, organize a Conference on Negro Studies (Herskovits Papers, Leland to Herskovits 1/10/39). The idea for such a session was important because the Social Science Research Council (SSRC) had upstaged the ACLS in acting as an informal advisor to Myrdal and in recommending scholars to conduct research for his study. Moreover, Myrdal's theoretical approach to the Negro in America differed significantly from the ACLS's humanistic perspective. In his memorandum to Frederick P. Keppel, president of the Carnegie Corporation, Myrdal emphasized the need for placing the "Negro problem" in the context of American society. He wrote that it was essential to recognize black peoples' plight in relation to the American social, political, and economic order. He explicitly excluded attention to the life and culture of black people outside the United States, even for background information. Myrdal concluded: "The actual situation, and pending changes and present tendencies involved in the situation, should be the concentration points. Historical development should be included only insofar as it is absolutely necessary to explain the actual situation" (Myrdal 1939: 10).

This paradigm opposed Herskovits's insistence on New World Negroes being seen as a laboratory for studying the process of cultural change. He held that the way in which human societies intermingled was critical to understanding the concept of culture. The problem for researchers was the absence of controlled conditions for examining this hypothesis. Unlike the biologist who can observe the process of heredity by crossing various plants and animals at will, the anthropologist cannot manipulate people for scientific purposes. Herskovits thought, however, "If we find a people of a known cultural background, who have been presented with known cultural alternatives and have accepted some and rejected others, we may obtain light on the implications of their action in studying what they have done" (Herskovits 1930: 145–150). For him, New World Negroes could be scrutinized to determine what happens to culture under stress and to discover what is discarded and what is retained. This inquiry became all the more significant if retention of African customs was found to be fairly constant among Negroes in different parts of the New World.

Both Myrdal and Herskovits proposed means of studying Afro-Americans that departed from the work of black scholars. Myrdal began from the premise that black peoples' lives were governed almost entirely by American values. On the other hand, Herskovits was chiefly concerned with the intricacies of black life to elucidate the method of culture change. They overlooked the notion of dual consciousness put forth by W. E. B. Du Bois (1903).

In preparing for the Conference on Negro Studies, Herskovits drafted a memorandum outlining its objectives. He recommended that the participants be scholars "whose studies are from a long term point of view rather than pointed toward immediate attempts at solution of the race problem" (Herskovits Papers, Herskovits to Leland 1/10/39). It was the issue of race, however, especially segregation, that faced the conference from the beginning and that would be responsible in large measure for the Committee on Negro Studies' demise. Herskovits, moreover, stressed the need for "Negro research to range beyond the boundaries of the United States, encompassing not only the critical areas of West Africa, but also other parts of the New World wherein Negroes live" (Herskovits, 1939). The degree of acculturation by New World Negro societies held theoretical importance for several disciplines, according to Herskovits. He suggested a preliminary conference as the logical step toward establishing a coordinating Committee for Negro Studies within the ACLS.

Such a conference would naturally include black scholars working in the field of Negro Studies. Because the meeting would be held in Washington, D.C., ACLS headquarters, it posed the dilemma of securing housing and dining for an interracial group (ACLS Papers, Leland to Herskovits 1/12/39; Herskovits Papers, Herskovits to Graves 12/19/39). Herskovits, who had been on the Howard University faculty in 1925, contacted his former colleague, Ralph Bunche, to arrange for the conference there. This step would avoid the problem of racial segregation in the nation's capital. Bunche duly took care of all the details (Herskovits Papers, Bunche to Herskovits 3/16/40). It is interesting to note that although Herskovits was willing to use Bunche's good offices for the meeting, he opposed inviting him to join the Committee on Negro Studies. Herskovits remarked that "Bunche has not produced for many years as we have hoped he would, and I do not think he ought to be included" (Herskovits Papers, Herskovits to Graves 12/1/39).

ACLS secretary-treasurer, Mortimer Graves, thought that the conference should be delayed until the release of Myrdal's report. Herskovits responded that the Myrdal project should not stand in its way. For him, this was all the more reason to hold the meeting as planned. "With the kind of analysis of Negro Studies now being carried on, there might go very well an investigation into the kinds of scholarly work being done on the Negro," he stated, "so that we would have the field entirely canvassed and be prepared to make recommendations in light of any report that would be turned in by Myrdal." Herskovits anticipated that the Myrdal study would have important implications for the direction of work in Negro Studies. As a field innovator, he wanted to be positioned to influence trends to complement his own research. He was setting boundaries for the nascent field of African Studies, creating a system of interpretation, and developing a school of followers. Herskovits surmised: "There is no doubt in my mind that we will be in a much more strategic position to encourage the continuation of scientific work in the field of Negro Studies if we are organized and ready prior to the appearance of the report" (Herskovits Papers, Herskovits to Graves 12/1/39).

The conference on Negro Studies was held March 29 and 30, 1940, at Howard University, with twenty-three scholars in attendance, of whom about half were black. The disciplines of physical and cultural anthropology, history, political science, sociology, economics, psychology, philosophy, literature, and the arts were represented. The purpose was to allow a small group of scholars to exchange information on the state of research and to suggest measures to stimulate and improve study of the Negro, especially through interdisciplinary cooperation (Herskovits 1941: 5). Waldo G. Leland, who had become ACLS director, defined Negro Studies as "the effect . . . upon American culture of the transfer of African cultures and civilization to a new world where, in a new physical, social, and human environment, they have had a part in producing what we now call American civilization or American culture." He declared that American scholarship could no longer concentrate exclusively on Western civilization and that it must broaden its base to include world cultures. He charged the conference to explore the requirements of Negro Studies and the best strategy to implement them in a systematic manner (Herskovits 1941: 12–13).

D. H. Daugherty, an ACLS member, added that Negro Studies possessed coherence even though inquiry was pursued in different disciplines, each with its own problems, methods, and materials. He asserted that Negro Studies required special attention because of the cultural patterns created by black people in different environments. The promotion of scholarship in this field dictated cross-disciplinary collaboration to develop and apply fresh techniques to both old and new sources (1941: 12–13).

Six scholars, four of them black, read papers at the conference on the following topics: Latin America, bibliographical problems, historical research, linguistics, African cultural survivals, and African economic research. General discussion followed each presentation, as well as at the end of the meeting. Lawrence D. Reddick, curator of the New York Public Library's Schomburg Collection, in addition to his comments on the need for guides to research materials on the Negro and for microfilming black newspapers published in the United States before 1900, raised an issue that became the committee's nemesis. He called for a frontal assault on racial bias in American scholarship and on the social barriers to research, especially for black scholars in the south where most of them were located (1941: 29–30).

Taking these and other suggestions into account, the conference recommended that a permanent body be established to foster research in Negro Studies across disciplines, such a group strives to dismantle obstacles impeding scholarly work by Negro students, microfilm centers be created to ease access to documents crucial to studying Negro history, significant interdisciplinary work in the field be published, valid scientific materials be popularized in a dignified manner to destroy racial stereotypes, and a panel be organized as a clearinghouse for funding projects. To these ends, the ACLS Executive Committee sanctioned a standing Committee on Negro Studies, consisting of Melville J. Herskovits (Chairman), Sterling Brown (Howard University), Otto Klineberg (Columbia University), Richard Pattee (U.S. State Department), Lawrence D. Reddick (Schomburg Collection), Lorenzo D. Turner (Fisk University), Donald Young (SSRC), and D. H. Daugherty (ACLS Secretary for the Committee). Of the eight committee members, three (Brown, Reddick, and Turner) were black (1941: 6–8).

The Committee on Negro Studies was to function as a development panel to encourage research and teaching in an emerging field. Its first task was to prepare a report on the status of research on the Negro. The committee planned to referee proposals before the ACLS for work in this area. It would have little money of its own to fund large projects and would have to seek financial support of this kind elsewhere (Herskovits Papers, Daugherty to Herskovits, 5/13/41).

Given the war raging in Europe, which also involved the African continent, Herskovits had an additional agenda for the Committee on Negro Studies. He worried about the disruption of work in African Studies, which remained his top priority. The journal *Africa* had to suspend publication in 1940. He expressed the desire "to have some group in this country carrying on in this field" (ACLS Papers, Herskovits to Leland 9/18/40). For Herskovits, Negro Studies, broadly defined to include black people throughout the New World, was inextricably linked to African Studies. He saw the delineation of key topics for African research being guided by the presence of African survivals in the New World. He reflected: "When a culture is under pressure from another way of life . . . ranks are closed and sanctions and institutions of the focal aspect (cultural focus) come to take on great . . . importance. In such a situation, the focal aspect thus becomes that part of the culture where we find the greatest resistance to change" (Herskovits 1948: 3–7). The discovery of this cultural focus among African descendants in the New World would pay handsome methodological dividends to African Studies. It would isolate specific New World practices for more intensive investigation in Africa.

To strengthen the Committee on Negro Studies as the main validating agency and to entrench himself as the dean of this new field, Herskovits proposed a Joint Committee on African and Negro Studies that would be responsible to the Conference Board of the Associated Research Councils (which consisted of the ACLS, SSRC, and the National Research Council). The Associated Research Councils embraced the range of scholarly research in the United States, as it represented the humanistic, social science, and scientific and technical disciplines. The aims of Herskovits's Joint Committee would be to (1) seek work in the field, (2) compile a roster of scholarly projects, (3) disseminate it to inform researchers with similar interests in different disciplines, and (4) serve as an advisory board to the research councils in evaluating proposals for funding (Herskovits 1944). Such a powerful committee would have given Herskovits as chairman a virtual barony over all research projects in the United States on the Negro. This plan was thwarted, however, by the SSRC's refusal to endorse it. Although the SSRC had supported some projects on the Negro, it did not have a specific committee in the field of African or Negro Studies. The SSRC did not seem to recognize the importance of research in this area. Moreover, it had declined participation in the Phelps-Stokes-funded "Encyclopedia of the Negro" project (Herskovits Papers, Herskovits to Leland 5/17/44 and Leland to Herskovits 4/4/34).

As a result of the SSRC's failure to sponsor a joint panel, the Committee on Negro Studies was retained solely within the ACLS. Its emphasis would be primarily on humanistic studies, such as language, literature, the arts, history, and so on. What is more, it would function simply as an advisory group rather than as an operating one similar to ACLS standing committees. It would acquire useful information, make suggestions, and assist other organizations to implement important projects (*ACLS Bulletin* 1945: 20). Accordingly, the Committee on Negro Studies redefined its objectives as the recovery and preservation of the history of the Negro in the New World, the identification and study of black New World populations and their African antecedents, and the survey of Negro art, literature, and language. It

210

planned as its immediate goal a list of American researchers engaged in Negro studies and the assembling, analyzing, and microfilming of black newspapers printed in the United States prior to 1900 (*ACLS Bulletin* 1945: 83, Minutes 11/10–11/44).

The Committee on Negro Studies—with a yearly budget of about $900 for its meetings in Washington, D.C., and clerical expenses— recorded three major accomplishments during its nine-year tenure. It drafted a roster of scholars working in Negro Studies, supervised the microfilming of black newspapers, and published a guide to materials on the Negro in the National Archives. Armistead S. Pride, Journalism School Director at Lincoln University in Jefferson City, Missouri, ad- ministered the microfilming project with a $9000 grant from the Gen- eral Education Board. Paul Lewinson of the National Archives prepared the guide, which surveyed significant groups of government documents pertaining to the Negro (*ACLS Bulletin* 1947: 78, Minutes, 2/7/46, and Lewinson 1947).

Although the committee had set its parameters as the Negro in the New World, its success came in activities relating to black people in the United States. It performed an invaluable service in assembling and making more widely available the black newspapers. This effort was singularly important because it brought a resource to the fore- ground that scholars could use to investigate the life and thought of Afro-Americans. White scholars in particular had ignored the role of black people in American society. They had not searched for expres- sions of black opinion on the assumption that little evidence existed. Lewinson's guide, moreover, specified government records from which researchers could gather a more accurate composite of the black experience in this country.

This trend, while crucial in developing a base for Negro Studies, generated friction within the committee, eventually leading to its demise. The committee in 1946 contemplated a series of conferences, each with greater emphasis on the black scholar's standing in Amer- ican scholarship. At first, it planned to canvass the opportunities for research in Negro Studies within specific disciplines. It hoped that pa- pers from a meeting on this theme would be published in the journals of appropriate learned societies. This undertaking would alert re- searchers to areas of Negro Studies begging investigation and would further demonstrate the significance of the field (Minutes 2/7/46).

These plans did not materialize, and the committee shifted to preparations for a conference on scholarship by and about Negroes (*ACLS Bulletin* 1949: 146). This meeting was to have four panel discussions on the Negro as subject and scholar in literature and language, music, history, and humanistic scholarship in general. The black committee members took primary responsibility for writing a series of memoranda to detail the potential benefits from such a conference. Sterling Brown assessed the research needs of Afro-American culture. He proposed the study and analysis of jazz, the blues, and Negro folklore, as well as an examination of the relationship between minstrelsy, jazz, ragtime, and vaudeville. He also suggested the writing of monographs on black artists and the reproduction of their works, together with a survey of early Negro shows and showmen. Lawrence D. Reddick sought better descriptions of and access to archival materials. Kenneth W. Porter, a white committee member appointed in 1946, broached the question of American bondage from the slaves' vantage, relations between Negroes and Indians, biographies of little known but important Negroes, more substantive analysis of key slave revolts, and local and state histories of Negroes (Minutes 2/14/48).

The committee circulated these memoranda among scholars active in the field and received glowing responses from them. For example, Rayford W. Logan generally agreed with all of Porter's suggestions, while Luther Porter Jackson advised more attention to local documents such as deeds, wills, marriage licenses, and court records (Herskovits Papers, Misc. Letters 1947). This discussion indicated the growing influence of black committee members, especially as the group telescoped its work on the United States. Reddick even demanded greater black representation on the committee, but Donald Young insisted that race not be a consideration for committee assignment (Herskovits Papers, Daugherty to Herskovits 4/4/47).

Although its personnel had often changed, Herskovits remained chairman throughout the committee's existence, and its black membership was always outnumbered. Herskovits was, in his biographer's words, "a fascinating and complicated person; brilliant, but at times obdurate; competitive, but extremely generous to friends; confident when he was in full control of a situation, but sometimes insecure when he felt he was not" (Simpson 1973: 7). Because he was losing his influence, especially over the direction of its work, Herskovits even thought of dismissing the whole panel. Daugherty, the committee's secretary, cautioned that such a drastic move would create much misunderstanding and ill-will. They agreed to continue the committee but with several personnel changes. Lorenzo D. Turner and Kenneth W. Porter would be replaced by more "cooperative" members (Herskovits Papers, Daugherty to Herskovits 7/18/48). It is possible that although Reddick was pushing for a stronger black presence, his dismissal would have been too politically sensitive.

The ACLS's Board of Directors soon questioned why the committee had not assumed larger planning activities on more wide-ranging ideas. Despite its reservations, the board voted in 1949 to continue the committee for another year with an $850 budget. The group immediately floundered on its inability to carry out its planned conference "The Negro as Scholar and as Subject of Scholarship." The meeting as proposed was fraught with problems, primarily because it sought to challenge the white academic establishment. It intended to assess the black scholar's ability to publish in journals of learned societies, evaluate their participation in white scholarly organizations, and probe conditions for research by Negroes (Herskovits Papers, Daugherty to Herskovits 1/6/50, and *ACLS Bulletin* 1950: 44–45).

These potentially explosive topics tore the committee apart. They arose at a time when civil rights was becoming a hot issue in this country, when Cold War tensions between the United States and the Soviet Union dampened anything that might weaken America's global image, and when the two most prominent champions of black history and culture, W. E. B. Du Bois and Paul Robeson, were being scorned by anticommunist hysteria. Herskovits expressed grave doubts about sponsoring such a controversial meeting. He informed Daugherty: "The more I think about the conference the less enthusiastic I am about it." He continued: "I cannot quite see what our committee could do in integrating the Negro scholar in the general community." Herskovits was not alone in his reservations about the conference. Sterling Brown, a black committee member, did not think that attention should be called to the black scholar as such (Herskovits Papers, Herskovits to Daugherty 1/23/50). Both Herskovits and Brown, whatever their reasons, acquiesced to the second-class status of black scholars, who were confined to the periphery of American scholarship.

Herskovits's hesitancy to fight racial segregation in American scholarship did not translate into condoning racism, although as chairman of the Committee on Negro Studies he might have supported measures to ease its sting. During his career, he made a stellar contribution to race relations by dispelling the myth that New World Negroes lacked a respectable past. He demonstrated through his work that no single society or segment therein had a monopoly on culture (Mintz 1964: 49–50). He contested the biological definition of race, thereby challenging assumptions that black people were inherently inferior (Herskovits 1924: 207–210; 1925: 204–208; 1946: 349; 1966: 7).

Herskovits had a long-standing interest in American race relations. From 1928 to 1932, he summarized developments in the area for the *American Journal of Sociology* (Merriam 1964: 85). Some of his earliest essays appeared in the Urban League's journal, *Opportunity*, and in the NAACP's *Crisis Magazine* (Whitten and Szwed 1970: 55–56). His efforts on behalf of race relations were those of a detached intellectual, however, and not an activist. In large measure, he was a gradualist on ameliorating racial conditions in this country. He stressed the scientific as opposed to the practical aspects of his research. At the Twentieth Anniversary Meeting of the Association for the Study of Negro Life and History, 1935, he stated: "experience has taught us that in matters requiring scientific study, the longest way around is most often the shortest route to a given point. . . . More preoccupation with the background of Negro life . . . may be the way to achieve happier results in the practical problems of race and racial relations with which we are all, as citizens, concerned" (Herskovits 1936: 30). He held that there was a danger in abandoning a broader perspective for ad hoc solutions. "This has been especially true in the United States," he wrote, "when for many years an almost exclusive preoccupation with action programs discouraged the type of broad research which characterizes the Afro-American field. For even in the short view, the broader base of comprehension that the results of Afroamerican studies can give those whose task is to frame policies for practical procedures would, of itself, justify the position that such studies *must be held distinct* from remedial programs in the troubled field of race relations" (Herskovits 1946: 340; emphasis added).

Herskovits was pulled by many forces during his chairmanship of the Committee on Negro Studies, particularly as the pattern of anthropological research shifted and as African Studies achieved visibility as a respectable area of scholarship. Anthropologists in general were discarding the study of New World Negroes as a distinct ethnic category for the model of "plantation society" that valued the systems under which they labored more highly than their historical backgrounds (Whitten and Szwed 1970: 29–30). Because Herskovits's work in the New World hinged on his African research and given his position as Director of the first African Studies Program in the United States, began at Northwestern University in 1948, he increasingly turned his attention to Africa during the late 1940s (Merriam 1964: 85–87). Moreover, the end of World War II meant that the African continent could again become the object of research. These developments, in large part, help to explain the Committee on Negro Studies' collapse.

At its March 17, 1950 meeting, the committee reviewed its work and recommended its own dissolution. It decided that Negro studies was too broad and imprecise a rubric for effective operation. It suggested that its goals might be achieved more efficiently by other ACLS panels. Although the decision as transmitted in the official record was not to abandon an interdisciplinary approach to studying Afro-american life and culture, the group was uncertain about identifying research on black people as "Negro Studies." After all, they concluded there were no academic departments of "Negro Studies." "Ideally," they reasoned, "Negro history is 'history,' Negro music is 'music,' and Negro art is 'art.'" The committee did admit, nevertheless, that the traditional disciplines had ignored the history and culture of black people. It therefore recommended that its work be absorbed by appropriate ACLS committees, that ad hoc committees be appointed as necessary, and that scholarship on the Negro be assessed periodically to avoid similar neglect in the future (*ACLS Bulletin* 1951: 41–42). It is ironic that the committee opposed isolating scholarly inquiry on the Negro, while it refused to challenge the segregation that burdened black scholars. What is more, there is little if any evidence that the ACLS observed its suggestions following the committee's termination.

In a span of only nine years, the committee had drifted from the idea of coherence in Negro Studies to the notion of unmanageability. It appears, however, that it was more Herskovits's inability to harness the group itself than the field of inquiry that was at issue. In an essay on the development of Afroamerican (Negro) Studies, published in 1951, he described it as a young field. The 1930s was a period when scientific problems were defined; the 1940s marked an era of conceptual and methodological refinement, while the 1950s would be a decade of intensive research. He concluded: "In its present state, the young area of research may be said to be fairly on its way" (Herskovits 1951: 123, 147). But he had to measure the demands on his time and energy for two emerging fields, Negro and African Studies. It appears, moreover, that the committee had deviated from his theory of Negro Studies as it focused more on black Americans. It had also considered some very pragmatic matters, such as the black scholar's plight.

The Committee on Negro Studies's dissolution was not an idle gesture, and it involved more than the official explanation for its demise. The decision to disband the group was carefully orchestrated as revealed in Herskovits's letter to Daugherty, wherein he disclosed that "certainly the fact that we were able to talk over procedures the night before made it possible for us to vote with a sureness that would otherwise not have been possible" (Herskovits Papers, Herskovits to Daugherty 3/22/50). Herskovits later did express some reservations about the action. "Whether what we did, on second thought, is the best thing we could have done," he reflected to Daugherty, "is something I am not as sure of now as I was earlier. However, I am of no two minds about the fact that the Committee *as constituted* was certainly not the best that we could have had to do the job that perhaps needs doing" (Herskovits Papers, Herskovits to Daugherty 2/15/51; emphasis added).

Conflict within the Committee on Negro Studies prevented it from entrenching in American scholarship either the black scholar or the study of Afro-American life and culture. There were substantive differences over both the definition of Negro Studies and the ability to remove the impediments that left the black scholar on the fringes of the intellectual domain. These disparities grew out of priorities, especially those of the committee's chairman, Melville J. Herskovits. He was devoted, above all, to African Studies, a field that he helped to innovate, and to the "scientific" appraisal of race relations.

Bibliography

American Council of Learned Societies Bulletin (1945–1951). Washington, D.C.

American Council of Learned Societies Papers, Manuscript Division (n.d.) Washington, DC: Library of Congress.

Aptheker, H. (1978). *The Correspondence of W. E. B. Du Bois,* (vol 3). Amherst: University of Massachusetts Press.

DuBois, W. E. B. (1903). *The Souls of Black Folk.* Chicago: McClurg.

Fitchett, E. H. (1950). "The free Negro in Charleston, South Carolina." Ph.D. dissertation, University of Chicago.

Garraty, J.A. (1974). *Encyclopedia of American Biography.* New York: Harper & Row.

Herskovits, F. S. (1966). *The New World Negro.* Bloomington: University of Indiana Press.

Herskovits, M. J. Papers. Northwestern University of Library of African Studies. Evanston, IL.

———. (1951). "The present status and needs of AfroAmerican research." *Journal of Negro History* 36: 123–147.

———. (1948). "The contribution of Afro-American studies to Africanist research," *American Anthropologist* 50: 1–10.

———. (1946). "Problem, method and theory in AfroAmerican studies," *Phylon* 7: 337–354.

———. (1944). "Memorandum on a Joint Committee on African and Negro Studies," Herskovits Papers.

———. (1941). "The interdisciplinary aspects of Negro studies," *American Council of Learned Societies Bulletin* 32: 339–447.

———. (1939). "Memorandum on the desirability of holding a Conference on Negro Studies," Herskovits Papers.

———. (1936). "The significance of West Africa for Negro research," *Journal of Negro History* 21: 15–30.

———. (1930). "The Negro in the New World: the statement of a problem," *American Anthropologist* 32:145–155.

———. (1925). "The color line," *American Mercury* 6: 204–208.

———. (1924). "What is a race?" *American Mercury* 2: 207–210.

Lewinson, P. (1947). *A Guide to Documents in the National Archives: For Negro Studies.* Washington, DC: American Council of Learned Societies Committee on Negro Studies Publication I.

Merriam, A. P. (1964). "Obituary: Melville J. Herskovits, 1895–1963," *American Anthropologist* 66: 83–91.

Mintz, S. (1964). "Melville J. Herskovits and Caribbean Studies: A Retrospective Tribute." *Caribbean Studies* 4:42–51.

Minutes of the American Council of Learned Societies Committee on Negro Studies. Herskovits Papers.

Myrdal, G. (1944). *An American Dilemma: The Negro Problem and Modern Democracy* (2 volumes). New York: Harper & Row.

———. (1939). "Memorandum of Gunnar Myrdal to Frederick P. Keppel," Carnegie-Myrdal Study of the Negro in American Papers. Schomburg Collection. Microfilm Reel, No. 9. New York City.

Simpson, G. E. (1973). *Melville J. Herskovits.* New York: Columbia Univ. Press.

Whitten, N. E., and J. F. Szwed (1970). *Afro-American Anthropology: Contemporary Perspectives.* New York: Macmillan.

Winston, M. (1971). "Through the back door: academic racism and the Negro scholar in historical perspective," *Daedalus* 100: 678–719.

CHAPTER 16

Culture, Leadership, and Intellectual Thought: A Critical Examination of Selected Historical Adult Education Ideologies by African American Educators

Andrew Smallwood

SYNOPSIS

To explore African American life historically, examining the role lead-ing African American individuals and their various contributions is important. These men and women served as advocates for voicing the concerns, hopes, and frustrations for black people in the United States. A key mechanism for improving opportunities for African Americans has been through educational advancement. In this study, I will identify selected twentieth-century African Americans that have specifically written about the education of African American adults. The purpose of this study is to discover to what degree did previous black educators build their concepts around the specific conditions of African Americans?

Obviously, the social, political, and economic forces contributing to poverty and overall marginality of underrepresented people helped to shape the need for adults to seek education outside of a formal set-ting to effectively address their community needs. Issues have gener-ally centered around human rights and a need for adults to either function in their jobs adequately or to be accepted as members of society.

Adult education has served as the catalyst for the liberation and empowerment of the adult population—liberation from the oppres-sive forces that keep people confused and unsure of themselves and their talents and abilities. The field of adult education can be defined as the systematic study of adults in a particular context (setting) for the purpose of sharing knowledge and facilitating the learning process to achieve a goal or set of goals. The purpose of the knowledge learned will be dependent upon both the context and the need of the population being served.

The research query raised in this study will address the following: (1) How did this black educator view culture; (2) What did this scholar view as the critical issues for educating African American adults; (3) What philosophical or practical concept did these African American adult educators make to the field and function of adult education; and (4) What do black educators identify as the existing problems that negatively impact African American adult education?

The purpose of this research is two-fold: 1) it serves to integrate the role of African American contributions to the field of adult education from their cultural perspective; 2) it allows me the opportunity to do a pilot study gathering preliminary and secondary data. The process of collecting and organizing data and its analysis can be a tool for future research.

The key focus of this research project is to construct a framework to examine the views of selected black intellectuals, and their position on an educational approach. In order to do this we must examine the historical context that influenced the conditions these black intellectual leaders faced. For this paper I chose to select three main areas: history, adult education, and policy, to examine how selected black intellectuals viewed these issues.

Throughout this discussion the terms African American, black, and Negro will be used interchangeably, referring to descendants of continental Africa. John Henrik Clarke (1980) puts this issue of terminology in perspective: "Black or Blackness, tells you how you look without telling you where you are, whereas Africa, or African, relates you to land, history, and culture. No people are spiritually and culturally secure until it answers only to a name of its own choosing, a name that instantaneously relates the people to the past, present, and future."[1]

The different use of terms also reflects the social context of the time period these authors lived in, when referring to African descended people. A desire for self-defined terms has served as a means for cultural affirmation, to combat racism and cultural annihilation. Another reason for the use of these terms interchangeably throughout this paper is that it prevents a redundancy in the compositional form, thus, for these reasons, I will employ the aforementioned terms in referring to African descended people.

History

In defining history, Karenga (1993) states that the function of African American history is for the "rescue and reconstruction" of lost and suppressed information related to contributions of African people world wide. By examining the views of these black educators on the relevance of history can provide further insight to their philosophical views and education approaches for African American people.[2]

Upon examination of the historical contributions of African American adults in the larger society and the field, there has been a failure to recognize their contributions. Education being no different, I will offer a brief historical discussion of adult education for African Americans.

Historical Overview African American Adult Education

Neufeldt and McGee (1990) states that to make the distinction between what Whitaker refers to as "broad and narrow" definitions of education is important.[3] The teaching of enslaved blacks labor-intensive skills might fit a broader definition of education versus classroom instruction as a formal activity.[4]

During slavery, Whitaker (1990) states no more than 5 percent of the slave population had any form of basic education (reading and/or writing), there is an important distinction to be made in the education of enslaved versus free blacks during the late 1700s and early 1800s. Enslaved blacks were educated for the purpose of performing manual labor, which did not include basic literacy skills.[5] During the pre-civil war era, some black newspapers sponsored literary societies, while Black churches sponsored learning for the purpose of moral development. Also addressed is the fact that in the south these activities were allowed as a security measure, rather than for intellectual enlightenment of enslaved and free blacks.

These societies continued, but with the advent of Abolitionism, a more hostile climate existed for slaves and free blacks alike, limiting the "approved" educational opportunities from the 1830s up to the Civil War.[6] During the Civil War and after, the black church and the federal government were responsible for educating African Americans.[7] Many southern black churches were led by self-educated free blacks who established schools in the Civil War south through the existing structure of black churches.[8] The Union Army, upon encountering slaves and free blacks in the south, offered rehabilitation services that included education. At the same time former slaves were recruited into the Army and received military training necessary to form black companies.[9]

According to Lovett (1990), after the Civil War, education was seen as a means for social control, in fear of black retaliation from institutional enslavement. Because of differences in purpose and mission between black churches and white missionaries, these educational programs also differed in the degree of independence they would provide their black constituency.[10]

At the center of the examination of African American adult education is the issue of control. Therefore, black autonomy of educational activities became a key issue during the post-Civil War era in the United States. Given societal pressures, education for blacks was viewed as a way to combat hostile forces which directly reflected the needs of African Americans in general. Given the importance of the post-Civil War era, augmented forces that led to segregation, racial, and economic discrimination against blacks. The need for what W. E. B. Du Bois coined "the talented tenth" became crucial in the quest for African American autonomy from societal oppression. Most of the leaders from this time period were born into families that were enslaved, and these individuals received first hand accounts of the problems facing blacks in society as they made a difficult adjustment towards freedom.[11]

Adult Education

A definition for adult education often varies with the context, purpose, and philosophy of the facilitator/educator. In *The Handbook of Adult Education* (1990), John Dewey provides a description of adult education in a liberal context: ". . . [it] is the aim of progressive education to take part in correcting unfair privilege and unfair depriva-tion, not to perpetuate them."[12] Education for social action familiar to grass roots movements enables groups of adults to negotiate power from an existing hierarchy and raise the concerns of a community.

Adult education in a more conservative context of a formal insti-tutional setting can be defined as: the training and retraining of a par-ticular work force so that they may perform their job function more effectively. The American Society for Training and Development de-fined the human resource development function of adult education as "identifying, assessing, and through planned learning, helping de-velop the key competencies which enable individuals to perform cur-rent or future jobs."[13]

In examining adult education, noting that different individuals have had different definitions for what purpose it should serve is im-portant. Before World War II, Morse Cartwright emphasized liberal education for individual transformation, whereas, Joseph Hart and Eduard Lindeman strongly favored adult education for social action. After World War II, definitions of adult education crystallized into three groups: 1) economic development expressed in Comprehensive Employment and Training Act (CETA) and Job Training Partnership Act (JPTA) programs; 2) social movements such as the civil rights movement's education programs; and 3) liberal education to help in-dividual adults as members of society to become productive.

Adult educators emphasizing social change such as, Paulo Freire, recognize the historical and present marginalization and hegemony imposed by institutions on oppressed people throughout the world. "Marginalization" refers to the contributions of oppressed people to society are considered at best marginal and at the worst irrelevant by society. Hegemony is the imposition of power through cultural values, politics, and economics for and social aspects of life. Oppressed peo-ple, including women as a whole, are generally considered members of racial and ethnic minority groups, undereducated people, and low-income groups. Social change in adult education describes the process of assisting these people in negotiating power from institu-tions, so they can take control of their lives and improve their condi-tion. Knowledge is not considered neutral, and education is used to correct forms of existing patterns of inequality in society. The per-spective of social change states: 1) many societies require an "under-class" of people to support the political and economic structure; and

2) there will always be an unequal distribution of resources to ensure that those in power remain in power. Adult education for social change enables the oppressed people to recognize both their potential and their resources, and addresses their needs via the transfer of knowledge so that the existing inequality will cease.

Public Policy

In defining public policy Anderson (1979) states: ". . . it is a purposive course of action followed by an actor or set of actors in dealing with a problem or matter of concern."[14] The exercise and negotiation of power through institutions was and continues to be an important step in the operationalization of any education program for African Americans. Examination of this area becomes important to understanding the individuals in this study and how the larger forces of institutions influenced their views.

Purpose of Research

Being the first group of highly educated African Americans and given their place in history one could argue, their views are unfettered by technological and socially constructed influences, which maintain inequality among the races. For this reason, I chose to conduct an historical overview of African American adult education.

Given the well documented history of defacto and dejure segregation, leading to the unequal distribution of resources in American public education, a need developed for African American community leaders to take action in analyzing problems, defining strategies, and implementing solutions. This need meant understanding and redefining the role of continental African American people in society through educational activities.

The call for African American adults to be educated about their history, according to Clarke (1980), goes back to the beginning of the twentieth century. During this period, scholars such as Alain Locke, Carter Woodson, and Mary McLeod Bethune took the position that the contributions of African Americans in the diaspora were both important and worthy of further study.[15] Locke, a philosopher and advocate

224

of African American adult education, saw the importance for blacks to understand their culture and history in the global perspective: "The study of racial and group history of group contributions to culture, or even of specific group problems is sound and constructively educative. In fact, these emphases have been found to be magnets of interest and galvanizers of the adult education program groups. . . . Social education is an unavoidable aspect of adult education, and an inescapable obligation of adult educators."[16]

Development of the Modern Black Studies Movement

During the 1960s, the civil rights movement helped society to re-examine the way issues of race and culture are addressed. Karenga (1993) discusses the significance of African American leaders such as Malcolm X and Martin Luther King, Jr., who served as catalysts for social change that would eventually lead to the new approaches to social science research in black communities across America.[17] Anderson (1990) also notes that the contributions of Black scholars such as Carter Woodson, W. E. B. Du Bois, and Cheikh Anta Diop, prior to the 1960s, provided scholarship that not only studied the condition of black people but did so with the insight of the black experience. The problem with "traditional" scholarship is that it interpreted the black experience from the paradigm of the white experience, values, and norms.[18]

Thus, during the mid-1960s, poor research, curriculum exclusion of blacks, and social protest resulted in blacks raising issues regarding the role that educational institutions played in depicting the contributions of various ethnic and racial groups to world history. Karenga (1993) sees the birth of the Black Studies movement was directly out of the student movement of the 1960s. He divides the student movement into four "thrusts": 1) the civil rights movement in the south from 1960 to 1964; 2) the free speech movement out of the University of California at Berkeley from 1964 to 1965; 3) the Vietnam War protests starting in 1965; and 4) the Black Power movement from 1966 to 1969, in which racially, self-conscious, and activist black students sought to change the relationship of the university to both black students and the black community.[19] As a result, a group of black students in the San Francisco Bay Area specifically raised the issue of the inclusion of blacks in the traditional college curriculum at San Francisco State College. It was at SFSC that the first Black Studies program was founded in 1966 as a direct result of student protest over the failure of the college to incorporate blacks in the curriculum.[20] In 1969, Harvard established the second Black Studies program, which gave an indirect validation to the black studies movement in higher education. During the next several years many more institutions formed programs or departments in Black Studies. Anderson also states that though many of these units are autonomous with concepts, theoretical perspectives, and ideology of their own, they are considered interdisciplinary since they borrow from and contribute to existing disciplines. Stewart (1992) agrees and provides an analysis of Black Studies by examining the linkages with traditional disciplines and how they have shaped the field.[21] By exploring the views of leaders in the African American community, we may be able to put into perspective the role education has had historically for African Americans. Many of these intellectual/race advocates had varying ideas on what the problems facing blacks were, as well as how to address them. Perhaps, the impact of culture on these individuals operationalized them in strategies and tactics in advancing black adult education.

Given the nature of this research, there is disciplinary overlap between adult education and Black Studies, whereas, the use of literature in both fields can create a mutually beneficial discourse bringing theoretical concepts with effective educational approaches for the development of educational needs related to culture.

Historical Development of Education Related to the Evolution of Black Studies

"Black Studies" in higher education refers to an academic unit within the college/university structure that offers courses that locate the contributions of people of African descent throughout the diaspora. This term is often used interchangeably with the terms Africana Studies, African Diaspora Studies, Pan-African, Africology, and Afro-American Studies. Variations of this term are due in part to political, ideological, and sociological factors specific to institutions and people that make policy decisions. Generally, these terms are used interchangeably by researchers and practitioners to reflect the study of black people in their environment.

According to Clarke-Hine (1990), the Black Studies unit within the university structure are categorized as either departments, programs, centers, or institutes. Clarke-Hine states that departments are autonomous academic units that hire faculty and grant tenure, offer degrees, and maintain an administrative budget. Programs generally offer majors or minors but hire faculty through joint appointments in other academic departments. Centers and institutes are administrative units that place an emphasis on scholarship rather than undergraduate teaching and may also provide cultural and social development. Hine also mentions the fact that the mixed mission of Black Studies centers often confuses the perception of their function on the college campus.[22]

Harris (1990) divides the growth of the Black Studies movement into four stages. The first stage (circa 1890 to 1945) consisted of various organizations attempting to document the history and culture of descendants from Africa.[23] During this time, Carter Woodson founded the Association for the Study of Negro Life and History, *The Journal of Negro History,* and became the exponent of Negro History Week now called Black History Month. Also during this time, W. E. B. Du Bois wrote books, scholarly articles, and called for a one-hundred-year study of black life in America to accurately research their development.

The second stage (circa 1945 to 1965) witnessed the contributions of traditional scholarship to the examination of African Americans in the United States. During this stage, researchers studied migration patterns, conditions of the black family and the role of blacks in a post-World War II America from a white male perspective. At the end of this period the civil rights movement had a major impact on the scholarship about blacks as black students entering predominantly white colleges found that the curriculum did not reflect the role and the contributions of African Americans nationally or internationally in the development of civilization. Harris explains: "Together with many black scholars from the first stage of Africana studies, black college students challenged the prevailing orthodoxies on predominantly white campuses. They demanded the employment of black professors and the establishment of Africana Studies programs."[24] Reasons for these programs, according to Harris, were and still are, a means of recovering knowledge of African culture and history for the purpose of resisting the dominance of Western culture in American education.

The establishment of new Black Studies programs aided in the transition to the third stage (1965 to 1985) in which professionals sought to legitimize and institutionalize the emerging modern field of Black Studies via new research approaches to acquire new knowledge. The emphasis was for scholars to research the experience of blacks by using black cultural paradigm to produce an accurate analysis of black community.

In sum, this stage marked a shift from using a Eurocentric approach or paradigm to an Afrocentric approach to study black people. This shift meant that black thoughts, ideas, and culture were the frame in which research would be conducted, analyzed, and interpreted about black people.

Finally, the fourth stage (from the mid-1980s to the present) involves the development of theory, analysis, and interpretation of research. This development would include the standardization in the field via the organization of programs, centers, and departments of Black studies, to adopt and implement a unified curriculum. For the purpose of this essay, the fourth stage in the development of the field of Black Studies will be examined in order to address how it has defined itself in the last twenty years and what have been the emerging schools of thought.

CARTER G. WOODSON

Biographical Sketch

Carter Godwin Woodson, born in 1875, is recognized for his contributions to the field of history and his advocacy for the inclusion of African Americans to United States and world history. Considered by many a scholar/activist, Woodson was known as a strong advocate for a balanced examination of Africana culture. Born to the parents of slaves, Scally (1985) points out that, Woodson's knowledge of slavery as a youth comes from first hand accounts of conditions from parents and members of the rural Virginia community he grew up in.[25] A significant impact on Woodson's education early is the association with Oliver Jones, while mining coal as an eighteen-year-old in West Virginia. Jones, a cook from Richmond, Virginia, had an extensive library collection. After working in the mines he would open his home to miners for eating and drinking.[26] Woodson's access to this extensive collection along with discussions of slavery and current conditions for blacks and family influences probably instilled in him a proud cultural identification that continued throughout the rest of his life.

Woodson's college matriculation takes a long and winding path as he attends several colleges: Berea College for two-thirds of a year, Lincoln University in Pennsylvania for a brief stay, and the University of Chicago in 1901 and 1902. Between schools, Carter Woodson spent time teaching in Chicago, the Philippines, Virginia, and Washington, D.C.[27] Eventually, Woodson received his Bachelor of Literature from Berea College in 1903, his M.A. from the University of Chicago in 1908, and his doctorate in History from Harvard in 1912.[28]

Among his noted contributions were establishing the idea for "Negro History Week" in 1925, which has now become known as Black History Month; the Association for the Study of Negro Life and History for scholarly publications; and the Negro History Bulletin for lay reading. Additionally, Woodson published important books such as *The Education of the Negro Prior to 1861* (1915), *The History of the Negro Church* (1921), *The Mis-education of the Negro* (1933), along with other works.[29]

Philosophical Ideas and Thoughts

History

Woodson maintained a strong desire to fight against the notions that black people made no significant contributions to American history. In his book *The Mis-education of the Negro* (1933), his criticism of education particularly during the Civil War pointed to the fact that the teaching of European history was highlighted while the contributions of Africans was seen at the bottom of the anthropological ladder: "In history of course, the Negro had no place in this curriculum. He was pictured as a human being, of lower order, unable to subject passion to reason, and therefore useful only when made the hewer of wood and the drawer of water for others."[30] Woodson chose a research agenda that would bring to the forefront the contributions of black people in America in the area of higher education and beyond through scholarly publications, journals, lectures, and books that could be used in black schools to teach history. His passion for recognition of the role of culture led him to found Negro History Week for the recognition of cultural contributions of African people. Scally finds this particularly significant for the 1920s since, given the negative connotations placed on Africa, cultural identification was unheard of at that time.

Adult Education

Woodson became a living example for bringing theoretical concepts to practice as his organizing skills to seek educational outlets to correct false images. He believed in a form of education that should do more than promote knowledge for knowledge sake: "Real education means to inspire people to live more abundantly, to learn to begin with life as [people] find it and make it better, but the instruction so far given to negroes in college and universities has worked to the contrary."[31] Woodson's involvement in both higher education and public education, and black organizations represented a systematic effort to change curricular and approaches to education on a larger level.

Policy

Given that Woodson was well aware of the role of formal education in distorting the role of Africa, there is a possibility that he was rather suspect of affiliating the Association for the Study of Negro Life and history with mainstream institutions like the university or a political organization.[32] The issue that needs to be explored further is how does one attempt to shape policy from the outside? Part of how Woodson addressed this issue was in the role of social networks with people of demonstrating a similar commitment to improving the conditions for blacks at that time. As a result, he may have helped to influence educational policy related to curriculum development. Scally mentions that the American Council on Education in 1944 made several curriculum changes in textbooks that inaccurately represented the contributions of other countries in historical events and that would have been attributed to the efforts of Carter G. Woodson.[33] Further investigation is needed to explore the role of policy in shaping and being shaped by Woodson.

ALAIN LOCKE

Biographical Sketch

Alain Locke was born in Philadelphia in 1886. His father was a member of the second graduating class of law students at Howard University. His parents value for quality education led him to attending schools in the Philadelphia area that were part of the educational reform taking place at that time.[34]

Locke graduated with a degree in Philosophy in 1907 from Harvard University after which he received a Rhodes Scholarship to study at Oxford University in England. Locke wrote on adult education and participated in various activities such as a conference funded by the Carnegie Foundation, the Atlanta and Harlem adult educational programs of the mid-1930s, and eventually became president of the Adult Education Association of America. He continued publishing and lecturing until his death in 1954, and his contribution to the field of adult education, particularly as it relates to African Americans, is a significant legacy to the field.

Philosophical Ideas and Thoughts

History

When Locke looked at Black history he began in Africa and then discussed the role of slavery in examining the conditions for African Americans. In his book *The Negro in America* (1993) he offers an outline of postslavery conditions, self-maintenance, confusion and set back, problems of tenant farming, loss of civil rights, and mass migration to cities that resulted in economic discrimination in employment opportunities and housing segregation as contributing to the problems faced by African Americans in society. "Certainly the past of the Negro in America has been an epical adventure, pursued against great odds and opposition but favored, almost providentially at critical times by saving alliances with the forces of moral and social liberalism all combines to achieve a gradually ascending scale of achievement and progress."[35]

Locke recognized the suffering and depravity experienced by blacks in the United States that resulted in their being negatively stereotyped in society and presented them with a unique place in society. Thus, examination of black life should examine the positive, unrecognized contributions to society that deserve further study. In 1933, he posed a positive view of the future for African Americans who, with white help, were working towards improving conditions for the black community.[36]

Adult Education

In Locke's discussion of history, he mentions the importance of educational opportunities for blacks coming from sympathetic whites, such as the northern missionaries that founded schools during slavery to eradicate illiteracy and develop leadership among blacks. In postslavery times, he discussed the importance of key figures, such as northern philanthropists, southern liberals, and Booker T. Washington, who fought to improve education of the freed slaves during reconstruction and the late 1800s.[37]

Policy

Locke discusses the role of segregation policies and discrimination in labor as being crucial factors related to race relations. The traditional policies of southern aristocracy ultimately contributed to force poor whites into competition with liberated slaves and created the inequality of segregation. According to Locke, the lack of contact resulted in cultural ignorance about blacks, which contributed to distrust, suspicion, and hatred of blacks by whites in the postslavery era.[38]

Locke mentions that a way to combat the effects of segregation would be for blacks to exercise their full rights as citizens through the power of voting to put people in place to advocate their equality in society.[39] Locke also stresses the importance and recognition of the unique cultural contributions and values of African Americans distinct from whites. "Both by temperament and group policy, the negro has been conformist throughout his history in this country. His values, his ideals, his objectives, have been pecularily and unreservedly American."[40] Locke goes on to note that strong racial identification has been done only as a means to combat racism in society, rather than to celebrate racial pride. From this stance, Locke appears to advocate strong cultural identification that goes beyond the pressures of societal discrimination.

MARY MCLEOD BETHUNE

Biographical Sketch

Mary McLeod Bethune was born the fifteenth of seventeen children to slave parents in Mayesville, South Carolina, in 1875. Bethune attended a Presbyterian middle school in Mayesville and, according to Lerner (1973), she described her family as religious, hard working, loving, and ambitious, with her mother being her greatest influence.

After attending the mission school she was given a scholarship by a white dressmaker, Mary Crissman, to attend Scotia Seminary in North Carolina. Scotia (now called Barber-Scotia) served as a Presbyterian school for black girls stressing religious and industrial education.[41] According to McCluskey (1994), the "'heart, head, hand' educational philosophy of Scotia, which eschewed purely intellectual knowledge in favor of a combination of religious, intellectual, and practical learning, became the basis of the philosophy that later guided Bethune's own school for black girls."[42] Students at Scotia were required to work in the school laundry or kitchen, which reflected a Bible-based curriculum to fight the societal belief that black women were immoral based on their role in slavery.[43] (Working in the laundry combated this belief system because it promoted ethics and frugality of black women. Furthermore, it helped to promote self-worth and self-esteem necessary for women to advance beyond the limitations of negative stereo-types.)

Bethune, after graduation, attended the Moody Bible Institute in Chicago after which she seeks to become a missionary on the African continent. After being turned down, Bethune leaves for Augusta, Georgia, to work with Lucy Craft Laney at the Haines Institute for Black Girls.[44] The Haines Institute proved to be a major influence for her: "From this dynamic pioneer in Negro education, I got a new vision; my life's work lay not in Africa, but in my own country."[45]

Lefall and Sims (1976) discuss how Bethune, with little money, opened the Daytona Educational And Industrial Training School for Negro Girls in 1904, which later merged with the all boys Cookman Institute from Jacksonville Florida to form the Bethune-Cookman College in 1923. While in the position as the first African American woman college president, Bethune established a reputation as a dogged fund raiser, educator, organizer, and advocate for black women's issues. Among her accomplishments were: director of the Division of Negro Affairs in the National Youth Administration under President Franklin D. Roosevelt, founder of the National Council of Negro Women (1935), president of the Association for the Study of Negro Life and History (1945), president of the National Association of Colored Women, and recipient of the NAACP's Spingarn medal for advancement of racial equality among her many other accomplishments.[46]

Philosophical Thoughts and Ideas

History

Throughout many of her speeches, Bethune draws on historical references from both the Bible and black culture, giving the impression that knowledge of the past was important in addressing the current issues. In an undated speech titled *A Century of Progress of Negro Women,* Bethune looks back at the role of women: "One hundred years ago [the negro woman] was the most pathetic figure on the American continent. She was not a person, in the opinion of many, but a thing—a thing whose personality had no claim to the respect of mankind."[47]

Adult Education

Her view of education is intertwined with both cultural identity as a black woman and her strong Christian values. She sees black women as having been treated harshly by society, yet, in spite of this fact,

234

with their great talents they have managed to overcome obstacles through education to achieve success. In the same speech she refers to other black women, such as, Charlotte Hawkins Brown, Nannie Helen Burroughs, Julia Jackson Harris, and Estelle Ancrum Forster, who were educators in leadership positions around the country. Having founded an educational institution with both traditional and non-traditional students, Bethune demonstrates her staunch advocacy for the education of adults.

Policy

As a leader, fund raiser, and supporter of interracial cooperation for improving conditions for African Americans, there is a possibility that Bethune recognized the importance of power and the affect it had in shaping educational opportunities in society:

> When the Ballot was [made] available to the Womanhood of America, the sister of the darker hue was not slow to take advantage. In the section where the Negro could gain access to the voting booth, the intelligent forward-looking element of the Race's women have taken hold of political issues with an enthusiasm and mental acumen that might well set worthy examples for other groups. Oftimes she has led the struggle toward moral improvement and political record, and has compelled her reluctant brother to follow her determined lead.[48]

Having spoken to both black and white audiences, she was able to position herself to serve as an advocate for the various issues affecting the quality of the African African experience. Having conferred with President Roosevelt, she achieved a level of political access unparalleled by many of her contemporaries, both male and female.

CONCLUSION

From this study, the fact that culture had a significant impact leading black proponents of adult education is evident. During the late nineteenth and early twentieth centuries, African Americans experienced racism resulting in segregation and leading to the inequality of participation in American society. Thus, education has been important in overcoming the social stratification based on race and class in society.

Having been the best educated of their group, leading black educators began taking steps in promoting educational access to adults with limited education, while proposing changes in curriculum and policy that would provide a more accurate representation of African American contributions to society. The research presented here reveals areas that deserve further investigation about black educators. What has become apparent is that each author translated his or her observations into a plan of action that would address the problems of African American people for the benefit of the entire society.

Bibliography

Anderson, James E. (1979). *Public Policy-Making Decisions and Their Implementation.* New York: Holt, Rinehart and Winston.

Anderson, Talmadge, ed. (1990). *Black Studies: Theory Method and Cultural Perspectives.* Pullman: Washington State University Press.

Bethune, M. M. Papers, 1923–1955 (n.d.). Amistad Research Center. New Orleans, LA: Tulane University.

Chateauvert, M. (1988). "The Third Step: Anna Julia Cooper and Black Education in the District of Columbia, 1910–1960," in *Sage: A Scholarly Journal on Black Women*, Student Supplement.

Clarke, John Henrik (1980). "Africana Studies: A Decade of Change, Challenge and Conflict," in J. E. Turner, ed., *The Next Decade: Theoretical and Research Issues in Africana Studies.* Ithica, NY: Cornell University Press.

———. (1973). "Education in the making of the Black Urban Ghetto," in James Hastings, ed., *Black Manifesto for Education.* New York: William Morrow.

Franklin, John Hope (1985). *George Washington Williams.* Chicago: University of Chicago Press.

Goggin, Jacqueline (1993). *Carter G. Woodson: A Life in Black History.* Baton Rouge: Louisiana State University Press.

Green, Lorenzo Johnston and Arvarh E. Strickland, eds. (1989). *Working with Carter G. Woodson, the Father of Black History: A Diary, 1928–1930.* Baton Rouge: Louisiana State University.

Harris, L., ed. (1989). *The Philosophy of Alain Locke.* Philadelphia, PA: Temple University Press.

Harris, Robert, Leonard Hine, Darlene Clark, and Nellie Mckay (1990). *Three Essays, Black Studies in the United States.* New York: The Ford Foundation.

Hayden, Robert C. and Eugene E. Du Bois (1972). "A Drum Major for Black Adult Education: Alain L. Locke," *Western Journal of Black Studies* 1(4): 293–296.

Hutchinson, L.D. (1981). *A Voice From the South by a Black Woman.* Washington, DC: Smithsonian Associates and the Anacostia Neighborhood Museum.

Karenga, Maylana (1993). *Introduction to Black Studies.* Los Angeles: University of Sankore Press.

———. (1988). "Black Studies and the Problematic of Paradigm: The Philosophical Dimension," *Journal of Black Studies* 18(4): 395–414.

Leffall, D. C., and J. L. Sims (1976). "Mary McLeod Bethune—The Educator; Also Including a Selected Annotated Bibliography," *Journal of Negro Education* 45 (Summer): 342–359.

Lerner, Gerda, ed. (1973). *Black Women in White America: A Documentary History.* New York: Pantheon Books.

Linnemann, Russell, ed. (1982). *Alain Locke: Reflection On a Modern Man.* Baton Rouge: Louisiana State University.

Locke, Alain (1933). *Negro in America.* Chicago: The American Library Association.

Lovett, Bobby L. (1990). "Black Adult Education during the Civil War," in Harvey F. Neufeldt and Leo McGee, eds., *The Education of the Afican American Adult: A Historical Overview.* Westport, CT: Greenwood Press.

McCluskey, Audrey T. (1994). "Multiple Consciousness in the Leadership of Mary McLeod Bethune," *National Women's Studies Association Journal* 6(1): 69–81.

———. (1989). "Mary McLeod Bethune and the Education of Black Girls," *Sex Roles* 21(1): 113–126.

Merriam, Sharon B., and Phyllis M. Cunningham, eds. (1990). *Handbook of Adult Continuing Education.* San Francisco, CA: Jossey Bass.

Neufeldt, Harvey G., and Leo Mcgee, eds. (1990). *The Education of the African American Adult: A Historical Overview.* Westport, CT: Greenwood Press.

Scally, Mary Anthony (1985). *Carter G. Woodson: A Bio-Bibliography.* Westport, CT: Greenwood Press.

Stewart, James B. (1992). "Reaching for Higher Ground: Toward an Understanding of Black/Africana Studies," *The Afrocentric Scholar* 1 (May): 1–63.

Washington, Johnny (1994). *A Journey into the Philosophy of Alain Locke.* Westport, CT: Greenwood Press.

———. (1986). *Alain Locke and Philosophy: A Quest for Cultural Pluralism.* Westport, CT: Greenwood Press.

Whitaker, L. H. (1990). "Adult Education within the Slave Community," in Harvey F. Neufeldt and Leo McGee, eds., *The Education of the Afican American Adult: A Historical Overview.* Westport, CT: Greenwood Press.

Woodson, Carter G. (1936). *African Background Outlined.* New York: Negro University Press.

———. (1933, reprint 1972). *Mis-education of the Negro*. Washington, DC: Associated Publishers.

———. (1922). *The Negro in Our History*, 11th ed. Washington, DC: Associated Publishers.

———. (1921). *The History of the Negro Church*. Washington, DC: Associated Publishers.

———. (1915). *The Education of the Negro Prior to 1861*. New York: Putnam's.

Notes

1. John Henrik Clarke, "Africana Studies: A Decade of Change, Challenge and Conflict," in James Turner, ed., *The Next Decade: Theoretical and Research Issues in Africana Studies* (Ithica, NY: Cornell University 1980), p. 31.
2. Maulana Karenga, *Introduction to Black Studies* (Los Angeles: University of Sankore Press 1993), p. 69.
3. Harvey G. Neufeldt and Leo Mcgee, eds., *The Education of the African American Adult: A Historical Overview* (Westport, CT: Greenwood Press 1990), p. vii.
4. Ibid., p. viii.
5. Ibid., p. 9.
6. Ibid., pp. 18–19.
7. Ibid., p. 36.
8. Ibid., p. 37.
9. Ibid., p. 38.
10. Ibid., pp. 45–46.
11. William E. B. Du Bois, "The Talented Tenth," in Ulysses Lee, ed., *The Negro Problem: A Series of Articles by Representative American Negroes of Today* (New York: Arno Press and *New York Times* 1969).
12. Sharan B. Merriam and Phyllis M. Cunningham, eds., *Handbook of Adult Continuing Education* (San Francisco: Jossey Bass 1990), p. 13.
13. Ibid., p. 426.
14. James E. Anderson, *Public Policy-Making Decisions and their Implementation* (New York: Holt, Rinehart and Winston 1979), p. 3.
15. Clarke, "Africana Studies: A Decade of Change, Challenge and Conflict."
16. Alain Locke, *Negro in America* (Chicago: The American Library Association 1933), p. 225.
17. Karenga, *Introduction to Black Studies*, pp. 167–168, 175–176, 269.
18. Talmadge Anderson, *Black Studies: Theory Method and Cultural Methodology* (Pullman: Washington State University Press 1990).
19. Karenga, *Introduction to Black Studies*, pp. 4–10.
20. Anderson, *Black Studies: Theory Method and Cultural Methodology*.
21. James B. Stewart, "Reaching for Higher Ground: Toward an Understanding of Black/Africana Studies," *The Afrocentric Scholar* 1:1 (1992).
22. Robert Harris, Darlene Clarke-Hine, and Nellie Mckay, *Three Essays, Black Studies in the United States* (New York: The Ford Foundation 1990).
23. Ibid.
24. Ibid., p. 10.
25. Mary Anthony Scally, *Carter G. Woodson: A Bio-Bibliography* (Westport, CT: Greenwood Press 1985), p. 4.
26. Ibid., p. 5.

27. Ibid., p. 6–7.
28. Ibid., p. 9.
29. Ibid., p. xvi.
30. Carter G. Woodson, *Mis-education of the Negro* (Washington, DC: Associated Publishers 1972, original printing 1933), p. 89.
31. Ibid., p. 29.
32. J. Goggin, *Carter G. Woodson: A Life in Black History* (Baton Rouge: Louisiana State University Press 1993), p. xiv.
33. Ibid., p. 19.
34. Robert C. Hayden and Eugene E. Du Bois, "A Drum Major for Black Adult Education: Alain L. Locke," in *The Western Journal of Black Studies* 1:4 (1972): 293.
35. Locke, *Negro in America,* p. 10.
36. Ibid., p. 48.
37. Ibid., pp. 28–30.
38. Ibid., p. 32.
39. Ibid., p. 34.
40. Ibid., p. 39.
41. Audrey T. McCluskey, "Mary McLeod Bethune and the Education of Black Girls," *Sex Roles* 21:1 (1989): 114.
42. Gerda Lerner, ed., *Black Women in White America: A Documentary History* (New York: Pantheon Books 1973), p. 73.
43. Ibid., p. 73.
44. McCluskey, "Mary McLeod Bethune and the Education of Black Girls": 115.
45. Lerner, *Black Women in White America,* p. 137.
46. Dolores C. Leffall and Janet L. Sims, "Mary McLeod Bethune—The Educator; Also Including a Selected Annotated Bibliography," *Journal of Negro Education,* 45 (Summer 1976): 344.
47. Mary McLeod Bethune Papers, 1923–1942, "A Century of Programs of Negro Women" (New Orleans, LA: Amistad Research Center), box 2, folder 14, p. 1.
48. Ibid., p. 4.

239

CHAPTER 17

A Literary and Critical Analysis of the Role of Hoyt W. Fuller (1927–1981), *Negro Digest* and *Black World* *Magazine*, during the Black Arts Movement, 1960–1976

Julius E. Thompson

This paper will explore the life and the works of the major African American literary editor, Hoyt W. Fuller, in the United States during the critical period of the black freedom struggle and the Black Arts movement, from 1960 to 1976. It was under his leadership that this publication became the premier organ for many black writers during the height of the civil rights movement, and the related artistic and literary developments in the Black Arts movement. Fuller, with the support of a small staff in Chicago, Illinois, offices of *Negro Digest* and later *Black World*, was able to attract local, regional, national, and international writers, artists, and cultural activists to the publication because of his unique abilities to forge a progressive publishing outlook and vision for black literature, politics, economics, and culture; while generally remaining faithful to the need for a diversity of black voices to reflect on the printed page, the complexities of black life in America, and abroad.[1]

Fuller, born in Atlanta, Georgia, in 1927, was educated at Wayne State University. His career was centered in the field of journalism, and he served as a features editor for the Detroit *Michigan Chronicle* from 1951 to 1954; an associate editor for *Ebony* from 1954 to 1957; as a correspondent in the late 1950's for the *Haagse Post*, a Dutch newspaper based in Amsterdam, Holland; and as an assistant editor for *Collier's Encyclopedia*, New York City, from 1960 to 1961. This rich background of work enabled Fuller to travel widely in the United

States, Europe, and Africa. His international concerns on the black experience in many countries is evident from his career positions.[2]

Contemporary writers, scholars, and activists point to his *Negro Digest* and *Black World* period as being highly significant to helping people understand the central role of black culture and literature in the lives of black people, and in their struggle over time in overcoming oppression in American society, and in other countries around the world. Perhaps the black critic and scholar, Addison Gayle states it best, when he noted in 1981, that Fuller "was probably the founder of the black esthetic movement and articulated—in his writings and the lectures—its aims, positions and goals better than anyone else." For Gayle, the black esthetic can be viewed as "basically a literary movement that suggested that within black culture there were those norms from which literature could be analyzed and evaluated."[3]

Within the context of the Black Aesthetic and the Black Arts movement, Hoyt W. Fuller emerged as perhaps the most important literary and cultural editor of the period, due to his editorship of the *Negro Digest* and *Black World* magazine. Although John H. Johnson was the creator (publisher and editor) of both magazines, extending first from November 1942 to October 1951, and again from May 1961 to April 1976, Fuller actually performed the major functions and duties of producing the monthly magazine in the 1960s and the 1970s.[4] But, in the background stood Johnson, who appears to have had a more active interest in producing, *Ebony, Jet*, and other dimensions of the Johnson Publishing Company, rather than in the *Negro Digest* or *Black World* in the later years.[5]

Fuller became a major influence in the Black Arts movement because he was able to move *Negro Digest/Black World* from basically being a *Reader's Digest*, to a more radical black periodical, which stressed the new mood of black writers, artists, and the community during the 1960s and early 1970s. The interest, of course, was a positive one and tied the journal to the civil rights and Black Power movements of the period. Economically, *Negro Digest* and *Black World* could depend on the strengths of Johnson Publishing and its large distribution system in this country and its ability to reach foreign markets. Because of these factors, Fuller could also offer a modest payment for work published by scholars, poets, short story writers, and others published in these periodicals. Only a handful of other Black Arts publications could afford to do so. In fact, among the major black organizations of the period, such as the *Journal of Black Poetry*, *Soulbook*, and *Black Dialogue*, authors received copies (generally two) of their published work. Few black literary magazines could boast of a circulation as large as *Negro Digest/Black World*, which reached 54,174, by 1971.[6] All of these factors as well as the intellectual vision of Fuller helped to make him a dominant force in the African American cultural life of the era.[7]

Scholar Donald Franklin Joyce noted in 1976 that Fuller's vision for *Negro Digest/Black World* included a focus on:

> . . . [O]riginal articles, essays, short fiction, and poetry by aspiring and seasoned Afro-American, African, Afro-Caribbean, and white writers, scholars, and intellectuals. As the 1960s progressed, Fuller fashioned the magazine into one of eloquent and articulate thought on Afro-Americans, with such new regular features of his own "Perspectives." Fuller's column, which included notes on books, writers, artists, and the arts, was an invaluable source to the librarian, scholar, and intellectual interested in Afro-Americana and African.[8]

Fuller's great success with *Negro Digest/Black World* was enhanced by his ability to attract a diverse group of black writers from throughout the world to the magazine. Being located in Chicago also helped him because many of the most important writers, scholars, and artists of the Black Arts movement, including Gwendolyn Brooks, Don L. Lee (Haki R. Madhubuti), Carolyn M. Rodgers, Carol A. Parks (assistant editor to Fuller), Sterling Plumpp, Angela Jackson, Johari M. Amini, Jim Cunningham, Phillip M. Royster, Sam Greenlee, George E. Kent and others lived there. Chicago was also a major powerhouse of black political strength, extending from the roles of blacks in the Democratic party, to the separatist ideologies of the Nation of Islam, and other groups.[9] Thus, Fuller operated from one of the top five nerve centers of the black Americans in this country.

Who did Fuller select to be published in the *Negro Digest/Black World*? An examination of forty issues of the journal between 1968 to 1971 and 1975, is revealing.[10] In total, as suggested by table 3.1, for these years 881 writers, artists, scholars, students, and community activists appeared in *Negro Digest/Black World*. The range of total numbers by years are as follows: 1968 (six issues), 170; 1969 (8 issues), 128; 1971 (nine issues), 185; and 1975 (ten issues), 176.[11] Table 3.2 notes the range of authors who were published in the organiza-

Table 3.1

Contributors to *Negro Digest/Black World* For Forty Months During 1968 to 1971 and 1975

881	Authors	159	Book Reviews
262	Articles	26	Letters
304	Poems	40	Cartoons
50	Short Stories	18	Reports
3	Plays		

Table 3.2

Authors in *Negro Digest/Black World* with Two or More Publications during Forty Select Months from 1968 to 1971 and 1975

Published Two Times	Men	Women
	Houston A. Baker, Jr.	Toni Cade Bambara
	Peter Bailey	Gwendolyn Brooks
	Sebastian Clarke	Liz Gant
	Stanley Crouch	Alicia L. Johnson
	Frank Marshall Davis	June Jordan
	Tom C. Dent	Carole A. Parks
	Sam Greenlee	Ann Allen Shockley
	Nathan Hare	
	Michael S. Harper	
	William Melvin Kelley	
	John O. Killens	
	Woodie King	
	Loften Mitchell	
	A. X. Nicholas	
	Huel Perkins	

Published Three Times	Men	Women
	S. E. Anderson	Barbara Mahone McBain
	Carr	Ellease Southerland
	Harold Cruse	
	Melvin Dixon	
	Robert L. Harris, Jr.	
	Etheridge Knight	
	C. L. R. James	
	Olumo (Jim Cummingham)	
	Askia Muhammad Toure	
	Quincy Troupe	

continued

Table 3.2 *(Continued)*

Published Four Times	Men	Women
	Stephen A. Henderson	Audre Lorde
	Ted Joans	Mary Helen Washington
	Octave Lilly, Jr.	
	Richard A. Long	
	Larry Neal	
	Frank Lamont Phillips	
	Ishmael Reed	
	Kalamu ya Salaam	
	James W. Thompson	
	Darwin T. Turner	
	John A. Williams	
	Marvin X	

Published Five Times	Men	Women
	Conrad Kent Rivers	Angela Jackson
		Sonia Sanchez

Published Six Times	Men	Women
	Ed Bullins	Eugenia Collier
	James A. Emanuel	Sarah Webster Fabio
	Philip M. Royster	

Published Seven or More Times	Men	Women
	John Henrik Clarke (7)	Mari Evans (7)
	LeRoi Jones [Amiri Baraka] (7)	Carolyn F. Gerald (7)
	David Llorens (7)	Johari Amini (11)
	Ron Welburn (7)	Julia Fields (11)
	Isaac Black (8)	Carolyn Rodgers (16)
	Zack Gilbert (8)	Nikki Giovanni (17)
	Sterling D. Plumpp (9)	
	Keorapetse Kgositsile (10)	
	Don L. Lee [Haki R. Madhubuti] (11)	
	Morrie (11)	
	Dudley Randall (11)	
	Hoyt W. Fuller (28)	

tion between two and five times, or more during this period. *Negro Digest/Black World* was an open journal; writers from throughout the United States and many foreign countries, especially in the Caribbean and Africa, or black writers who lived in Europe, were published by Fuller in the late 1960s and early 1970s, with African American men having the dominant voice in *Negro Digest/Black World*. They composed fifty-four individuals of 72 percent of the authors who were published two or more times in the forty issues reviewed here. Women numbered twenty-one or 28 percent of the total.

Yet, Fuller had a select list of authors who appeared frequently in the journal, four or more times during these years. This group numbered forty authors, twenty-eight men (70 percent), and twelve women (30 percent). Tables 3.3 and 3.4 highlight their major literary interests and region of the country in which they were generally associated with during the late 1960s and early 1970s. This list includes a significant number of leading black authors of the period. New York City with fifteen authors (or 37.5 percent), and Chicago with eleven authors, (or 27.5 percent), are well represented among this group of writers who were published in the journal. Fuller had special interest in the younger writers—Johari Amini, Zack Gilbert, Angela Jackson, Keokapetse Kgositsile (a South African black poet), Don L. Lee, Sterling D. Plumpp, Carolyn Rodgers, Ed Bullins, Nikki Giovanni, LeRoi Jones (Amiri Baraka), Audre Lorde, Larry Neal, Sonia Sanchez, James W. Thompson, and Ron Welburn—who lived in Chicago and New York City, two of the national cultural centers of the United States. Older writers that also appeared frequently in *Negro Digest/Black World* were John Henrik Clarke, James A. Emanuel, Ted Joans, and John A. Williams. Fuller was also impressed with the work of the writers who lived in Detroit—Dudley Randall, James W. Thompson, and Mary Helen Washington; San Francisco— Ed Bullins and Marvin X; Oakland, California—Sara Webster Fabio and Ishmael Reed; and New Orleans, Louisiana—Octave Lilly, Jr. and Kalamu ya Salaam. Other writers on his favorite list included Mari Evans, from Indianapolis, Indiana; Eugenia Collier, Baltimore, Maryland; Stephen A. Henderson, Washington, D.C.; Richard A. Long, Hampton, Virginia and later Atlanta, Georgia; and among others, Darwin Turner, in Iowa. At the top of Fuller's list were several reviewers in the forty issues who appeared nine or more times in the

Table 3.3

Geographical Distribution of Forty Leading Authors for Forty Months in *Negro Digest/Black World*, during 1968 to 1971 and 1975

Author/Major Literary Art Forms	Region of the Country
Amini, Johari, *poet, essayist*	Chicago
Black, Isaac J., *poet, playwright*	New York City
Bullins, Ed, *playwrite, poet, essayist*	San Francisco, CA and New York City
Clarke, John Henrik, *historian, essayist, poet*	New York City
Collier, Eugenia, *essayist, short story writer, poet*	Baltimore, MD
Emanuel, James A., *poet, essayist, short story writer*	New York City
Evans, Mari, *poet, essayist, short story writer*	Indianapolis, IN
Fabio, Sarah Webster, *poet, essayist*	Oakland, CA
Fields, Julia, *poet, essayist, short story writer*	Virginia and North Carolina
Fuller, Hoyt W., *editor, essayist*	Chicago
Gerald, Carolyn F., *essayist, poet*	Philadelphia, PA
Gilbert, Zack, *poet*	Chicago
Giovanni, Nikki, *poet, essayist, short story writer, critic*	New York City
Henderson, Stephen A., *essayist, critic*	Washington, DC
Jackson, Angela, *poet, essayist, short story writer*	Chicago
Joans, Ted, *poet, essayist*	New York City, Europe, and Africa
Jones, LeRoi [Amiri Baraka], *poet, essayist, short story writer, novelist*	New York City and Newark, NJ
Kgositsile, Keokapetse, *poet, essayist, short story writer*	Chicago
Lee, Don L. [Haki R. Madhubuti], *poet, essayist*	Chicago
Lilly, Octave Jr., *poet, essayist*	New Orleans, LA
Llorens, David, *essayist*	Chicago
Long, Richard A., *poet, essayist, critic*	Virginia and Atlanta, GA
Lorde, Audre, *poet, essayist*	New York City
Morrie, *artist*	Chicago
Neal, Larry, *poet, essayist, critic*	Philadelphia, PA and New York City
Phillips, Frank Lamont, *poet, essayist*	New York City
Plumpp, Sterling D., *poet, essayist, critic*	Chicago
Randall, Dudley, *poet, essayist, critic*	Detroit, MI
Reed, Ishmael, *poet, essayist, critic, novelist*	Berkeley and Oakland, CA
Rivers, Conrad Kent, *poet*	New York City
Rodgers, Carolyn, *poet, essayist, critic*	Chicago
Royster, Philip M, *poet, essayist*	Chicago
Salaam, Kalamu ya, *poet, essayist, critic*	New Orleans, LA
Sanchez, Sonia, *poet, essayist, critic*	San Francisco, CA and New York City

Table 3.3 *(Continued)*

Author/Major Literary Art Forms	Region of the Country
Thompson, James W., *poet, novelist*	Detroit, MI and New York City
Turner, Darwin T., *essayist, critic*	Iowa
Washington, Mary Helen, *essayist, critic*	Cleveland, OH and Detroit, MI
Williams, John A., *poet, novelist, essayist, critic*	New York City
X, Marvin, *poet, essayist*	San Francisco, CA

Table 3.4

Geographical Distribution by City of Forty Leading Authors in *Negro Digest/Black World* for Forty Months, during 1968 to 1971 and 1975

Region of the Country	Author
Chicago	Johari Amini
	Hoyt W. Fuller
	Zack Gilbert
	Angela Jackson
	Keokapetse Kgositsile
	Don L. Lee [Haki R. Madhubuti]
	David Llorens
	Morrie
	Sterling D. Plumpp
	Carolyn Rodgers
	Philip M. Royster
New York City	Isaac J. Black
	Ed Bullins
	John Henrik Clarke
	James A. Emanuel
	Nikki Giovanni
	Ted Joans
	LeRoi Jones [Amiri Baraka]
	Audre Lorde
	Larry Neal
	Frank Lamont Phillips
	Conrad Kent Rivers
	Sonia Sanchez
	James W. Thompson
	Ron Welburn
	John A. Williams
Detroit, MI	Dudley Randall
	James W. Thompson
	Mary Helen Washington

continued

247

Table 3.4 *(Continued)*	
Region of the Country	**Author**
San Francisco, CA	Ed Bullins
	Sonia Sanchez
	Marvin X
New Orleans, LA	Octave Lilly, Jr.
	Kalamu ya Salaam
Philadelphia, PA	Carolyn F. Gerald
	Larry Neal
Oakland, CA	Sarah Webster Fabio
	Ishmael Reed
Virginia/North Carolina	Julie Fields
	Richard A. Long
Cleveland, OH	Mary Helen Washington
Baltimore, MD	Eugenia Collier
Indianapolis, IN	Mari Evans
Atlanta, GA	Richard A. Long
Iowa	Dartin T. Turner

pages of *Negro Digest/Black World*. This group included: Johari Amini (11), Julie Fields (11), Fuller (28), Nikki Giovanni (17), Keorapetse Kgositsile (10), Don L. Lee (11), Morrie (a cartoonist, 11), Sterling D. Plumpp (9), Dudley Randall (11), and Carolyn Rodgers (16). This latter group was very dedicated to submitting articles, reviews, poetry, and short stories to *Negro Digest/Black World*. Of the ten figures on this list, eight lived and worked in Chicago during this period. This factor reflects the chief importance of Chicago writers to the base of operations at the *Negro Digest/Black World*, and the major importance of many Chicago area black writers to the Black Arts movement.[11]

In essence, the greatest achievement of Fuller was his editorship of *Negro Digest/Black World*, from the 1960s to the 1970s, as the leading African American literary journal of the Black Arts movement. This is the central theme which emerges in tables 3.5 and 3.6 by twenty-eight critics and eighteen special dedications to Fuller, by individuals and organizations, who have written or sponsored pro-

Table 3.5

The Critics On Hoyt W. Fuller

Name Date	Comment
Arnold Adoff 1973	"Through his work on the magazine [*Negro Digest/Black World*], he has presented and encouraged hundreds of black American writers, and played a major role in the development of contemporary black literature."
Afro-American Writing 1985	"Responding to the challenge of reviving the Johnson Publishing Company's *Negro Digest*, he turned that magazine into a major forum of original black world opinion, an achievement duly commemorated by the change of the name of the magazine to *Black World* in 1970."
Houston A. Baker, Jr. 1980	"Foremost here was *Negro Digest*, edited by Hoyt Fuller of Chicago. The name change which *Negro Digest* underwent during the sixties captured the spirit of the times: it was retitled *Black World*."
Amiri Baraka 1976	"How black is *Black World*?"
C. W. Bigsby 1980	"In the renamed *Black World*, Hoyt Fuller sustained a continuous assault on white critics and those black writers who failed to accept their historic role in the revolution."
Black Books Bulletin 1971	"Hoyt W. Fuller as a man is much like the publication he edits—*Black World*. He is diverse, serious, competent, impatient, intellectually challenging, community oriented, and intimately concerned about the welfare and survival of African people and the world which we occupy. . . . I would imagine that his strongest assets are the ones least known—those of stabilizer and teacher. This is to say that his influence as a blackman and his quiet movements throughout the world reflecting such has pushed writers to dedicate books to him, artists to paint his portrait and poets to write lines of him. By the force of his personality and seriousness, he demands of others who are in his context to face themselves and their predicament."
Gwendolyn Brooks 1987	"Hoyt Fuller, innovator, scholar, persuasive influence, never presented himself as a god, never wished to

continued

Table 3.5 *(Continued)*

Name Date	Comment
	stand away from the rest of us. Multitalented and enacting, he involved himself with youth and age. He was cleanly committed. He subscribed to the quality of Afrikan glory. In the interests of its preservation, in behalf of its regeneration, he Watched, he Warned, he Warded Off.
	He hammered us high, he hoisted us in Black self-believing. He was hinge and hi-fi and Home. He was hunter-host, hope. Is."
Herb Boyd 1985	"As an editor and writer, Fuller—who was reared in Detroit and studied at Wayne State University—had few equals in the country, and even more astounding was his broad network of communications. Fuller was in touch with hundreds of writers, both here and in the Third World; and it made little difference to him if you were established or just beginning to knot your ideas together. My own first literary attempts to reach a national and international audience came under his stewardship."
Eugenia Collier 1987	"In the summer of 1969, I met Hoyt Fuller. Richard Long had invited us both to be consultants at a workshop in Atlanta University. I was anxious to meet Hoyt, for I greatly admired his work as editor of *Negro Digest*. For some reason, I pictured him as a short, squat, hyperactive little man with piercing eyes behind round gold-rimmed glasses. The moment I saw that tall, beautiful man in the black turtleneck, his quietly intelligent eyes gazing at the students, his smooth voice sharing with them the products of a brilliant mind, I knew that Hoyt Fuller would be a friend and a positive influence on all my life. And so he has been. The force of his personality, the depth of his convictions provided a dynamic which, perhaps more than any other single factor, nurtured the black aesthetic. Certainly the fact of his existence as a pivot on which turned the entire direction of my life. This change in direction accelerated immediately after the Atlanta meeting."
Gerald Early 1993	"Hoyt Fuller . . . was an editor, writer, teacher, and one of the leading lights of the Black Aesthetic movement in the late sixties and early seventies."

250

Table 3.5 *(Continued)*

Name Date	Comment
Carolyn Fowler 1981	This important writer notes that on the death of *Black World* in 1976, and the creation of the *First World Foundation*: "We were concerned that a vital forum in the black community was no longer available and there was a feeling that the guiding spirit behind that forum had always been Hoyt Fuller. . . . Hoyt had been the guiding light of artistic and literary flowering in the black community since the '60s and we felt he and his visions were needed."
Addison Gayle 1981	"For the 1960s and 1970s Hoyt was the voice of young black writers across the country who dared to differ esthetically and politically with what had been the mainstream of American literature." [Furthermore, according to Gayle, Fuller] "was probably the founder of the black esthetic movement and articulated—in his writings and lectures—its aims, positions, and goals better than anyone else." [Gayle defines the black esthetic as] "basically a literary movement that suggested that within black culture there were those norms from which literature could be analyzed and evaluated."
Paula Giddings 1981	Believes that Hoyt Fuller was successful in turning "the magazine into the voice of the new black movement."
Dorothy Gilliam 1981	This black woman journalist notes that Fuller, along with Bob Marley (who also died in 1981), "leave legacies very worthy of note at a time when many blacks appear to have forgotten what 'the struggle' was all about. . . . Fuller . . . made the black revolution as popular in words as the activists made it on the streets. He was a mentor for many black writers and artists recognized as the new wave among their peers. He was a fulcrum for the development of a rich new body of literature on black consciousness firmly rooted in a positive identification with the African past—and present. Both epitomized the revolutionary spirit of the 1960s. They didn't fade in the 70s. They pressed on into the uncertain 80s. Losing both of them in one week was enough to suggest the end of an era."
Vincent Harding 1987	This important historian wrote on the historical importance of *Negro Digest/Black World*: "I think all of us need to remember the crucial role it played throughout a ten- to fifteen-year period in the revival of

continued

Table 3.5 *(Continued)*	
Name **Date**	**Comment**
	black history." Harding goes on to note that under Hoyt Fuller's "editorship the magazine became a major vehicle for discussion, analysis and hard debate within the black intellectual community. As such, it performed several important roles for the black history movement. First, it opened its pages to several kinds of black historians. The academy-based heirs of Woodson were solidly and regularly represented through such men as John Hope Franklin and Benjamin Quarles. It also provided a vehicle for those outside of the academies who had much to contribute, such people as John Henrik Clarke, Harold Lawrence, John A. Williams, Sterling Stuckey, and Harold Cruse. Interestingly, by now all of them are inside the academy. Both *Ebony* and *Negro Digest/Black World* provided places for some of the younger academics like me, who chose in the late 1960s not to address our primary work to the white academic journals. Instead, we chose to return to our people, in a hopefully clarified way, the knowledge and, therefore, the power we had received from them. . . . A second major contribution made by *Negro Digest* was its use of excerpts from books by black authors, many of them excerpts on black history. . . . Finally, among the many signal contribution of *Negro Digest* to the struggle for black history was the magazine's self-consciously interdisciplinary approach."
Robert L. Harris, Jr. 1976	"*Black World*, one of our most influential journals, has ceased publication with the April issue of this year. Its demise is a tragic loss, particularly for the black intellectual and artistic communities and therefore for our people as a whole. Through its pages, we have been informed of important political, artistic, and intellectual developments. It has been one of the few forums available for discussing on a principled level a wide range of opinion about crucial issues, affecting black people. *Black World* has supported young and established black writers in numerous fields. The loss of this journal deprives us of an indispensable educational tool for *Black World*, under the editorship of Hoyt Fuller, clearly established itself as the premier defender of African values in America."
Stephen E. Henderson 1969	Viewed Hoyt Fuller as "the urbane, articulate managing editor of *Negro Digest*."

Table 3.5 *(Continued)*

Name Date	Comment
Abby Arthur Johnson and Ronald M. Johnson 1979	The publication lasting the longest [during the 1960s and early 1970s] survived on the largess of its publisher, John H. Johnson. Existing on a relatively stable base of support, *Negro Digest/Black World* became not only the oldest but the most significant of such journals. Much credit goes to Hoyt Fuller, who can be numbered among the most influential editors of black little magazines. By his involvement in the black arts movement, he transformed *Negro Digest* from a popular commercial publication to a pacesetting small journal."
John H. Johnson 1981	Observes that Hoyt Fuller was "an usually gifted journalist who used the power of his intellect and talent for the education and enlightenment of others."
Randall Kennedy 1990	Suggests that *Negro Digest/Black World* was "the most vibrant and widely-read black literary-political journal of the past forty years. . . . Hoyt Fuller . . . fashioned it into a distinctive literary-political forum for black nationalist, pan-Africanist, and other self-consciously politicized cultural tendencies. . . . *Black World* was the nation's most widely-read black literary magazine."
George E. Kent 1987	"The selves of Hoyt W. Fuller that I in varying degrees knew are of profound meaning for our community. Most prominent and most clearly sustained was the self of the man-engaged-by-history. But also visible were the man of individual aspirations and the private man who had put himself together in his own distinctive way, a fact recognized by those who habitually addressed him as Mr. Fuller . . . [h]is published works show that his talent was outstanding."
Richard A. Long 1981	"Fuller became the single most important figure among writers of the black arts movement."
Carole A. Parks 1987	"Hoyt Fuller was a brilliant man, an accomplished journalist, editor, critic, essayist, creative writer, speaker, teacher—a veritable fountain of wisdom on almost any subject. There are probably as many perspectives on why he was so magnetic as there are people who sought his counsel. He touched each of us differently, and each of us felt uniquely special in those eyes whose vision we respected beyond almost any other. In retrospect, I believe that what we really appreciated was Hoyt's simplicity. . . . He brought this

continued

253

Table 3.5 *(Continued)*

Name Date	Comment
	same Black consciousness to *Negro Digest/Black World* and *First World*. Above all, Hoyt wanted the magazines to risk. He used them to encourage us—the young in particular—to study different ways for gaining more control over our lives, for participating in the world, for exploring and acting upon our imaginations. He gave writers a respected forum where they could experiment with old molds, fire and twist a cold language into new forms, turn traditional images upside down or inside out until we got the feel again of making something out of our selves."
Ishmael Reed 1976	"As in most things, you don't know how hard it is to put out a magazine until you've tried. That's why we are unhappy to learn that *Black World*, the country's largest literary magazine, has ceased publication. *Black World*, edited by Hoyt Fuller, was a model of efficient operation. Mr. Fuller was among the first to acknowledge the explosion of poetry by Afro-Americans in the late 1960s. His magazine served as a bulletin for an international community of writers. It seemed, however, the more Mr. Fuller began to devote his time to organizing a literary festival in Nigeria, *Black World* came under the influence of a local Royal family replete with Queen Mother and Jr. Prince." Seventeen years later, this important writer lists Hoyt Fuller in the "tradition of Chicago writers who place their pens in the service of the common people . . ."
Kalamu ya Salaam 1987	"Hoyt Fuller was my literary 'main man,' my beacon and archetypal embodiment of commitment to promulgating a 'Black aesthetic'—a frequently misinterpreted concept which, nonetheless, critically impacted the work of those of us who sought to produce a creative and engaged literature anchored in the African-American experience. In many ways for many years, Hoyt was our preeminent emcee as well as critic. He championed as well as published our work, first in *Negro Digest*, then *Black World* and finally in *First World*, an amazing span of over fifteen years of constant literary activity. A male midwife for countless poets, fictionalists, essayists, dramatists, and critics, Hoyt delivered the first writings of many of us to the world, helped bring them to life: washed them off with his critical editorial eye and shaped out fledgling scribblings into print."

254

Table 3.5 *(Continued)*

Name Date	Comment
Charlotte Wilhite 1972	In a review of Fuller's first book, this critic notes: "*Journey to Africa*, leaves one with a flicker of hope and happiness. . . . [This book] is Hoyt Fuller's personal recollection of his search for strength which would enable him to live as a black man in white America. In route, he learns of the attitude held by whites and blacks alike toward Africa and Africans both in the Homeland and those of us divorced by history, miles, and miseducation. . . . *Journey to Africa* is no ordinary textbook on African affairs. It does not masquerade as being an 'objective' analysis of Africa and Africans today. It is instead a very subjective and highly emotional (can it be otherwise?) analysis of our future as a people both in Africa and America. We are taken on a journey from the Unreal, i.e., dig that shiny black limousine parked out front—to the Real, i.e., bro, that's a shiny black hearse. *Journey to Africa* says it ain't got to be that way."
John A. Williams 1976	Observed in the mid-1970s that he had been "sandbagged" at *Black World*, when Hoyt Fuller accepted one of his essays on black publishing, but then unknown to Williams, had Dudley Randall write "a rebuttal" to his essay. Williams writes, "I did not know that Randall was going to comment on it. I wasn't told. Nor was I given a chance to respond to Randall's article, point by point."

Table 3.6

Works Dedicated to Hoyt W. Fuller

Name Date	Work
African Studies and Research Center, Cornell University, Ithaca, New York Oct. 5–6, 1984	Commemorative Colloquium In Honor of Hoyt W. Fuller Writer, Editor, Literary Critic (Conference Theme: The role of the Black Writer in the American Social Fabric: Confronting Issues of Philosophic and Theoretical (literary) Criticism.
Houston A. Baker, Jr. 1987	"Moonlit Chambers and Sibylline Leaves, or, How 'The Black Aesthetic' Changed My Life"

continued

Table 3.6 *(Continued)*

Name Date	Comment
Gwendolyn Brooks, ed. 1971	*Jump Bad, A New Chicago Anthology* (Detroit, MI: Broadside Press 1971); ("Great editor, warm educator").
1987	"Seeds for the Coming Hell and Health Together."
Kiarri T. H. Cheatwood, ed. 1991	Noted at the front of the book: "The 10th Anniversary of the Mysterious Deaths (May 11, 1981) of Hoyt W. Fuller and Bob Marley," in *The Race: Matters Concerning Pan-Afrikan History, Culture, and Genocide* (Richmond, VA: Native Sun Publishers 1991).
Eugenia Collier 1987	"Some Thoughts On the Black Aesthetic."
Mari Evans, ed. 1984	*Black Women Writers (1950–1980): A Critical Evaluation* (New York: Anchor Press/Doubleday 1984).
1987	"For Hoyt," a poem.
Carolyn Fowler, compiler 1976	*Black Arts and Black Aesthetics: A Bibliography* (Atlanta, GA. Carolyn Fowler 1976). ("To the Memory of Hoyt W. Fuller, September 10, 1923–May 11, 1981, who gave us the word.")
Addison Gayle 1987	"Hoyt Fuller and the Black Aesthetic."
Robert L. Harris 1981	"Hoyt W. Fuller's Challenge."
George E. Kent 1987	"Glimpses of Hoyt W. Fuller."
Keorapetse Kgositsile 1971	My Name Is Afrika (Garden City, NY: Anchor Books/Doubleday 1971).
Woodie King, ed. 1972	*Black Short Story Anthology* (New York: Columbia University Press 1972).
Jewel C. Latimore [Johari Amini] 1971	*Let's Go Some Where* (Chicago: Third World Press 1970).
Richard A. Long 1987	"Watching Just the Same: Some Recollections of Hoyt."

Table 3.6 *(Continued)*

Name Date	Comment
Carole A. Parks, ed. 1987	*Nommo: A Literary Legacy of Chicago (1967–1987): An OBAC Anthology* (Chicago: The OBAC Writers' Workshop/OBAC House 1987).
1987	"Consciously Hoyt: Colleague, Mentor, Friend."
Carolyn M. Rodgers 1971	"For H. W. Fuller," a poem.
Kalamu ya Salaam 1987	"Making the Most of the Middle Passage."
1987	"Our World Is Less Full Now that Mr. Fuller Is Gone," a poem.
Kharlos Wimberli 1987	"The Shadows of Your Frown," a poem.

grams on the editor, or by dedicated books, articles, and poems in his honor and memory.[12] Fuller was also important in promoting the Black Aesthetic movement, and in publishing black poets, since, according to writer Jennifer Jordan, "of all the writers of the Black Arts movement, the poets were the strongest advocates of the Black Aesthetic."[13]

Hoyt W. Fuller's place in the literary and social history of the 1960s and 1970s is a secure one. This position is based on his leadership role as the leading black literary editor of the period, and on his ability to promote a Pan-African perspective among black writers everywhere. He was always able to help promote the work of the older generation of black writers, while molding and mentoring many in the circles of the younger generation of new thinkers and writers who emerged in the 1960s and 1970s. Thus, his intellectual ability allowed him to be a leader among black writers, as well as being an activist in the daily struggle of African Americans to bring about change and reform in American life, with a commitment to advance the lives of black people who lived in other parts of the world.

Preserving the Memory

(For Hoyt W. Fuller, 1923–1981)

A giant
Falls,
The forest
Does not
Hear.
Soon
The skies
Are clear,
Another speed
Rises from
The soil
And Time
Waits.[14]

—Julius E. Thompson

Bibliography

Alhamisi, Ahmed and Hurun Kofi Wangara, eds. (1969). *Black Arts: An Anthology of Black Creations*. Detroit, MI: Black Arts Publications.

Bailey, Leanead Pack, ed. (1974). *Broadside Authors and Artists An Illustrated Biographical Directory*. Detroit, MI: Broadside Press.

Chapman, Abraham, ed. (1972). *New Black Voices*. New York: New American Library.

Cook, Mercer and Stephen E. Henderson (1969). *The Militant Black Writer in Africa and the United States*. Madison: University of Wisconsin Press.

Fowler, Carolyn (1974). "A Contemporary American Genre: Pamphlet/Manifesto Poetry," *Black World* 23 (June): 4–19.

Gayle, Addison, Jr., ed. (1985). *The Black Aesthetic*. Garden City, NY: Anchor Books.

George, Nelson (1989). *The Death of Rhythm and Blues*. New York: E.P. Dutton.

———. (1985). *Where Did Our Love Go? The Rise and Fall of the Motown Sound*, selected bibliography. New York: St. Martin's Press.

Johnson, Abby Arthur and Ronald M. Johnson (1979). *Propaganda and Aesthetics: The Literary Politics of Afro-American Magazines in the Twentieth Century*. Amherst: University of Massachusetts Press.

Jones, Leroi and Larry Neal, eds. (1968). *Black Fire: An Anthology of Afro-American Writing*. New York: William Morrow and Company.

Madhubuti, Haki R. (1971). *Dynamite Voices: Black Poets of the 1960s*. Detroit, MI: Broadside Press.

Page, James A., ed. (1977). *Selected Black American Authors*. Boston: G. K. Hall.

Parks, Carole A., ed. (1987). *Nommo: A Literary Legacy of Black Chicago (1967–1987)*. Chicago: The Organization of Black American Culture Writer's Workshop.

Randall, Dudley (1975). *Broadside Memories: Poets I have Known*. Detroit, MI: Broadside Press.

———. (1970). "Broadside Press: A Personal Chronicle," in Floyd B. Barbaur, ed., *The Black Seventies*. Boston: Porter Sargent, p. 139–148.

Redmond, Eugene B. (1976). *Drumvoices, The Mission of Afro-American Poetry: A Critical History*. Garden City, NY: Anchor Press/Doubleday.

Notes

1. Donald Franklin Joyce, "Magazines of Afro-Americans," *Americans Libraries* 7:11 (December 1976): 678, 681–682.
2. Ann Allen Shockley and Sue P. Chandler, compilers, *Living Black American Authors: A Biographical Directory* (New York: R. K. Bowker 1973), pp. 52–53; Clare D. Kinsman, ed., *Contemporary Guide to Current Authors and Their Works*, vols. 53–56 (Detroit, MI: Gale Research 1975), p. 208; William C. Matney, ed., *Who's Among Black Americans, 1975–76* (Northbrook, IL: Who's Who Among Black Americans 1976), p. 220; James A. Page, compiler, *Selected Black American Authors: An Illustrated Bibliography* (Boston: G. K. Hall 1977), pp. 93–94.
3. *New York Times*, May 13, 1981.
4. Joyce, "Magazines," p. 681.
5. Donald Franklin Joyce, *Black Book Publishers in the United States: A Historical Directory of the Presses, 1817–1990* (New York: Greenwood Press 1991), pp. 135–139; John H. Johnson with Lerone Bennett, Jr., *Succeeding Against the Odds: The Autobiography of A Great American Businessman* (New York: Amstad Press 1989).
6. Joyce, "Magazines": 682.
7. David Lionel Smith, "The Black Arts Movement and Its Critics," *American Literary History* 3:1 (1991): 95; Larry Neal, "The Social Background of the Black Arts Movement," *The Black Scholar* 18 (January/February 1987): 20.
8. Joyce, "Magazines": 681–682.
9. D. H. Melhem, *Heroism in the New Black Poetry: Introductions and Interviews* (Lexington: University of Kentucky Press 1990), p. 83; Nicholas Lemann, *The Promised Land: The Great Black Migration and How It Changed America* (New York: Knopf 1991); Kenneth O'Reilly, *"Racial Matters," the FBI's Secret File on Black America, 1960–1972* (New York: The Free Press 1971), pp. 274–277.
10. The issues surveyed for this data were *Negro Digest*, April, May, July, August, September, October, and November 1968; January, February, April, August, September, October, November, and December 1969; January and April 1970. *Black World*, June, July, September, October, November, December 1970; February, March, May, June, July, September, October, November, and December 1971; and January and December 1975.

11. Eugene B. Redmond, *Drumvoices: The Mission of Afro-American Poetry, A Critical History* (Garden City, NY: Anchor Books/Doubleday 1976), pp. 386–394.

12. Arnold Adoff, ed., *The Poetry of Black America: Anthology of the 20th Century* (New York: HarperCollins), p. 524; James A. Page and Jae Min Roh, compilers, *Selected Black American, African, and Caribbean Authors: A Bio-Biography* (Littleton, CO: Libraries Unlimited 1985), p. 99; Houston A. Baker, Jr., *The Journey Back: Issues in Black Literature and Criticism* (Chicago: University of Chicago Press 1980), p. 119; Amiri Baraka, "How Black Is Black World?" *Yardbird Reader* V (1976): 13–17; C. W. Bigsby, *The Second Black Renaissance: Essays in Black Literature* (Westport, CN: Greenwood Press 1980), p. 50; *"Black Books Bulletin* Interviews Hoyt W. Fuller," *Black Books Bulletin* 1:1 (1971): 19; Gwendolyn Brooks, "Seeds for the Coming Hell and Health Together," in Carole A. Parks, ed., *Nommo: A Literary Legacy of Black Chicago (1967–1987): An OBAC Anthology* (Chicago: OBAC Writers Workshop 1987), p. 304; Herb Boyd, *Metro* [Detroit] *Times* 5:32 (May 29, 1985); Gerald Early, ed., *Speech and Poetry: The African-American Essay and Its Cultural Content, From Polemics to Pulpit*, vol. 2 (Hopewell, NJ: Ecco Press 1993), p. 443; Carolyn Fowler quoted in the *Washington Post* (May 14, 1981): C–6; Addison Gayle quoted in the *New York Times* (May 13, 1987): 19; Paula Giddings, quoted in the *New York Times* (May 13, 1987); Dorothy Gilliam, *The Washington Post* (May 16, 1981): D–I; Eugenia Collier, "Some Thoughts on The Black Aesthetic," in Parks, *Nommo*, p. 332; Vincent Harding, "Power From Our People: The Sources of the Modern Revival of Black History," *The Black Scholar* 18:1 (January/February 1987): 10; Robert L. Harris, Jr., "Black World Magazine Discontinued," *The Black Scholar* 7:7 (April 1976): 38; Mercer Cook and Stephen E. Henderson, *The Militant Black Writer in Africa and the United States* (Madison, WI: University of Wisconsin Press 1969), p. 78; Abby Arthur Johnson and Ronald Mayberry Johnson, *Propaganda And Aesthetic: The Literary Politics of Afro-American Magazines in the Twentieth Century* (Amherst: University of Massachusetts Press 1979), p. 203–204; John H. Johnson, quoted in C. Gerald Fraser, "Hoyt W. Fuller, A Literary Critic and Editor of Black Publications," *New York Times* (May 13, 1981): 19; Randall Kennedy, "Making It: A Review of Succeeding Against the Odds," by John H. Johnson with Lerone Bennett, Jr., in *Reconstruction* (Winter 1996): 32, 66; George E. Kent, "Glimpses of Hoyt W. Fuller," in Parks, *Nommo*, pp. 331, 333; Ishmael Reed, "You Can't Be a Literary Magazine and Hate Writers," *Yardbird Reader* V (1976): 18–20, and *Airing Dirty Laundry* (Reading, MA: Addison-Wesley 1993), p. 104–105; Kalamu ya Salaam, "Making the Most of the Middle Passage," in Parks, *Nommo*, p. 307; Charlotte Wilhite, in a review of Hoyt W. Fuller, "Journey To Africa," *Black Books Bulletin* 1:2 (1972): 42–45; John A. Williams, "Sandbagging at Black World," *Yardbird Reader* V (1976): 11–12. See also: Africana Studies and Research Center, Commemorative Colloquium in Honor of Hoyt W. Fuller (Ithica, NY: Africana Studies and Research Center, October 5–6, 1984); Houston A. Baker, Jr., "Moonlit Chambers and Sibylline Leaves, or How 'The Black Aesthetic' Changed My Life," in Parks, *Nommo*, p. 314–319; Gwendolyn Brooks, ed., *The Race: Matters Concerning Pan-African History, Culture and Genocide* (Richmond, VA: Native Sun Publishers 1991), pp. iv–v; Mari Evans, ed., *Black Women Writers (1950–1980): A Critical Evaluation* (New York: Anchor Press/Doubleday 1984), p. vii, and "For Hoyt," in Parks, *Nommo*, 300–301; Carolyn Fowler, *Black Arts and Black Aesthetics: A Bibliography* (Atlanta, GA: Carolyn Fowler 1976), p. iii; Addison Gayle, "Hoyt Fuller and the Black Aesthetic," in Parks, *Nommo*, p. 310–313; Robert L. Harris, "Hoyt W. Fuller's Challenge, in Parks, *Nommo*, p. 297–299; Woodie King, ed., *Black Short Story Anthology* (New York: Columbia University Press 1972), p. vii;

Keorapetse Kgositsile, *My Name Is Afrika* (Garden City, NY: Anchor Books/Doubleday 1971), p. iii; Richard A. Long, "Watching Just the Same: Some Recollections of Hoyt," in Parks, *Nommo*, pp. 326–330; Jewel C. Latimore [Johari Amini], *Let's Go Some Where* (Chicago: Third World Press 1970), p. iii; Carolyn M. Rodgers, "For H. W. Fuller," in Dudley Randall, ed., *The Black Poets* (New York: Bantam Books 1971), p. 262, and in Parks, *Nommo*, p. 75; Kalamu ya Salaam, "Our World Is Less Full Now That Mr. Fuller Is Gone," in Parks, *Nommo*, p. 309; Kharlos Wimberli, "The Shadows of Your Frown," in Parks, *Nommo*, p. 76.

13. Jennifer Jordan, "Cultural Nationalism in the 1960s: Politics and Poetry," in Adolph Reed, Jr., ed., *Race, Politics, and Culture, Critical Essays On the Radicalism of the 1960s* (Westport, CT: Greenwood Press, 1986), p. 39.

14. Julius E. Thompson, "Preserving the Memory," *Black American Literature Forum* 23:3 (1989): 500.

CHAPTER 18

Charles H. Wesley, African American Historiography and Black Studies: An Historical Overview

James L. Conyers, Jr.

INTRODUCTION

Charles Harris Wesley was a cited and prolific historian, educator-administrator, African Methodist Episcopal minister, public speaker, and activist. Rarely are individuals of his caliber studied with precision and accuracy. His primary research emphasis was in the discipline of history-economics. Within the discipline of history, he was one of the early African American pioneers in the academy of higher learning, who promoted the teaching, researching, and writing of black American history.

Although much of his work was interdisciplinary, Wesley consistently focused his content analysis on African continental and diasporic phenomena. More precisely, with his disciplinary training in history, Wesley consistently attempted to describe and evaluate the paradox of African American history and culture. Earl Thorpe notes Wesley's ideas and philosophy of history, in the following manner: "History is not the story of men and women of one race or color and the neglect and omission of the men and women of another race or color. It is neither the glorification of white people nor black people, but it is the story of the people irrespective of race or color."[1]

Yet, with the prolific rate of producing scholarly works in the form of books, articles, book reviews, and monographs, Wesley, like many of his contemporaries, was limited and confronted with the auspices of individual and institutional racism. Darlene Clark Hine elaborates on this point, by noting:

> In spite of limited opportunities and professional ostracism, many black historians nevertheless researched and wrote exemplary works on the Afro-American historical experience. Scholars such as Carter G. Woodson, Benjamin Quarles, John Hope Franklin, W. E. B. Du Bois, Lorenzo Greene, Charles H. Wesley, A.A. Taylor, and Helen Edmonds persevered in the face of adversity to make the world see black Americans as actors and creators of history instead of so many hapless victims of forces beyond their control.[2]

In general, Melvin Drimmer's analysis is of merit, when he identifies how race is one of the central themes of Americana history and culture, which is an issue that has been destructive, divisive, persistent, and permanent.[3]

Despite the aforementioned limitations and domestic constraints placed on African Americans during the turn of the twentieth century; the subject of this study is an example of the intellectual tradition of black social scientists, who emerged during the first thirty years of this century. Wesley, in some cases, can be seen as the hybridity of W. E. B. Du Bois and Carter G. Woodson: Du Bois a valiant scholar activist; and Woodson an ideological maverick and precursor of African American revisionist history.[4] Henceforth, this commentary analysis is presented to establish a context to study Charles H. Wesley, in place, space, and time, from an interpretative analysis.

This essay seeks to conduct a historical overview of Charles H. Wesley, examining themes of African American historiography and Black Studies, relevant to the intellectual ideas and philosophy of the subject. Certainly, one could write an exhaustive literary, intellectual, or full-scale biography on this subject.[5] Although, essays produced on the subject matter are minimal, if not available at all. I have edited a volume *Charles H. Wesley: The Intellectual Tradition of a Black Historian* (1997). But, there are also two dissertations on the subject: 1) Janette Hoston Harris, *Charles H. Wesley, Educator, and Historian: 1891–1947*; and 2) Lathardus Goggins, *The Evolution of Central State College under Dr. Charles from 1942–1965: An Historical Analysis.* Of the two studies, Harris's study is the only biographical sketch of the subject, covering the first fifty-six years of his life. In addition, there are numerous entries on Wesley, located in African American history reference books.

With pointing out these studies conducted on Wesley, I contend that additional studies are necessary to examine his ideas and philosophy, in order to address the axiological base of transitional change in African American historiography and the evolution of Black Studies.[6] Moreover, then, the aim and objective of this study is to provide an alternative epistemological framework, studying Wesley's common-sense approach and critical analysis in writing Africana history and culture.

METHODOLOGY

Procedure, methodology, and theory are the scholarly characteristics that distinguish the rigorous aspects of Wesley's scholarship. Reflective of his contribution to the intellectual tradition of African American history, the data retrieved for this study is derived from secondary sources and bibliography. Sources used to compile this biographical profile are: 1) questionnaires and interviews with key resource personnel who personally knew Wesley. Included in this group is his wife, the late Dr. Dorothy Porter-Wesley; and 2) bibliographical data from African American historical reference guides, from the Alpha Phi Alpha Fraternity archive files, and the Hallie Q. Brown Memorial Library at Central State University.

Therefore, the thematic issues and schemes of African American historiography and Black Studies are examined in this study, in order to represent the intersubjective bias of this writer, and attributes that also distinguish Wesley's attentiveness to creativity and academic rigor.

SOCIAL ECOLOGY

Wesley was born in 1891, in Louisville, Kentucky, to Charles and Matilda Wesley. His parents were free blacks, who could easily be identified within the black middle-class strata.[7] Again, the purpose of the Wesley's social ecology gives reference to: examining the social environmental characteristics and identifying those environmental factors that shaped and formatted his ideas, philosophies, memory, and ethos. Table 3.7 is a detailed biographical sketch of Wesley's educational and occupational status.

264

Table 3.7

Biographical Sketch and Social Ecology of Charles Harris Wesley

Year	Event
1891	Wesley is born on December 2, to Matilda and Charles Snowden Wesley, Louisville, KY.
1904–1906	Attends and graduates from Central High School.
1906–1907	Attends Fisk College Prepatory School.
1907–1911	Attends and graduates from Fisk University; awarded a B.A. in Classics.
1911–1913	Attends and graduates from Yale University with a M.A. in History-Economics.
1913	Accepts a teaching position as Instructor of History and Modern Language at Howard University.
1915–1916	Attends Howard University Law School.
1914–1937	Ordained and serves as Minister of the African Methodist Church.
1920–1925	Attends and graduates from Harvard University with a Doctorate of Philosophy in History.
1921–1942	Promoted to Professor and Head of the History Department, Howard University.
1928	Awarded Honorary Doctorate of Divinity, Wilberforce University.
1930–1931	First African American to be awarded a Guggenheim Fellowship.
1931–1940	General president of Alpha Phi Alpha Fraternity Inc.
1932	Awarded an Honorary Doctorate of LL, Allen University, Columbia, SC.
1941–1987	Historian of Alpha Phi Alpha Fraternity Inc.
1942–1947	President of Wilberforce University.
1943	Awarded an Honorary Doctorate of LL, Virginia State University, Petersburg, VA.

continued

Table 3.7

Year	Event
1946	Awarded an Honorary Doctorate of LL, Morris Brown College.
1947–1950	Becomes president of Central State University.
1950–1965	President of the Association for the Study of Negro Life and History (ASNLH).
1961	Awarded an Honorary Doctorate of Pedagogy, Morgan State College.
1964	First African American to be Awarded an Honorary Doctorate of LL, from the University of Cincinnati.
1965–1972	Executive Director of the ASNLH.
1967	Awarded an Honorary Doctorate of LL, from Tuskegee University.
1974–1976	Director, Afro-American Historical and Cultural Museum.[8]
1987	Wesley passed away on August 16.

By 1904, Wesley was attending Fisk Preparatory, and in 1907, he became a student at Fisk University, majoring in classics. His extracurricula activities included participation on the Fisk debating team, the Fisk Jubilee Glee Club, and membership on the Fisk University football team. He graduated in 1911 and was immediately accepted to Yale University and majored in history and economics for a masters degree. In 1913, he completed his masters degree and began his teaching career at Howard University in the department of history. Gradually, Wesley moved through the academic ranks of tenure and promotion, becoming a full professor of history in 1921.

That same year he pursued a doctorate in history at Harvard University. By 1925, he became the third African American in the United States to earn a doctorate in history from Harvard. In the latter part of his life, he retired from teaching and administration, but still served in the capacity of the executive administrator of the Association for the Study of Afro-American Life and History and the Philadelphia Afro-American Museum.

HISTORICAL OVERVIEW

The year 1891 is an historical period that illustrates African Americans' collective capacity to locate a niche in the public sphere of economic, political, and social life. Again, this historical overview is relevant to studying Wesley, because it allows the reader to develop an aesthetic regarding the social and political implications of the subject.

Moreover, "between the years of the late 1870s and early 1890s, more than fifty African Americans had been elected to the North Carolina and South Carolina state legislatures."[9] Additionally, in 1890, the "In re Green decision, the United States Supreme Court sanctions control of elections by state officials, thus weakening federal protection for southern black votes. In the case *Louisville, New Orleans, and Texas Railway* v. *Mississippi*, the court permits states to segregate public transportation and facilities."[10]

Other historical events of relevance that occur in 1891 are:

1. August 12 to November 1; the constitutional convention in Mississippi adopted the literacy and understanding tests as devices to disfranchise Negroes.[11]
2. Dr. Daniel Hale Williams founds Provident Hospital, with the first training school for Black nurses in the United States.[12]
3. The number of African Americans being lynched in the United States is reported to be estimated at 112, most of these casualties and victims are reported to be located in southern states.[13]

During the preceding years from 1895 to 1896, African American historiography was taking shape and format towards black autonomy. In 1895, Booker T. Washington delivered his Atlanta Compromise speech at the Cotton States International Exposition. Equally important, W. E. B. Du Bois was the first African American to receive a doctorate from Harvard University. Finally, Frederick Douglass died in Washington, D.C.[14]

In 1896, the U.S. Supreme Court upheld the concept of separate but equal, concerning public facilities for African Americans in the case of *Plessy* v. *Ferguson*. The National Association of Colored Women, led by Mary Church Terrell was organized and established in Washington, D.C.; and W. E. B. Du Bois published the *Suppression of the African Slave Trade*, which is considered one of the first sociological studies conducted in the United States.[15]

In summary, this historical chronology is presented to identify the climate and environmental factors that shaped and formatted Wesley's ecology. Again, in studying the historical periods during his birth and adolescent stage illustrate that he was born during a period of struggle; in which, African Americans were confronted with migration out of the south, lynching, Jim Crow laws, and other consequences of subordinate group status, whereas, blacks were consistently agitating for social equality.

AFRICAN AMERICAN HISTORIOGRAPHY

Generally, most historical studies of African Americans is extensively descriptive, lacking critical analysis, and contextual clarification. Historiography then takes shape and form articulated through the worldview and ideas of the historian's intersubjective analysis. John Cannon notes:

> With the growth of the civil rights movement in the United States and the increasing anger of Afro-Americans against the slavery-derived term "Negro," the expression black historiography arose in the 1960s to describe writings by persons of African descent about the part played by blacks in the history of North America. The expression is occasionally widened to include work on the African Diaspora and is sometimes applied to the study of writing by sympathetic whites on the black experience in the New World. . . . Black historiography as an adjunct to Afro-American nationalism developed before the American Civil War in such works as Martin R. Delany's *The Condition, Elevation, Emigration and Destiny of the Colored People of the United States, Politically Considered* (Philadelphia 1852). Yet integration into American life through the examination of patriotic episodes in the Afro-American past was also an important motive of black historians at this time; for example, William C. Nell's *The Colored Patriots of the American Revolution* (Boston 1855).[16]

Relative to the subject in this study, Wesley was successful in fulfilling literary merit; a sound knowledge of the philosophy of history; advanced training and competence in historical methodology, with emphasis on the use of sources and documentation; and a critical analysis in his interpretative analysis of historical events and occurrences.[17]

Wesley produced an abundance of scholarship in several genres of knowledge, ranging from biographies, social histories, and cultural histories to intellectual studies. His biographical studies are: *Richard Allen: An Apostle of Freedom*; *The History of Prince Hall Grand Lodge of Free and Accepted Masons of the State of Ohio, 1849–1960*; and *A Biography of Henry Arthur Callis*. Still, to this date, the biography of Richard Allen is the definitive study of Allen and the A.M.E. Church. His publication of social historical studies consisted of: *Negro Labor in the United States*; *The History of Alpha Phi Alpha Fraternity Incorporated*; *The Collapse of the Confederacy*; and *The History of Sigma Pi Phi*. In summary, Wesley published over twenty books and over one hundred scholarly articles. Majority of his articles were published in the *Journal of Negro History*. His impact on the transitional development of African American historiography, is ever lasting.

In the broad sense of historiography, Conal Furray and Michael J. Salevoris, offer a working definition of this term: ". . . the writing of history. In modern usage, however, the word refers to the study of the way history has been written and is written—the history of historical writing, if you will. When you study historiography you do not study the event of the past directly, but the changing interpretations of those events in the works of the individual historians."[18] Therefore, much of Wesley's scholarship contended to confront and challenge the cultural hegemonic views and depictions of African people. Rudwick and Meier point out Wesley's reservations concerning the perspective and presentation of African Americans: "Historians, he noted, had minimized the contributions of non-Anglo-Saxon peoples to the richness and diversity of culture in this nation of nations."[19] In fact, noted and late historian Benjamin Quarles discusses the problems in American historiography, whereas African Americans are consistently located on the margins of world history:

> Until recent times, the role of the Afro-American in our national life was thought to be hardly worth considering. An intellectual white flight held sway; most writers in the social sciences and the humanities, whatever their individual specialties, assumed that they knew as much about blacks as they needed to know or as their readers cared to learn. With this static image, the black was considered something of an intruder, if not indeed an outsider. In many quarters he was regarded as an exotic, an offshoot, hardly "a piece of the continent, a part of the maine." Certainly, he was underplayed in American history and letters.[20]

To supplement this citation, Kusmer notes that scholars who engaged in black history research used holistic methodologies, as they pertained to conducting regional and community studies.[21] Primarily, borrowing or employing tools from disciplines such as sociology, economics, anthropology, and political science. William H. Harris adds: "Despite the richness of the historiography on Afro-Americans during the past decade, much remains to be done. . . . Historians of the past have always emphasized the importance of charisma among black leaders. But over concentration on charisma deflects our minds and makes it difficult for us to see that these leaders, despite their styles, were involved in the difficult work of creating institutions and organizations of permanence."[22] Such is the case with Wesley, whereas, the ontological base of his scholarship was historiographic, he consistently sought for, and used tools of analysis, which located his scholarship as having a interdisciplinary perspective. Indeed, Wesley research was cutting-edge scholarship that transcended the enterprise of African American historiography.

BLACK STUDIES

The intellectual tradition of African American studies has its roots in the 1800s.[23] Contemporary Black Studies scholars articulate that Africa is the conceptual formation in the process to describe and evaluate Africana diasporic phenomena. Thorpe cites Wesley, by stating:

> Laying down the lines along which the history of the United States and the Western world should be rendered, Wesley declared that 1) History should be reconstructed so that Africa . . . shall have its proper place; 2) History should be reconstructed so that Negroes shall be known on a higher level than that of jokes and minstrels; 3) History should be reconstructed so that Negroes shall appear not only as the recipients of liberty, but as the winners of it, not only for themselves, but also for others; and 4) History should be reconstructed so that Negroes shall be regarded as Americans.[24]

Indeed, Wesley can be considered a precursor to the Black Studies movement. During his tenure period at Howard University and Central State University, he developed sound undergraduate and graduate curricular on the study of the Africana continental and diaspora;

and focused on the recruitment of prolific scholars who expressed an interest like himself on studying the black experience in America from an alternative epistemological framework. Therefore, Black Studies, is not so much a collection of antidotes and information on African Americans as it is this body of knowledge—the concept being augmented by Wesley—is a systematic academic holistic discipline, which seeks to study Africana phenomena from an intersubjective perspective as subjects.

Academically, Wesley's primary training was in history; he consistently struggled with presenting an alternative epistemology of African American life, history, and culture. Molefi Asante is correct when he states: "An alternative framework suggests that other definitional assumptions can provide a new paradigm for the examination of education within the American society."[25] More importantly, the organizational structure of Black Studies evolves during the 1960s at San Francisco State College. Rudwick and Meier note that upon Wesley accepting his first teaching position at Howard University, "he quickly introduced special lectures that focused on the contributions of African Americans to America's civilization, and that Wesley was among a growing number of Howard University faculty who were interested in offering courses on the African American experience."[26] In an historical perspective, the antecedents to Black Studies has an intellectual history that dates back to the 1800s, with pioneering lay and trained historians such as William Cooper Nell and George Washington Williams.

In Thorpe's classical study entitled, *Black Historians*, he places Wesley within the intellectual tradition of Black Studies: "Charles H. Wesley is placed with the Middle Group of black historians because of his prominent role in establishing the field of Afro-American studies, and because his general attitude toward the place and importance of black history with that of Woodson and Du Bois."[27]

Overall, Wesley's multidisciplinary approach to examining African American history and culture postures his ideological repertoire, within the intellectual tradition of Black Studies. Yet, being confronted with adversity and institutional and individual racism, Wesley's rigor, efforts, tenacity, body of research scholarship, and ideas and philosophies concerning African American historiography are the antecedents to the disciplinary boundaries of Black Studies.

CONCLUSION

The purpose of this essay was to examine thematic issues and schemes of Charles H. Wesley, with emphasis on African American historiography and Black Studies. Composition and format of this study is an historical overview of the subject. Simply put, Wesley, like other prolific African American historians, deserves scholarly treatment of his writings, ideas, and philosophies, as they pertained to study of African American history and culture. In particular, Wesley has made lasting contributions to African American revisionist history and the disciplinary matrix of Black Studies theory and methodology.

A salient and critical point of discussion lies in the fact that Wesley worked against the odds of institutional and individual racism because he committed his professional career to advancing humanistic interpretative analysis, and a scientific qualitative-quantitative methodology of studying Africana kinship and culture. Nevertheless, the aim and objective of the cause and view of African Americans was his primary goal and concern. Still, this essay is an overview of his life, and is limited to addressing contextuality of the limitations and obstacles that confronted, and still confront, black scholars.

Lerone Bennett challenges our ethos and creativity by addressing the dialectic of the either-or controversy. Mentioning this philosophic thought, in relation to Wesley is necessary in attempting to understand how this black historian did not accept conventional wisdom as his world-view of describing and evaluating African Americans history and culture.

Notes

1. Earl Thorpe, *Black Historians: A Critique* (New York: William & Morrow 1969), p. 136.
2. Darlene Clarke Hine, ed., *The State of Afro-American History* (Baton Rouge: Louisiana State University Press 1986), p. ix.
3. Melvin Drimmer, *Issues in Black History* (Dubuque, IA: Kendall Hunt 1987), p. 1.
4. E. A. Johnson, *A School History of the Negro Race in America from 1619 to 1890* (Philadelphia, PA: Sherman and Co. 1891).
5. See Arnold Rampersaud, "Biography and Afro-American Culture," in Houston Baker and Patricia Redmond, eds., *Afro-American Literary Tradition in the 1980s* (Chicago: University of Chicago Press 1989).

6. James L. Conyers, Jr., ed., *Charles H. Wesley: The Intellectual Tradition of A Black Historian* (New York: Garland Publishing 1997), p. ix-x.
7. Elliott Rudwick and August Meier, *Black Historians and the Historical Profession* (Urbana: University of Illinois Press 1986), p. 77.
8. Conyers, *Charles H. Wesley: The Intellectual Tradition of a Black Historian*, pp. 315–316; James L. Conyers, Jr., "An Intellectual Biography of Charles H. Wesley: An Oral History," *The Negro Educational Review*, 67:3–4 (July–October 1996): 204–209; Francille Rusan Wilson, entry essay on Charles H. Wesley, in Jack Salzman, David Lionel Smith, and Cornel West, eds., *Encyclopedia of African American Culture and History* (New York: Simon Schuster Macmillan 1996), vol. 5, pp. 2802–2803; and Janette Hoston Harris, "Charles H. Wesley, Educator, and Historian 1891–1947," Ph.D. dissertation, Howard University, 1975.
9. Michael L. Levine, *African Americans and Civil Rights* (Phoenix, AZ: Oryx 1996), p. 109.
10. Ibid., p. 27.
11. Alton Hornsby, *Chronology of African American History: Significant Events and People from 1619 to the Present* (Detroit, MI: Gale Research Incorporated 1991), p. 52.
12. Levine, *African Americans and Civil Rights*, p. 21.
13. Ibid.
14. Hornsby, *Chronology of African American History,* p. 55.
15. Ibid.
16. John Cannon, ed., *The Blackwell Dictionary of Historians* (New York: Blackwell Reference 1988), p. 41.
17. Thorpe, *Black Historians: A Critique*, p. vi.
18. Conal Furray and Michael Salevouris, *The Methods and Skills of History: A Practical Guide* (Wheeling, IL: Harlan Davidson 1988), p. 223.
19. Rudwick and Meier, *Black Historians and the Historical Profession*, p. 79.
20. Benjamin Quarles, *Black Mosaic: Essays in Afro-American History and Historiography* (Amherst: The University of Massachusetts Press 1988), p. 181.
21. Kenneth Kusmer, ed., *Overviews, Theory and Historiography,* vol. 9 (New York: Garland 1991).
22. William H. Harris, "Trends and Needs in Afro-American Historiography," in Darlene Clark Hine, ed., *The State of Afro-American History* (Baton Rouge: Louisiana State University Press 1986), p. 150.
23. James L. Conyers, Jr., "African American Studies: Locating a Niche in the Public Sphere of Higher Education," in James L. Conyers, Jr., ed., *Africana Studies: A Disciplinary Quest for Both Theory and Method* (Jefferson, NC: McFarland Publishing 1997), p. 130.
24. Thorpe, *Black Historians*, p. 136.
25. Molefi Kete Asante, "The Afrocentric Idea in Education," *Journal of Negro Education* 60:2 (1991): 171.
26. See Wilson's entry essay on Charles H. Wesley, *Encyclopedia of African American Culture and History*, p. 2803.
27. Thorpe, *Black Historians*, p. 134.

273

Index

Index